Arming the Defence Forces

ARMING THE DEFENCE FORCES

Col. (Retd.) R.K. Gaur (ASC)

SUMIT ENTERPRISES
NEW DELHI - 110002

Published by :
SUMIT ENTERPRISES
4649 B/21, Ansari Road,
Daryaganj, New Delhi-110002
Phone : 011-23279353
Mob. : 9810217567
E-mail : sumit_enterprises2007@yahoo.com.in

ARMING THE DEFENCE FORCES

First Published 2013

ISBN 978-81-8420-314-1

PRINTED IN INDIA

Published by Sri Lokesh Kumar for Sumit Enterprises, New Delhi-110002, Typesset by Lucky Graphics, Printed at Sachin Printers.

Contents

Preface

The strength, type and structure of the armed forces have to take into account the security environment facing the nation, both conventional as well as nuclear. Indian Armed Forces have to be organised to fight on two fronts, as our unresolved border with China in the North and North East continues to pose a threat despite an improvement in relations. The long drawn 'Proxy War' in J & K and our strained relations with Pakistan are serious challenges facing the nation. India has also to plan for dealing with threats to its sea coast and island territories. The size and shape of the defence forces has to take into account the threat to the sealanes and its trade routes. The nonstate actors and terrorist groups are another factor to be considered.

The transformation of the US armed forces was initially promoted as nothing less than a fundamental shift in the way wars would be fought in the future and has often been re-ferred to as a "revolution in military affairs." Such far-reaching and ambitious aims natu-rally implied significant changes for the US defense industrial base; such potential changes, in turn, naturally catalyzed many questions. In particular, would new require-ments for network-centric warfare undermine the long-standing predominance of the US military's traditional suppliers and, thereby, shift defense work in favour of a new cadre of firms-particularly those drawn from the commercial information technology (IT) sector?

The book will provide a valuable reference, will contribute to the discussion about exploitation potentials of agent technology, armed forces and society in the defense industry and initiate implementation of further innovative applications and deployment exercises.

—Editor

1

Accessible Defence Force

A USABLE, ACCESSIBLE, FLEXIBLE DEFENCE FORCE

The Government's defence policy orientation as set out in the present bill is aimed at enhancing Sweden's defence capability by increasing the usability and accessibility of the country's armed forces. The Swedish Armed Forces must be deployable here and now and contribute to a greater extent than hitherto to Sweden's security and stability in the world. Enhanced operational accessibility and flexibility will enable the armed forces to respond to crises and conflicts more rapidly and effectively, even where these arise at short notice.

Operating alone or with others, the military defence system is responsible for defending Sweden and promoting our security, inside Sweden, in our immediate region and beyond. The whole of Sweden must be defended.

Increasing the number of usable, accessible units will strengthen Sweden's defence capability. We are building an accessible, usable and mobile Swedish operational defence force capable of undertaking missions using the same combat units, whether inside Sweden, in our immediate region or beyond.

Our preparedness must be continually adapted to current threat and risk levels in our region. Air and naval forces, including submarines, watch over sea approaches and airspace, and can rapidly be adapted to defence needs, both in Sweden and our immediate region. The national protection forces being developed in the Home Guard will receive better training and equipment than under the present home defence arrangements and will form an important part of Sweden's defence.

The battalion combat groups that will form the core of the Army's forces will be more mobile and flexible than at present, and will have high operational effectiveness. Like our naval and air defence forces, they can be rapidly deployed for missions in Sweden, the immediate region and beyond. Safeguarding our security does not stop at our borders. A security threat to a neighbouring country could have significant repercussions for Sweden. Through collaboration with others we can deal with challenges and threats before they reach our territory.

The Government's proposals in this bill set out the overall direction towards achieving a more usable and accessible defence force. The initiative will result in greater freedom of action in defence policy matters. The inherent flexibility of operational defence advocated by the Government will better equip the defence force to deal with a broad and changeable threat spectrum. In June 2008, an unanimous Defence Commission submitted its report *Försvar i användning* [Defence in Use]. The report contained specific proposals in a number of areas. These included a new principle with regard to personnel provision, rationalisation of the funding authorities, a transition from heavier to lighter combat units, far-reaching collaboration in the Baltic Sea area, measures to concretise civil-military coordination and better financial management of the Armed Forces.

The Commission further proposed a division between permanent and contract units, and that national service conscripts be barred from serving in any future operational organisation. These recommendations are fully in line with the shift in priorities that must be made if we are to create a usable defence force. The present bill is largely based on the Defence Commission's proposals.

RESTRUCTURING AND MODERNISATION

The Swedish Armed Forces' new operational organisation should be in place in 2014, although not all units are expected to be fully operational by then, mainly owing to a predicted shortage of personnel. The Government wishes to emphasise that the pace of the proposed development towards a more accessible defence force will be determined by the economic situation. The need to free up resources will be met by reforming and rationalising personnel, equipment and logistics supply systems and other support activities. As resources are freed up the new, more usable defence force will emerge, in which higher costs and raised ambitions in connection with operational activities are offeset by rationalisation and lowered ambitions in other areas. The orientation set out by the Government is thus subject to adjustment both as regards the pace of transition and capability, equipment, organisational and operational requirements. If necessary, the Government will submit any such adjustments to the Riksdag either in conjunction with the annual budget bill or in another bill.

The Government further intends to report back to the Riksdag on the measures and efficiency enhancements being planned and implemented as part of the continued reform in order to achieve the objectives proposed by the Government in the present bill. The Government also intends to present a description of the new personnel supply system, with *inter alia* longer fixed-term employment contracts, in an upcoming bill.

The Swedish Defence Forces will prioritise the development of usable and accessible army units incorporating flexible battalion combat groups capable of operating in Sweden, our immediate region and beyond; a new personnel supply system based primarily on contract soldiers; the ability to protect our national sovereignty; and the arming of existing weapons platforms. The focus will be on the operational benefits, now and in the future.

2

Arming the Indian Defence Forces

It needs to be understood that defence modernisation must imperatively respond to prevailing challenges and needs of our country. The technology environment is changing and unless the development cycle of new equipment is shortened, the Armed Forces will continue to remain in an operationally disadvantageous situation. In the present strategic scenario, the sources of assured military supplies have dwindled. At the same time, the availability of a variety of new and alternate equipment has added to the complexities of procurement. Added to this is the fact that the environment has become conflict prone and uncertain, with the result that the Forces have to be prepared to meet contingencies over a wide spectrum of conflict and a large physical area of operation. Therefore, in addition to the security challenges from external threats, we need to be prepared to combat internal challenges and tackle cross-border terrorism. We have to develop a national strategy and an integrated response to effectively deal with threats to our national security. This calls for an integrated politico-military strategy for projecting our national power and building capabilities, both economic and military.

STREAMLINING DEFENCE PROCUREMENTS

The defence reforms were carried out in 2001 to evolve integrated and joint structures for higher defence organization in order to face the emerging threats and consequently achieve the desired levels of modernization. These reforms have achieved some degree of maturity and have been periodically updated. Formation of HQ Integrated Defence Staff has been instrumental for a joint approach towards building military capability. Streamlining defence procurement procedures, involving private sector in defence-production, spurring research and development, taking long term perspective in defence planning and budgeting, up-gradation of quality of personnel in the armed forces and rationalization of manpower were among many of the key reforms recommended by the Group of Ministers Report of 2001. However; these need to be implemented fully, as lack of a central policy planning staff and absence of Chief of Defence Staff greatly inhibit integrated effort in defence modernization. A few instances of malpractices in defence purchases should not derail the entire procurement programme; instead the guilty should be given suitable punishment and the planned inductions continued. Today the entire decision making apparatus appears paralyzed once a scandal in the defence purchase is reported and the Capital budget for procurements remains unspent, adversely affecting the defence capability.

Technology Induction

At the present juncture, our armed forces are in transition from industrial age forces to knowledge age forces with a portion being equipped with the state-of-the art weapons. While the Army is more manpower intensive, the Navy and the Air Force are more technology intensive forces and are much better on the equipment profile. Availability of state-of-the art technology is dependent on international relations and strategic partnerships between us and the major militaries. A collaborative approach between the users, DRDO, the industry and foreign vendors is the only way ahead. We must transform our buyer-seller relationship to joint-ventures. Transfer of technology being undertaken at the HAL aircraft manufacturing factory and some of the other joint ventures with countries like Israel, Russia and France for various weapon systems is the right step from the earlier days of licensed production system. Defence Public Sector Units and DRDO must adopt time bound processes and adopt bold management practices and scrap the process if it does not conform to a reasonable time-frame, rather than seeking frequent time extension, as shelf-life of equipment is becoming shorter by the day due to obsolescence.

Precision Guided Munitions (PGMs)

Precision engagement is considered one of the most important aspects of the ongoing modernisation. And this is one of the niche capabilities which are being strengthened in our armed forces. The benefits of PGMs are well known. Precision weapons are a far more efficient substitute for heavy mass retaliation. They enable concentration of effects from geographically widely dispersed forces, contribute to reduced logistics tail, and help in reducing collateral damage. Therefore, increasing the accuracy and range of our missiles, and acquiring and developing a family of PGMs should receive greater attention in our armed forces.

However, long ranges of weapon platforms are of no use unless they are complemented by matching surveillance, target acquisition, battle damage assessment and weapon guidance capabilities. Therefore, besides ground based and air borne early warning systems, space based assets assume importance for imparting force-multiplication effects to air and surface forces. In addition, space is another area which is being used basically for communications and navigations and we are in the process of increasing our capabilities in this area too. Aerospace capabilities have a long gestation period. It is necessary to carry out cost-effective replacements and selective upgradation of existing systems. All platforms including transport support aircraft and helicopters with residual life must be upgraded, along with the weapon systems.

Surveillance and Night Vision Devices

With the change of battlefield scenario, Indian Army is now equipping itself with latest state of the art technology and looking for night vision equipment between 3000-5000 meters range. This would give a tactical advantage for our forces which would enhance their night fighting skills and improve surveillance and reconnaissance capabilities greatly, but the numbers are large and would take time for induction. Army feels that the night vision equipment will enhance combat potential to facilitate operations over 24 hours cycle. As a part of its modernization and upgrading weaponry, Indian Army has planned to equip all its battalions with night vision equipments but the progress is painfully slow. We need to push these on fast-track procurement procedure by intervention at the highest level.

'MBT-Arjun' Tank Production

The inordinate delay in the production of the ARJUN Tank and its design faults is a major cause of worry. Indian Defence Minister has admitted that frequent design modification and assembling format have also caused additional delay in its induction. His assurance that necessary steps have been taken to ensure the timely availability of all critical aggregates, is still far from the reality. The Ministry of Defence in regular intervals comes out with promising statements only to justify the public-sector defence undertakings and to secure uninterrupted financial grants. Meanwhile, we continue to import the Russian T-90 and T-72 tanks, which are far superior but involve huge expenditure on imports from foreign sources.

Modernisation of Field Artillery (155mm guns)

As part of the field artillery modernization programme, Army is looking to purchase artillery guns since mid-80s as well as increase domestic manufacture of field guns. Artillery modernization programme has been held hostage to various scandals and pressures and the Army is even considering buying older models of 130 mm guns as a desperate measure. Despite the Army repeatedly requesting for induction of 155 mm guns, due to irregularities in the procurement process and the unscrupulous role of middlemen and agents, this has not seen the light of day. It needs to be realized that even after giving the go-ahead, it takes at least five years for the equipment to reach the Army units since these products are not available off-the-shelf and the numbers to be inducted are large. This is a matter of serious concern and the operational readiness of the Army is jeopardized by continued inaction of the Government.

Building Maritime Capability

India's peninsular configuration invests her with an opportunity to project maritime power in the Indian Ocean. This enables her to protect its Sea-Lanes as also to interdict hostile shipping, which traverse through the Indian Ocean. The rationale for an extensive PLA Navy build-up, development of Gwadar port in Pakistan, surveillance outposts on Myanmar islands, and beefing of ports in Sri Lanka and Bangladesh by the Chinese, suggest an intention to use these during forays of the PLA Navy into the Indian ocean. India, therefore, needs to enhance its naval build –up and expedite induction of the planned aircraft-carrier, the Scorpene submarines and the Maritime surveillance aircraft. Whereas, India can meet some of the challenges independently, others require rallying together Indian Ocean region Navies.

BUILDING MILITARY CAPABILITY

The strength, type and structure of the armed forces have to take into account the security environment facing the nation, both conventional as well as nuclear. Indian Armed Forces have to be organised to fight on two fronts, as our unresolved border with China in the North and North East continues to pose a threat despite an improvement in relations. The long drawn 'Proxy War' in J & K and our strained relations with Pakistan are serious challenges facing the nation. India has also to plan for dealing with threats to its sea coast and island territories. The size and shape of the defence forces has to take into account the threat to the sea-lanes and its trade routes. The non-state actors and terrorist groups are another factor to be considered.

There is, therefore, a compelling need for India to undertake military modernisation especially when we compare the rapid investment in military hardware and infrastructure by China. This is more noticeable in the infrastructure in our border region, in the air and maritime capabilities. Over 96 per cent of China's nuclear arsenal has relevance only for its neighbours..China has been aggressively expanding its missile defence and aerospace power. Pakistan on the other hand is adding to its military power by diverting US aid meant for fighting the Taliban on the Pak-Afghan border. Post 9/11 Pakistan received 11 billion $ aid from the USA and 85 per cent of this has been spent on defence. Pakistan has been made a non-NATO ally and recipient of huge funds for counter-terrorism as part of Af-Pak strategy. It has also been transferred radars, Attack-helicopters, Harpoon missiles and F-16 aircraft, and has developed its nuclear capabilities significantly. Terrorism in Kashmir and elsewhere in India is supported by Pakistan. We must, therefore, have the capabilities to deter and defeat the external threats from our neighbours, as the war fighting potential of China and Pakistan has increased tremendously.

The other factors that determine military capability are the state of indigenous defence industry and the induction of new technology. Military capability takes time to be created and cannot be achieved in a hurry in times of war. Financial angle is another important consideration. Affordability and budgetary allocation in view of high costs of military equipment and manpower requirement have to be taken into account. The quality and speed of defence modernization is influenced to a large extent by political, economic, technological and strategic factors. The Indian approach to defence modernization is, therefore shaped by:-geo-political and geo-strategic environment; economic interests; technology constraints and imperatives; and social and cultural factors.

The security challenge facing India is diverse, complex and constantly evolving. Instability in our immediate and extended neighbourhood heightens the threat to our security. Indian strategic thinking is influenced by what happens in the Indian Ocean, West Asia, Central Asia and South-East Asia. Prime Minister Manmohan Singh during his address to Combined

Commanders' Conference in October 2005, had observed thus: "To meet national security challenge, our strategy has to be based on three broad pillars. First is to strengthen ourselves economically and technologically; second, to acquire adequate defence capability to counter and rebut threats to our security, and the third to seek partnerships both on the strategic front and on the economic and technological front to widen our policy and developmental options". Thus introduction of cuttingedge technologies, both in the field of defence and civil, becomes equally important. Even though preference to economic over military development is normally given, it is possible to proceed simultaneously in both the areas once a certain level in economic development and capabilities has been reached. Defence modernisation is therefore, a necessity for the armed forces. However, priorities at the national level vary because of competing needs of other important social sectors that need funds for development.

It is not the intention here to review the entire range of military modernisation that needs to be undertaken but to highlight a few of the important aspects which illustrate the existing status of modernization. This is being done in the succeeding paragraphs. Similarly a national strategy to fight tribal insurgencies, religious fundamentalism and Maoist activities needs to be formulated with a suitable mechanism for centralized control and synergy. This too would need to be examined comprehensively elsewhere as its detailed examination is outside the scope of this chapter.

Joint Doctrine

A joint military doctrine between the forces and other wings of the government is a must to conduct war and conflicts in all their complexities. Joint doctrine not only gives a common perspective but also provides an authoritative guidance for the Armed Forces on new military technologies which may be of use for future operations. Though what has been termed a 'Joint Military Doctrine' has been formulated and released by the Services from their individual perspectives, it is neither truly 'joint' nor fully integrated. The Army Doctrine envisages a number of taskoriented integrated Battle Groups penetrating adversary's territory from a cold start and executing their assigned tasks quickly within a short span before any international pressure can be brought to bear. However, Air Force and Naval Doctrines both emphasise the strategic reach of their respective services and the need to operate in joint service environment in order to achieve synergies of defenceeffort.

The Indian Navy was first off the block in achieving high speed connectivity between shore establishment ships, other naval platforms and even logistics installations. The Army has also made strides in Net-centric warfare and few of the formations have already been exercised. However, we have to factor the Chinese Ballistic Missile and anti-Satellite capabilities. Chinese counter-space capabilities are a threat to India's limited but valuable intelligence, surveillance, reconnaissance, and communication satellites. While China continues to improve its space assets, it indirectly also makes Pakistan a proxy space power because of the close cooperation between the two. India is still miles away from validating a Ballistic Missile Defence System. We urgently need to create an organization for overseeing the entire gamut of militarization of space with a national perspective and integrate the Doctrines of the three Services under the long awaited Chief of Defense Staff.Such a step would assist in setting out critical national priorities in the acquisition of military-hardware and ensure best utilization of funds. This would also act as the nodal-point for providing single-point military advice, as also sorting out inter-service differences and fixing responsibility.

Air Power

Air assets are best applied centrally and can be switched to other sectors speedily. The areas where IAF needs capability enhancement is its strike-forces, its Space–assets, AWACS, airlift aircraft, air-rescue and air defence. This would imply creating a composite capability to be able to strike strategic targets and sustain a rapid –reaction force in the Indian Ocean region. It would also necessitate expansion of air-ports and harbour infrastructure. It is well known that our defence budget allocation and our procurement policies have not been adequate to support our defence potential.

Budgetary Support

The future direction and pace of modernization would largely be dictated by budgetary constraints. Presently, the budget is at modest level of 2.3 per cent of the GDP. Even in current five years defence plan (2007 – 2012), the defence budget is expected to be around 2.5 per cent of the GDP. If there is a sustained growth of eight per cent and above in the economy then additional budget for the defence must be allotted. This is especially important in view of the rapid modernization and increased defence budgets of our adversaries. Pakistan military budget is at 3.5 per cent and China has 4.5 per cent of the GDP and both countries hide actual expenditures, such as pensions and new procurements under different heads. Additionally, PGMs, induction of force-multipliers, cyber security and achieving synergies in the field of information technology should continue to be the focus of our modernization programme. However, a long-term perspective, accountability in decision making, a firm financial commitment and fast–track procurements procedure will have to be adopted to actually achieve our planned defence capabilities, otherwise the funds will remain unspent, eroding our combat-edge adversely.

FIGHTING INTERNAL CHALLENGES

Challenges to internal security have been discussed at various forums and a national counter-terrorism centre and a national investigative agency have been established. These are commendable steps which need to be effectively implemented. However, what ultimately matters is the political will to act and good governance. An effective legal frame-work and modernization of Police Force along with fair and equitable economic development of all sections of Indian society, is equally necessary. The policy of appeasement needs to be replaced by a pro-active and Positive response, to emerging situations. The intelligence agencies will have to be made more accountable and the State response more professional for timely intervention. National response cannot be the sole responsibility of the Security Forces and the government. Each and every citizen and civil society as a whole, including its commercial and business institutions would need to be involved in strengthening our nation's security.

Restoring Combat Edge

We are yet to buy a single artillery gun in 23 years. We have an aging naval fleet and dwindling numbers of advance jet fighters. Therefore, there is a compelling need to give a greater impetus to procurement of critical equipment. India also has a bitter experience of foreign vendors not fulfilling their contractual commitments once full payments are made. They fail to provide accepted after-sale support, arbitrarily increase cost of spares, and decline to honour transfer of technology commitments. India's failure to negotiate foolproof contracts has allowed Russia to increase the cost of aircraft-carrier 'Gorshkov' manifold. Similar contractual flaws have resulted in delays in the deliveries of 'Hawk Trainers', T-90 tank kits, and 'Scorpene' submarines. It is essential that we develop critical technologies ourselves or enter joint-ventures with strategic partners. We also need to have professional teams to negotiate defence contracts. This would need the establishment of a dedicated Procurement Agency staffed by professionals, who are experts and are accountable to the Defence Minister. It is evident that the state of our defence modernization is unsatisfactory and there is urgent need for full implementation of the required institutional restructuring.

ROLE OF DEFENSE RESEARCH AND DEVELOPMENT

The political and economic context of DoD's basic research has changed dramatically. Industrial competition has become global, and the commercial market has become much larger than the military market. These changes have had several implications for defense-related research and development. First, the commercial sector is driving many, if not most, of the near-term advances in components and systems. Second, DoD must incorporate commercial products into defense systems, adding ruggedness and military specialization as an overlay, rather than developing military-specific components. Third, international competition and the desire for near-term profits have reduced longer-term investments by industry in many areas of basic and applied research.

These changes have affected one specific area, semiconductor integrated circuits (IC), which are a critical aspect of the information dominance and near-perfect SA on which the AAN is predicated. Similar examples could be cited in other technology areas, such as wireless communications and turbine engines. In 1976, U.S. military purchases accounted for 17 percent of IC sales worldwide ($700 million out of total sales of $4.2 billion)a significant market share that gave DoD leverage in defining product specifications and directions. In the next 20 years, the U.S. military market increased only marginally, to $1.1 billion, while the commercial market exploded to $160 billion. The military market now accounts for less than 1 percent of sales, and the commercial market has become the dominant force in setting IC product directions. Although lower prices have resulted, the DoD is now compelled to use commercial IC products and adapt them to meet military requirements, as necessary.

At the same time, competitive pressures have shortened industry's development horizons to one or two product cycles. As former director of defense research and engineering, Dr. Anita K. Jones, has observed, "... industry research and development horizons are increasingly near term." The horizon for the information technology industry sector, for example, is typically three years or less.

In a cycle that begins with S&T (science and technology) and runs through development and production to life-cycle support, DoD has little to gain by adding a few additional dollars to industry's profit-driven, near-term development. Except for requirements that are truly unique to defense applications, DoD can exert much more influence by leveraging its dollars either at the front end in the enabling S&T phase or at the back end by adapting commercial technology to meet DoD needs. Nevertheless, commercial industry remains dependent on the federal government for investments in long-term, higher risk S&T research. Historically, DoD has provided 15 to 20 percent of the total federal investment. In fiscal year 1997, expenditures by all of the services accounted for almost $8 billion in basic and applied research and advanced technology development. This amount represents 40 percent of federal spending for basic research and includes more than 70 percent of all federal investment in microelectronics and electrical engineering.

U.S. industry has become increasingly dependent on the crucial leverage of government-funded research conducted at universities and in federal laboratories.

Although DoD's research investment has declined in constant dollars, the percentage of the DoD budget has remained stable since World War II because the relationship with industry has served the needs of the DoD, the research community, and the commercial sector.

The imperatives of national defense have enabled DoD to invest directly in important new ideas with adequate resources to make a difference. Although this focused approach has not led to success in every project, it has led to enough successes to foster enormous progress in new technologies for both the military and commercial sectors.

Early-stage development of new technologies is almost always applicable to both sectors. Therefore, by investing wisely, DoD can influence the directions of research and guarantee an adequate research base for technologies to meet its future needs. DoD can also leverage its investments by coordinating teams drawn from federal laboratories, industry, and universities for demonstration projects to develop new defense applications based as much as possible on commercially available components and software. The S&T advantage of U.S. forces will increasingly depend on adaptations of commercial products with a defense overlay, rather than on expensive military-specific designs.

ARMY SCIENCE AND TECHNOLOGY PROGRAM

Army and DoD S&T programs include basic research (budget line item 6.1), which increases scientific understanding, applied research (budget line item 6.2), which identifies and exploits technology opportunities based on new knowledge and evaluates their technical feasibility to increase war-fighting capabilities, and advanced technology development (budget line item 6.3), which demonstrates applications to specific military systems, to speed the transition to maturity and insertion.

The Army share of DoD funding for research in all three categories. Like overall DoD investments, funding for research has remained a constant proportion of Army appropriations, although investment in constant real dollars has declined steadily since the end of the Cold War along with the rest of the defense budget.

The research and technology development needed for the AAN will require a cooperative effort. As the Army has fewer and fewer dollars to invest, it will become increasingly important for the Army to leverage the research activities of industry, government, and the other services. Army dollars should be invested principally in projects that will meet Army-specific requirements or that will be undertaken only if they are funded by the Army.

Strategic Research Objectives and S&T Objectives

The Army and DoD use the term "Strategic Research Objective" (SRO) to refer to an area of scientific research selected for emphasis because of its potential relevance to military operations, particularly for long-range, high payoff applications.

The relatively small number of Army (and DoD) SROs should not be confused with the roughly 200 Army Science and Technology Objectives (STOs). An STO states a specific, measurable technology advance funded by applied research or exploratory development dollars (budget line items 6.2 or 6.3) and is to be achieved by a specific fiscal year. By contrast, Army SROs focus and guide the S&T community on predominantly basic research (budget line item 6.1) that can be linked, although more tentatively than an STO, to Army requirements for technology development (DA, 1997c).

Strategic Research Objectives and AAN Situational Awareness

Based on the critical role of the technologies for enabling the near-perfect SA required to achieve "one-round, one-target" lethality for the AAN, as well as other operational efficiencies, including terrain awareness, operational energy management, and just-right logistics support, the committee believes that the current SROs in nanoscience, mobile wireless communications, intelligent systems, and compact power have the potential to support logistics burden reduction.

NANOSCIENCE

The historical trend of increasing computational power at decreasing cost (according to Moore's Law) has been based entirely on the integration of increasingly large numbers of metal-oxide-on-silicon semiconductor devices on a given area of silicon substrate. For this trend to continue beyond the presently perceived physical limits on decreasing the size of silicon-based transistors (e.g., approximately 50-nm gate widths for CMOS [complementary-metal oxide on silicon] devices), new device concepts and computing architectures will have to be invented. Decreasing the size of transistor devices below these physical limits is likely to involve quantum devices with scales on the order of electronic wave functions (1 to 10 nm) or devices based on Coulomb blockade effects.

DEVELOPMENT AND MODERNISATION OF INDIAN ARMY

The Indian Army is the largest branch of the armed forces of India and bears responsibility for land-based military operations. Its primary objectives include defending India from external aggression, maintaining peace and security within the country, patrolling borders and conducting counter-terrorist operations. It also conducts rescue and humanitarian operations during calamities and other disturbances. The President of India is the Commander-in-Chief of the Indian Army. With more than 1,130,000 soldiers in active service and about 1,800,000 reserve troops, the Indian Army is the world's second largest. It is a completely voluntary service and although a provision for military draft exists in the Indian constitution, it has never been imposed.

The Indian Army was formed soon after India gained independence in 1947 and retained most of the regiments of the British Indian Army. The Army is deployed in many of the world's conflict zones as a part of the United Nations Peacekeeping forces. The force is currently headed by the Chief of Army Staff, General Deepak Kapoor. Field Marshal is the highest attainable rank in the Indian Army and is conferred by the President of India, on advice of the Union Government, only in exceptional circumstances. Two officers have attained this rank so far.

Objectives

The Indian Army doctrine defines the role of the Indian Army as-"The Indian Army is the land component of the Indian Armed Forces which exist to uphold the ideals of the Constitution of India." As a major component of national power, along with the Indian Navy and the Indian Air Force, the roles of the Indian Army are as follows :

- Primary: Preserve national interests and safeguard sovereignty, territorial integrity and unity of India against any external threats by deterrence or by waging war.
- Secondary: Assist Government agencies to cope with 'proxy war' and other internal threats and provide aid to civil authority when requisitioned for the purpose."

History

Upon India gaining independence in 1947, the British Indian Army was divided into two parts to serve the newly created nations of Union of India and Islamic Republic of Pakistan.

Most units went to India; four Gurkha regiments were transferred to the British Army while the rest went to India.

FIRST KASHMIR WAR (1947)

Almost immediately after independence, tensions between India and Pakistan began to boil over, and the first of three full-scale wars between the two nations broke out over the then princely state of Kashmir. Upon the Maharaja of Kashmir's reluctance to accede to either India or Pakistan, an impatient Pakistan sponsored a 'tribal' invasion of parts of Kashmir. The men included Pakistan army regulars. Soon after, Pakistan sent in more of its troops to annex the State.

The Maharaja, Hari Singh, appealed to India, and to Lord Mountbatten, the Governor General, for help. He signed the Instrument of Accession and Kashmir acceded to India (a decision ratified by Britain). Immediately after, Indian troops were airlifted to Srinagar and repelled the invaders. This contingent included General Thimayya who distinguished himself in the operation and in years that followed, became a Chief of the Indian Army. An intense war was waged across the state and former comrades found themselves fighting each other. Both sides made some territorial gains and also suffered significant losses. An uneasy UN sponsored peace returned by the end of 1948 with Indian and Pakistani soldiers facing each other directly on the Line of Control, which has since divided Indian from Pakistani-held Kashmir. Tensions between India and Pakistan, largely over Kashmir, have never since been entirely eliminated.

PARTICIPATION IN UN PEACE-KEEPING OPERATIONS

Presently, the Indian army has dedicated one brigade of troops to the UN's standby arrangements. The large number of sustained troop commitments made by India has been praised for taking part in long and difficult operations. The Indian Army has participated in several UN peace-keeping operations, including the ones in Angola, Cambodia, Cyprus, Congo, El

Salvador, Namibia, Lebanon, Liberia, Mozambique, Rwanda, Somalia, Srilanka & Vietnam. The army had also provided a paramedical unit to facilitate the withdrawal of the sick and wounded in Korea.

Inclusion of Hyderabad (1948)

After the partition of India, the State of Hyderabad, a princely-state under the rule of a Nizam, chose to remain independent. The Nizam, refused to accede his state to the Union of India. The following stand-off between the Government of India and the Nizam ended on 12 September 1948 when India's then deputy-Prime Minister Sardar Vallabhai Patel ordered Indian troops to secure the state. Within 5 days of intense fighting, the Indian Army, backed by the Indian Air Force, successfully defeated Hyderabad State forces. The following day, the State of Hyderabad was proclaimed as a part of the Union of India. Major General Joyanto Nath Chaudhuri, who led the Operation Polo was appointed the Military Governor of Hyderabad (1948-1949) to restore law and order.

Goa, Daman and Diu Operation (1961)

Even though the British and French vacated all their colonial possessions in the Indian subcontinent, Goa, Daman and Diu remained under Portuguese control. On 12 December, 1961, after repeated Portuguese refusals to negotiate their leaving, New Delhi launched Operation Vijay and ordered a small contingent of its troops to invade the Portuguese territories and secure them. Unable to withstand the assault that lasted twenty-six hours, Goa, along with Daman and Diu (enclaves lying to the north of Maharashtra) joined India.

Sino-Indian Conflict (1962)

Since 1959, India followed a "forward policy" under which Indian border patrol units continuously pushed their posts forward deep into territory claimed by the People's Republic of China (PRC). Small-scale clashes between the Indian and Chinese forces broke out as India insisted on the disputed McMahon Line being regarded as the international border between the two countries. Despite heavy casualties, Indian troops did not retaliate the cross-border firing by Chinese troops. China's misinterpretation of India's true intentions in Tibet created more rifts between the two countries.

Buoyed by the success of its military operations in Hyderabad and Goa, India took a more aggressive stance towards its border disputes with China. In 1962, the Indian Army was ordered to move to the Thag La ridge located near the border between Bhutan and Arunachal Pradesh and about three miles (5 km) north of the disputed McMahon Line. Meanwhile, Chinese troops too had made incursions into Indian-held territory and tensions between the two reached a new high when Indian forces discovered a road constructed by China in Aksai Chin. After a series of failed negotiations, People's Liberation Army attacked Indian Army positions at the Thag La ridge. This move by China caught India by surprise and by October 12, Nehru gave orders for the Chinese to be expelled from Aksai Chin. However, poor coordination among various divisions of the Indian Army and the late decision to mobilize the Indian Air Force in vast numbers gave China a crucial tactical and strategic advantage over India. On October 20, Chinese soldiers attacked India in both the North-West and North-Eastern parts of the border and captured vast portions of Aksai Chin and Arunachal Pradesh.

As the fighting moved beyond disputed territories, China called on the Indian government to negotiate, however India remained determined to regain lost territory. With no peaceful agreement in sight, China unilaterally withdrew its forces from Arunachal Pradesh. The reasons for the withdrawal are disputed with India claiming various logistical problems for China and diplomatic support to it from the United States, while China stated that it still held territory that it had staked diplomatic claim upon. The dividing line between the Indian and Chinese forces was christened the Line of Actual Control.

The poor decisions made by India's military commanders, and, indeed, its political leadership, raised several questions. The Henderson-Brooks committee was soon set up by the

Government of India to determine the causes of the poor performance of the Indian Army. The report of committee apparently faulted much of the command of Indian Armed Forces and severely criticized the executive government for its failures on several fronts. The committee found that the major reason for the defeat was low deployment of troops on India's border with China even after hostilities began and also criticized the decision to not allow the Indian Air Force to target Chinese transport lines out of fear of Chinese aerial counter-attack on Indian civilian areas. Much of the blame was also targeted at the incompetence of then Defense Minister, Krishna Menon who resigned from his post soon after the war ended. Despite frequent calls for its release, the Henderson-Brooks report still remains classified.

Second Kashmir War (1965)

A second confrontation with Pakistan took place in 1965, largely over Kashmir. Pakistani President Ayub Khan launched *Operation Gibraltar* in August 1965 during which several Pakistani paramilitary troops infiltrated into Indian-administered Kashmir and tried to spark an anti-India rebellion. Pakistani leaders believed that India, which was still recovering from the disastrous Sino-Indian War, would be unable to deal with a military thrust and rebellion. However, the operation was a major failure since the Kashmiri people showed little support for such a rebellion and India quickly moved forces to drive the infiltrators out. Within a fortnight of the launch of the Indian counter-attack, most of the infiltrators had retreated back to Pakistan. Battered by the failure of Operation Gibraltar and expecting a major invasion by Indian forces across the border, Pakistan launched Operation Grand Slam on September 1, invading India's Chamb-Jaurian sector. In retaliation, the India's Army launched major offensive throughout its border with Pakistan, with Lahore as its prime target. Though the Indian Army's break through of the final phases of Pakistani defense was considerably delayed due to logistical issues, the conflict was largely seen as a debacle for the Pakistani Army. Initially, the Indian Army met with considerable success in the northern sector. After launching prolonged artillery barrages against Pakistan, India was able to capture three important mountain positions in Kashmir. By September 9, the Indian Army had made considerable in-roads into Pakistan. India had its largest haul of Pakistani tanks when the offensive of Pakistan's 1 Armoured Division was blunted at the Battle of Asal Uttar which took place on September 10 near Khemkaran. Six Pakistani Armoured Regiments took part in the battle against three Indian Armoured Regiments with inferior tanks. By the time the battle had ended, the 4th Indian Division had captured about 97 Pakistani tanks in either destroyed, or damaged, or in intact condition. This included 72 Patton tanks and 25 Chafees and Shermans. 32 of the 97 tanks, including 28 Pattons, were in running condition. In comparison, the Indians lost only 32 tanks at Khemkaran-Bhikkiwind. About fifteen of them were captured by the Pakistan Army, mostly Sherman tanks. Pakistan's overwhelming defeat at the decisive battle of Assal Uttar hastened the end of the conflict.

At the time of ceasefire declaration, India reported casualties of about 2,000 were killed. On the other hand, it was estimated that about 3,800 Pakistani soldiers were killed in the battle, 9,000 were wounded and about 2,000 were taken as prisoners of war. About 300 Pakistani tanks were either destroyed or captured by India and an additional 150 were permanently put out of service. India lost a total of 190 tanks during the conflict and about 100 more had to undergo repair. In all, India lost about half as many tanks as Pakistan lost during the war. Given India's advantageous position at the end of the war, the decision to return back to pre-war positions, following the Tashkent Declaration, caused an outcry among the polity in New Delhi. It was widely believed that India's decision to accept the ceasefire was due to political factors, and not military, since it was facing considerable pressure from the United States and the UN to stop hostilities.

Bangladesh Liberation War (1971)

An independence movement broke out in East Pakistan which was brutally crushed by Pakistani forces. Due to large-scale atrocities against them, thousands of Bengalis took refuge in neighboring India causing a major refugee crisis there. In early 1971, India declared its full-support for the Bengali rebels, known as Mukti Bahini, and Indian agents were extensively involved in covert operations to aid them.

On November 20, 1971, Indian Army moved the 14 Punjab Battalion and 45 Cavalry into Garibpur, a strategically important town near India's border with East Pakistan, and successfully captured it. The following day, more clashes took place between Indian and Pakistani forces. Wary of India's growing involvement in the Bengali rebellion, the Pakistan Air Force (PAF) launched a pre-emptive strike on Indian military positions near its border with East Pakistan on December 3. The aerial operation, however, failed to accomplish its stated objectives and caused India to declare a full-scale war against Pakistan the same day. By midnight, the Indian Army, accompanied by Indian Air Force, launched major military thrust into East Pakistan. The Indian Army won several battles on the eastern front including the decisive of battle of Hilli, which was the only front where the Pakistani Army was able to buildup considerable resistance. India's massive early gains was largely attributed to the speed and flexibility with which Indian armoured divisions moved across East Pakistan.

Pakistan launched a counter-attack against India on the western front. On December 4, 1971, the A company of the 23rd Battalion of India's Punjab Regiment detected and intercepted the movement of the 51st Infantry Division of the Pakistani Army near Ramgarh, Rajasthan. The battle of Longewala ensued during which the A company, though being outnumbered, thwarted the Pakistani advance until the Indian Air Force directed its fighters to engage the Pakistani tanks. By the time the battle had ended, 34 Pakistani tanks and 50 armoured vehicles were either destroyed or abandoned. About 200 Pakistani troops were killed in action during the battle while only 2 Indian soldiers lost their lives.

Pakistan suffered another major defeat on the western front during the battle of Basantar which was fought from

December 4 to 16th. By the end of the battle, about 66 Pakistani tanks were destroyed and 40 more were captured. In return, Pakistani forces were able to destroy only 11 Indian tanks. None of the numerous Pakistani offensives on the Western front materialized. By December 16, Pakistan had lost sizable territory on both eastern and western fronts.

Under the command of Lt. General J.S Aurora, the three corps of the Indian Army, who had invaded East Pakistan, entered Dhaka and forced Pakistani forces to surrender on 16 December, 1971, one day after the conclusion of the battle of Basantar. After Pakistan's Lt. General A.A.K. Niazi signed the Instrument of Surrender, India took more than 90,000 Pakistani prisoners of war, which included about 38,000 armed forces personnel and 52,000 militia and bureaucrats of West Pakistani origin. At the time of the signing of the Instrument of Surrender, 9,000 Pakistani soldiers were killed-in-action while India suffered only 2,500 battle-related deaths. In addition, Pakistan lost 200 tanks during the battle compared to India's 80.

In 1972, the Simla Agreement was signed between the two countries and tensions simmered. However, there were occasional spurts in diplomatic tensions which culminated into increased military vigilance on both sides.

Siachen Conflict (1984)

The Siachen Glacier, though a part of the Kashmir region, is not officially demarcated. As a consequence, prior to the 1980s, neither India nor Pakistan maintained permanent military presence in the region. However, Pakistan started hosting a series of mountaineering expeditions to the glacier during the 1950s. By early 1980s, the government of Pakistan was granting special expedition permits to mountaineers and United States Army maps deliberately showed Siachen as a part of Pakistan. This practice gave rise to the contemporary meaning of the term *oropolitics*.

An irked India launched Operation Meghdoot in April 1984 during which the entire Kumaon Regiment of the Indian Army was airlifted to the glacier. Pakistani forces responded quickly and clashes between the two followed. Indian Army secured the strategic Sia La and Bilafond La mountain passes and by 1985, more than 1000 sq. miles of territory, claimed by Pakistan, was under Indian control.

The Indian Army continues to control more than 2/3rd of the glacier. Pakistan made several unsuccessful attempts to regain control over Siachen. In late 1987, Pakistan mobilized about 8,000 troops and garrisoned them near Khapalu, aiming to capture Bilafond La. However, they were thrown back after engaging the Indian Army personnel guarding Bilafond. During the battle, about 23 Indian soldiers lost their lives while more than 150 Pakistani troops perished. Further unsuccessful attempts to reclaim positions were launched by Pakistan in 1990, 1995, 1996 and 1999.

India continues to maintain a strong military presence in the region despite extremely inhospitable conditions and the conflict over Siachen is regularly cited as an example of mountain warfare. The highest peak in the Siachen glacier region, Siakangri, is strategically important for India because its immense altitude and proximity to the Karakoram Highway enables the Indian forces to keep check on any Pakistani or Chinese movement in the region. Maintaining control over Siachen poses several logistical challenges for the Indian Army. Several infrastructure projects were constructed in the region, including a helipad 21,000 feet (6,400 m) above the sea level. In 2004, Indian Army was spending an estimated US$2 million a day to support its personnel stationed in the region.

MANPOWER AND GROUND FORCES

As of 2005, India has the second largest military manpower in the world - at 3,773,300 personell, next only to China. Pakistan's manpower of 1,449,000 personell, although smaller in numbers, is proportionally higher than India in terms of their population ratios. Pakistan's ground forces are equipped with American or Chinese weapons like *FIM 92 Stinger* SAMs, *BGM-71 TOW* anti-tank missiles, *T-82* tanks and other equipments. Indian ground forces are equipped with mostly home-made and Soviet technologies like IR guided *9K35 Strela-10* SAMs, 3rd Gen IR guided *Nag* anti-tank missiles, UAVs and a large inventory of tanks and support vehicles. In terms of both numbers and equipments, Indian military dominates the Pakistani ground forces.

COMPARISON OF AIR FORCES

As of 2006, Indian Air Force (IAF) has over 170,000 personnel and 3,382 aircrafts, of which 1,330 are combat aircrafts operating off 61 airbases - making it the fourth largest air force in the world. India's strike fighters consist of Russian and French aircrafts like *Mikoyan MiG-29*, *Dassault Mirage 2000*, *Sukhoi Su-30* - the last one developed under dual licensing by HAL, India's aerospace industry in Bangalore.

In addition to these, Indian Air Force also owns ground attack aircrafts, reconnaissance aircrafts, UAVs and support helicopters - a majority of them either of Soviet or French origin. Pakistan Air Force (PAF) has about 530 combat aircrafts and 65,000 active personnel, operating out of 9 airbases. Its strike fighters consist of US, Chinese and ageing French fighters like *F-16 Fighting Falcon*, *JF-17 Thunder* and *Dassault Mirage ROSE-III*. It also has transport aircrafts like *Lockheed Martin C-130* and *Airbus A310*, however unlike India, there are no UAVs or reconnaissance aircrafts in the Pakistani Air Force.

NAVAL AND SEA BASED FORCES

After the overwhelming losses in the 1971 war against India, Pakistan rapidly increased the size of its naval fleet which doubled in the 1980s after a massive 3.2 billion dollar military and economic aid by US President *Ronald Reagan*. At present, Pakistan's navy owns over 45 vessels , most of them of US or European origin which include submarines, destroyers, frigates, patrol and mine warfare boats. It operates from its sole naval port in Karachi and sometimes from naval facilities in UK, USA and France.

It had recently been involved in various humanitarian operations during the 2005 Tsunami in South East Asia. Indian

Navy on the other hand, is a three dimensional naval force consisting of missile-capable warships, an aircraft carrier, mine sweepers and a host of marine aircrafts. Most of the warships in the Indian navy are indigenously built in its own dockyards. The navy operates from its major naval bases in Visakhapatnam, Mumbai, Goa and the Andaman Islands. Indian Navy has significant capabilities of being a true blue water Navy and is experienced both in war and peacekeeping operations in the Indian Ocean.

THE NUCLEAR CLUB

India tested a nuclear bomb in 1974 using materials from Canada and technical help from Soviet Union. However, the embargo on heavy water export from Canada after the test stalled India's nuclear ambitions till 1998, when it shocked the world by conducting five nuclear detonations termed as *Shakti* tests. The highest yield was by a 48 kiloton staged fusion device, which India claimed was a thermonuclear bomb but seismic data on the tests proved otherwise. In the same year 1998, Pakistan conducted a series of six nuclear detonations in a test termed as *Chagai*. The highest yield was reported to be about 25 kiloton from a two stage boosted device. At present Pakistan's nuclear stockpile is slated to be around 30-40 warheads while India possesses 70-100 warheads. The nuclearisation of India and Pakistan became a turning point in the history of conflicts between these two countries with high tensions but no war, not very much unlike the US vs USSR Cold War.

BALLISTIC AND CRUISE MISSILE PROLIFERATION

In the nuclear delivery front, both India and Pakistan have a series of ballistic and cruise missiles in addition to ground attack aircrafts. The maximum range among India's operational ballistic missiles is 2000 km achieved by Agni-2. India's Agni ballistic missiles are indigenously developed by its own missile defence industry known as *IGMDP*. The maximum range among Pakistan's missiles is by *Hatf V Gauri* which is reported to do over 2200 kms. Pakistan's Hatf missiles are based on North Korean *No-Dong* series of IRBMs. Both Pakistan's *Hatf* and India's *Agni* ballistic missiles are nuclear capable. India has also developed a supersonic cruise missile *BrahMos* which is by far the fastest cruise missile at Mach 2.6 and maximum range of 290 km. It is reported to be nuclear capable but it is not confirmed yet. On the Pakistan side, its *Babur* cruise missile has a reported range of 700 km and a maximum speed of 880 km/h (Mach 0.7). As with India *BrahMos*, *Babur* is also reported to be nuclear capable but there is no confirmation yet.

The Final Verdict

Both Pakistan and India are almost evenly matched head to head in nuclear and missile fronts, however India has strategic and technological superiority over the conventional forces of Pakistan. Indian Navy is larger in fleet and personnel size with a more varied range of ships including an aircraft carrier while Pakistan's Navy is smaller and has no aircraft carriers. Indian's IAF is equipped with highly capable fighters like 4.5th generation *Su-30*s and 4th gen *Mirage 2000*s which are technologically superior to Pakistan PAF's *F-16*s and *Mirage III*s. Additionally Indian pilots are better trained and more capable in air combat than Pakistani forces as was demonstrated by its various wars with Pakistan or joint exercises with US and UK. In the area of conventional ground forces both the Indian as well as Pakistani Army is well equipped and highly trained to survive in extremities of topography and climate in combat conditions, like wars in the high Himalayas.

If a purely conventional war were to take place between both these countries, India would most likely overpower Pakistan owing to its superior military technology and infrastructure, larger manpower, more territorial area and a strategic advantage in its sea and air forces. It must also be noted that a war between these two countries will matter more than India's conventional superiority as both these nations are nuclear powers on an equal deadlock. India has maintained a 'no first use' nuclear policy in the lines of a similar policy by China while Pakistan does not have any such policy, considering their only hope against India is in nuclear deterrance. It would be risky for India at the present scenario to go into any aggressive war against Pakistan as the repercussions would be serious a nuclear devastation for both countries.

Unfortunately India and Pakistan had adversarial relations since sixty years. After the Mumbai carnage Pakistan is under threat of pre-emptive strikes. Fourth Indo-Pakistan war could be triggered by another terrorist attack anywhere in India. This is a dangerous scenario. India and Pakistan have fought three wars, and war drums for the fourth war are getting louder.

It is in order therefore to comprehend Indian military capabilities, and Pakistan's ability to defend itself. Defense capability is an interplay of economic and military potential. Indian economy is booming, and its GDP growth is in double digits. The global recession has impacted Indian economy, but its defense capability remains intact. Military power and capabilities are sustained by economic and industrial potential. Geography, demography, population, oil resources and reserves, industrial capability including defense production, dollar reserves, self reliance, education, quality of manpower and leadership have a bearing on military power. Seven lakh Indian troops are tied down in Jammu and Kashmir. India has over one hundred billion dollar reserves. The West, Israel and Russia are India's weapon suppliers.

Indian Army has eighteen Corps with 34 Divisions including four Rapid Action Divisions, which would spear head ground offensives. Pakistan Army has ten Corps and twenty five divisions. Indian Army has eighteen Infantry, ten Mountain, three Armoured, and two Artillery Divisions. Besides it has five Infantry, one parachute, thirteen Air Defense, and four Engineering Brigades, designated as independent formations. In addition there are two Air Defense Groups, and fourteen Army Aviation Helicopter units. This is a sizeable force, capable of launching major offensives from several fronts.

The decentralized command structure will be an advantage, as compared to Pakistan's centralized Army command organization. Pakistan Army has an active force of 620,000 well trained personnel, with 528000 reservists, and 150000 para-military troops. Pakistan armed forces are seventh largest in the world. Pakistan Army's doctrine of "Offensive Defense", evolved by General Mirza Aslam Beg was put to test in 1989 in Exercise Zarb-e Momin.

The doctrine is to launch a sizeable offensive into enemy territory, rather than wait for enemy strikes or attacks. In case of Indian land offensive Pakistan Army and Air Force will respond with land and air offensives to gain and hold enemy territory. Before embarking on further offensive, gains shall be consolidated. In 1990 the Central Corps of Reserves was created to fight in the desert sectors , where enemy land offensives are expected. These dual capable formations trained for offensive and holding actions are fully mechanized.

Pakistan Army has ten Corps including the newly formed Strategic Corps. The Army has twenty six divisions (eight less than India). Two more divisions were raised as Corps reserves for V and XXXI Corps. Pakistan Army has two armoured divisions, and ten independent armoured brigades. Presently one hundred thousand troops are stationed on the Pak Afghan border to fight terror. Special Service Group-SSG comprises two airborne Brigades i.e. six battalions.

Pakistan Army has 360 helicopters, over two thousand heavy guns, and 3000 APC's. Its main anti-tank weapons are Tow, Tow Mk II, Bakter Shiken and FGM 148 ATGM. The Army Air Defence Command has S.A- 7 Grail, General Dynamics FIM-92 Stinger, GD FIM Red Eye, and ANZA Mk-I, Mk-II, Mk-III and HQ 2 B surface ti air missiles. Radar controlled Oerlikon is the standard Ack Ack weapon system.

The ballistic missile inventory of the Army is substantial. It comprises Ghauri III and Shaheen III IRB'S; medium range Ghauri I and II and Shaheen II, and short range Hatf I- B, Abdali, Ghaznavi, Shaheen I and M -11 missiles. All the ballistic missiles can carry nuclear war heads. Nuclear and conventional weapon capable Babur Cruise missile is the new addition to Pakistan's strategic weapon inventory. Number of ballistic missiles and war heads are almost the same as India has. So there is a parity in nuclear weapons, which is a deterrent.

Indian armor is of Russian origin. Out of 2295 Indian Army's Main Battle tanks, 2235 are of Russian origin. The main battle tanks are; 310 T-90-S Bishsma's (300 are on order), 1925 T-72M Ajeya's.. The T-90 and the T-72 have 125 mm smooth barrel guns. T-72 though old is the backbone of Indian Armor Corp's. 268 Ajeya's have been upgraded with Israeli Elbit thermal imaging systems. 1000 T-72 MBT's are awaiting up-gradation.

There have been several instances of T-72's gun barrel bursting. 124 Indian made Arjun (heavy 56 ton) MBT are on order. Sixty Arjun's are in operational service. Arjun's engine overheating problem has not been solved. Arjun has a 120 mm gun, but is unfit or desert operations. Pakistan Army is equally strong in armor, capable of giving a fitting response to any Indian military adventure.

Main Battle tanks Al-Khalid and Al-Zarrar are the backbone of Pakistan's armor Corp's. Both are Pakistan made. Pakistan's tank armory comprises :five hundred Al-Khalid MBT's; 320 Al-Zarrar type 85 II MBT's, 500 Al-Zarrar MBT's; 450 79II AP (Chinese-type 81 upgrade, and 570 T-80 UD MBT of Ukranian make. In addition Pakistan has 880 Type 59, which were procured from China in 1970.This makes a total of three thousand six hundred and twenty tanks.

All Pakistani MBT's except T-59's have 125 mm smooth barrel guns. Indian armor offensives in Kashmir, Punjab, and Sind would be effectively challenged by Pakistani armor and mechanized formations, depending on PAF's ability to keep the skies over the battle areas clear of Indian Air Force. India's modern air defense system has Israeli Arrow anti-missile missiles, and 90,000 surface to air missiles-SAM's. India has one hundred nuclear armed ballistic missiles (Agni-1 and Agni II), and Brahmos the new supersonic cruise missile. Indian Army is well trained, equipped and highly professional, and so is Pakistan Army. Air power is likely to play a key, if not a decisive role in any future major or minor India-Pakistan armed conflict. The aim of Indian pre-emptive strikes will be maximum destruction by surprise air attacks, combined with shock commando action. A possibe scenario is; intensive bombing of the target to be followed by attacks by armed helicopters and ground assault by heliborne Commandoes. An overview of Indian Air Force and Pakistan Air Force will help comprehension of IAF's offensive capabilities, and defensive capabilities of Pakistan Air Force.

Indian Air Force has 3000 aircraft including training, transport, helicopters and 800-1000 combat air craft, which operate from sixty air bases, including Farkhor airbase in Tajikistan.. Six hundred IAF's strike and air defense fighters are expected to be operational. Pakistan Air Force has 630 aircraft, which include 530 combat aircraft, with 400 operational at any time. In 1996 India signed an agreement with Russia for the purchase of 90 Su 30 Mk-1 multi-role fighter-bombers. In 2004 a multi-billion licence was signed for building additional 140. 240 Su30-Mk-1's were ordered, 120 are already in service. With a maximum speed of Mach 2.3 and range of 8000 Km with refueling and ability to carry tons of conventional munitions and nuclear weapons, it is a lethal and menacing weapon system for the strike and interception role.

Other IAF's advanced strike and combat aircraft are: 51 Mirage-2000 (of Kargil fame), 60 Mig-29's (for air defense), 250 old Mig-21's (110 have been refurbished with Israeli help), 47 Jaguars and 70 Mig-27's for ground attack. 220 LCA Teja's under manufacture at HAL Bangalore will start entering service in 2010... IAF's fighter pilots are well trained and have out shone American pilots during joint exercises.

Pakistan Air Force has 200 rebuilt Mirage- 3's (for night air defense) and Mirage-5's for the strike role. They can carry nuclear weapons. They have been upgraded with new weapon systems, radars, and avionics. Additionally the PAF has 42 F-16's, 150 F-7's including 55 latest F-7 PG's. Manufacture of 150 JF 17 Thunder fighters (jointly designed) is underway at Pakistan Aeronautical Complex Kamra. The JF -17 Thunder is a 4th generation fly by wire multi-role fighter aircraft. Eight are already in PAF service. An order has been placed with China for the purchase of 36 JF-10, a Mach 2.3 -5th generation multi-role fighter, comparable in performance to the Su-30 Mk-1 with the Indian Air Force. PAF is on Red Alert, and is maintaining full vigil to intercept and destroy IAF intruders.

During the recent air space violation, the IAF intruders were in the sights of PAF's F-16's, but were allowed to escape unscathed to avoid a major diplomatic crisis. PAF pilots and technicians are well trained, high professionals, who will be able to prove their mettle in the future battle with India. A comparison of Indian Navy and Pakistan Navy reveals that Pakistan Navy could inflict substantial damage to the Indian Navy. Indian Navy has 16 submarines; Pakistan Navy has ten, some are brand new. Indian Navy has 27 war ships, Pakistan Navy has ten. Indian Aircraft Carrier Veerat, will be a menace, and must be sunk by submarine or air attacks, if it attempts to block Pakistan's sea lanes or ports. It is hoped that better sense prevails and India desists from invading and attacking Pakistan. If it does, the consequences will be horrible for both the countries.

Manpower and Ground Forces

India has the second largest manpower in its military globally - at 3,773,300 personell (2005), next only to China. Pakistan has a much smaller manpower of 1,449,000 personell which is proportionally higher than India in terms of their population ratios. Pakistan's ground forces are equipped with American or Chinese weapons like FIM 92 Stinger SAMs, BGM-71 TOW anti-tank missiles, T-82 tanks and other equipments. Indian ground forces are equipped mostly by home-made or Soviet technologies like IR guided 9K35 Strela-10 SAMs, 3rd Gen IR guided Nag anti-tank missiles, UAVs and a large inventory of tanks and support vehicles. In terms of numbers and equipments, both Indian and Pakistani ground forces are on an closely equal footing.

Comparison of Air Forces

As of 2006, Indian Air Force (IAF) has over 170,000

personnel and 3,382 aircrafts of which 1,330 are combat aircrafts operating off 61 airbases - making it the fourth largest air force in the world. India's strike fighters consist of Russian and French aircrafts like Mikoyan MiG-29, Dassault Mirage 2000, Sukhoi Su-30 - the last one developed under dual licensing by HAL, India's aerospace industry in Bangalore.

In addition to these, India's air force owns ground attack aircrafts, reconnaissance aircrafts, UAVs and support helicopters - a majority of them either of Soviet or French origin. Pakistan Air Force (PAF) has about 530 combat aircrafts and over 65,000 active personnel, operating out of 9 airbases. Its strike fighters consist of US, Chinese and French fighters like F-16 Fighting Falcon, JF-17 Thunder and Dassault Mirage ROSE-III. It also has transport aircrafts like Lockheed Martin C-130 and Airbus A310, however there are no UAVs or reconnaissance aircrafts in the Pakistani Air Force.

Naval and Sea Based Forces

After the overwhelming losses in the 1971 war against India, Pakistan rapidly increased the size of its naval fleet which doubled in the 1980s after a massive 3.2 billion dollar military and economic aid by US President Ronald Reagan. At present, Pakistan's navy owns over 45 vessels , most of them of US or European origin which include submarines, destroyers, frigates, patrol and mine warfare boats. It operates from its sole naval port in Karachi and naval facilities in UK, USA and France.

It had recently been involved in various humanitarian operations during the 2005 Tsunami in South East Asia. Indian Navy on the other hand, is a three dimensional naval force consisting of missile-capable warships, an aircraft carrier, mine sweepers and a host of marine aircrafts; most of its warships indigenously built in its own dockyards. The navy operates from its major naval bases in Visakhapatnam, Mumbai, Goa and the Andaman Islands. Indian Navy has significant capabilities of being a true blue water Navy and is experienced both in war and peacekeeping operations in the Indian Ocean.

The Nuclear Club

India tested a nuclear bomb in 1974 using materials from Canada and technical help from Soviet Union. However the embargo in heavy water export from Canada after the test stalled India's nuclear ambitions till 1998, when it shocked the world by conducting five nuclear detonations termed as Shakti tests.

The highest yield was by a 48 kiloton staged fusion device, which India claimed was a thermonuclear bomb but seismic data on the tests proved otherwise. In the same year 1998, Pakistan conducted a series of six nuclear detonations in a test termed as Chagai.

The highest yield was reported to be about 25 kiloton from a two stage boosted device. At present Pakistan's nuclear stockpile is slated to be around 30-40 warheads while India possesses 70-100 warheads. The nuclearisation of India and Pakistan became a turning point in the history of conflicts between these two countries with high tensions but no war, not very much unlike the US vs USSR Cold War.

Ballistic and Cruise Missile Proliferation

In the nuclear delivery front, both India and Pakistan have a series of ballistic and cruise missiles in addition to ground attack aircrafts. The maximum range among India's operational ballistic missiles is 2000 km achieved by Agni-2. India's Agni ballistic missiles are indigenously developed by its own missile defence industry known as IGMDP.

The maximum range among Pakistan's missiles is by Hatf V Gauri which is reported to do over 2200 kms. Pakistan's Hatf missiles are based on North Korean No-Dong series of IRBMs. Both Pakistan's Hatf and India's Agni ballistic missiles are nuclear capable. India has also developed a supersonic cruise missile BrahMos which is by far the fastest cruise missile at Mach 2.6 and maximum range of 290 km. It is reported to be nuclear capable but it is not confirmed yet. On the Pakistan side, its Babur cruise missile has a reported range of 700 km and a maximum speed of 880 km/h (Mach 0.7). As with India

BrahMos, Babur is also reported to be nuclear capable but there is no confirmation yet.

The Final Verdict

Both Pakistan and India are almost evenly matched head to head in nuclear and missile fronts, however India has strategic and technological superiority over the conventional forces of Pakistan. Indian Navy is larger in fleet and personnel size with a more varied range of ships including an aircraft carrier while Pakistan's Navy is smaller and has no aircraft carriers. Indian's IAF is equipped with highly capable fighters like 4.5th generation Su-30s and 4th gen Mirage 2000s which are technologically superior to Pakistan PAF's F-16s and Mirage IIIs. Additionally Indian pilots are better trained and more capable in air combat than Pakistani forces as was demonstrated by its various wars with Pakistan or joint exercises with US and UK. In the area of conventional ground forces both the Indian as well as Pakistani Army is well equipped and highly trained to survive in extremities of topography and climate in combat conditions, like wars in the high Himalayas.

If a purely conventional war were to take place between both these countries, India would most likely overpower Pakistan owing to its superior military technology and infrastructure, larger manpower, more territorial area and a strategic advantage in its sea and air forces. It must also be noted that a war between these two countries will matter more than India's conventional superiority as both these nations are nuclear powers on an equal deadlock. India has maintained a 'no first use' nuclear policy on the lines of a similar policy by China while Pakistan does not have any such policy, considering their only hope against India is in nuclear deterrence. It would be risky for India at the present scenario to go into any aggressive war against Pakistan as the repercussions would be serious a nuclear devastation for both countries.

India's numerical and technical superiority in a conventional war is beyond question - therefore Pakistan's low nuclear threshold and maintenance of the first-use option.

However, in a surgical kind of strike being talked about in Indian and Pakistani circles, over Muridke or Muzaffarabad , cruise missiles are likely to be used. The Pakistani and Indian capability is evenly matched in these except for India's supersonic cruise missile with a speed of Mach 2.6 which is an obvious advantage in this kind of a strike, but it only has a range of 290 kms - enough to reach Muridke if launched from East Punjab but not much more. Pakistan's answer is the Babur cruise missile with a range of 700 km and a speed of Mach 0.7 - sub-sonic but pretty fast.

UAV's was the other Indian advantage which has recently been matched by Pakistan. With the evenly matched air, missile and nuclear capability, a surgical strike doesn't seem to be the best option. If India is to win, it will have to be a full-scale conventional war with both sides avoiding breaching the other's nuclear threshold.

3

Defence Force Preparedness

BACKGROUND

Under the Defence capability architecture, the force structure that is in place, when combined with its preparedness to undertake operations, delivers military capability. This allows for the separation of preparedness management (which relates to the current force-in-being) from the longer term investment processes associated with new capital equipment.

Preparedness is conceptually broken down into the components of 'readiness' and 'sustainability'. This division is intended to recognise the separate nature of the management processes underlying the achievement of military readiness and the many factors influencing the length of time for which a military force may sustain operations on a particular mission.

Preparedness of the Australian Defence Force (ADF) is managed as an integral part of the processes by which Defence plans, resources, evaluates and reports its performance. The Preparedness Management System (PMS) has been developed to manage preparedness and is intended to be a performance enhancement process. Preparedness outcomes are linked with a range of other outcomes sought by Defence, such as military capability development and contributing to the Government's international policy commitments. The management of preparedness involves the allocation of resources to achieve strategic policy objectives, in order to prepare for possible contingencies. It involves four phases: development, implementation, reporting, and review. The nature of preparedness means that many areas within Defence perform activities that are highly relevant to preparedness and, indeed, 'enable' it. The 2003–04 Defence Budget provides four capability outcomes (with a total budgeted price of $13 781 million) and two functional outcomes (with a total budgeted price of $616 million). All six are directed towards the defence of Australia and its interests.

The objective of the audit was to provide assurance to Parliament concerning the adequacy of Defence preparedness management systems and to identify possible areas for improvement. The audit focused on the systems and processes that Defence uses to manage preparedness. We did not review the preparedness levels of specific capabilities, nor did we cover capital acquisition processes. The audit included coverage of:

- preparedness system architecture;
- control and direction of preparedness;
- coordination among contributors to preparedness; and
- performance management of preparedness.

MANAGEMENT OF DEFENCE FORCE PREPAREDNESS

The ANAO found that the PMS provides a sound framework for preparedness planning down to the unit level. A number of linkages exist between Government strategic guidance, Defence operational planning and Service outputs. However, improvements could be made to the design of the system so as to strengthen and make more effective these linkages, which should result in better outcomes.

The PMS operates alongside operational planning arrangements which maintain more frequent review points for immediate planning of the use of ADF capability than the annual cycle of activities in the PMS. This means that, at operational levels, there are effectively two management systems working in tandem. While each system serves different purposes, there would be benefits to Defence in creating functional linkages between the two. This would enable the military task identification process in the PMS to be informed by the more frequent strategic assessments used in the immediate planning context, compared to using the current annual cycle in the PMS.

Defence is seeking to develop a common basis for military task definition that could be used across the Services. As a result, it has developed the Australian Joint Essential Task (ASJET) list. The ASJET list could be used to support consistent training and proficiency development, and to enhance consistency of approach across ADF units, a critical element in the conduct of joint operations. It could also contribute substantially to the interoperability of ADF units with those of other countries. This would enhance the PMS, as such cross-Service training and international interoperability aspects are not specifically developed in the present definitions of operational preparedness objectives.

At unit level, key preparedness management concepts and definitions are frequently understood in different ways. Also, at lower levels of capability management, there was found to be some latitude taken in determining actual numbers of force elements to be held at particular settings of Readiness Notice. Though individually minor, these differences, when aggregated, could lead to distortions in the reporting of overall preparedness.

The Directed Level of Capability (DLOC) assumes central importance as a standard for resourcing of preparedness in a financially constrained environment. It will be important to retain the concept of a Minimum Level of Capability (MLOC) so as to maintain a reality check on how difficult it may be to transition a force element from its resourced level of capability (DLOC) to the state of operational usefulness to perform particular tasks. Concerns should be raised where the DLOC status falls below the MLOC standard.

Management of the sustainment dimension of preparedness is subject to limited policy guidance. The arrangements for assessing sustainment requirements for core war-fighting needs, including reserve stockholding policies, are characterised by informal processes and complex planning structures. The deficiency reporting system is especially weak in sustainment aspects for the band of Military Response Options (MRO) with longer warning times (that is, greater than 365 days). Defence recognises the need to develop the PMS framework to incorporate a disciplined and coordinated assessment procedure for sustainment issues in the logistic and materiel areas.

CONTROL AND DIRECTION OF PREPAREDNESS

Defence governance systems and organisational structures generally facilitate preparedness planning and management. The Chief of the Defence Force Preparedness Directive (CPD), in combination with the Australian Theatre Operational Preparedness Requirement (ASTOPR) and the system of annually renegotiated Organisational Performance Agreements (OPA), create a coherent governance framework resourced and controlled through the Defence Management and Finance Plan (DMFP). The ANAO found that this framework provides a strong basis for policies, guidelines, directives and financial management arrangements to be devised to satisfy ADF preparedness requirements.

The information base on which capability controls and reporting takes place is a composite of judgments and assessments made at various levels in the Services, using different methodologies, different sources and deriving from variations in understandings about the meanings of some concepts in the PMS. The ANAO found that quantitative information is generally lacking. Information technology systems are not major suppliers of reporting data used for PMS purposes.

Although individual Services are giving attention to improving and standardizing reporting from their capability outputs, no consistent means are employed to workshop 'best practice' ways of calibrating and reporting preparedness across the Force Element Groups (FEG) and capability output managers, which are the source of much of the data. To enhance the quality of preparedness data and ensure greater consistency of information proceeding to higher levels, Defence should introduce greater standardisation of preparedness measures and systems applied across the ADF and also promulgate common terminology for use in preparing inputs to the PMS.

COORDINATION AMONG CONTRIBUTORS TO PREPAREDNESS

The Defence business model depends on the interlocking networks of customer supplier and service level arrangements between 'enabling groups' (the Defence Materiel Organisation (DMO) and the Corporate Services and Infrastructure Group (CSIG)) and the capability outcome groups. These present an incomplete picture of the underlying complexity of actual transactions. No mechanisms exist to map the range of interdependencies that have developed. The PMS only partly reflects them. Defence would benefit from mapping these interdependencies and identifying the implications for the architecture on the Defence preparedness arrangements.

The structures and supply arrangements in place between the ADF and enabling organisations that provide logistics and support services to meet preparedness requirements are not yet fully developed. The mechanisms for facilitating the contributions of the enabling groups to chosen levels of military preparedness need to be further developed if they are to play an effective role in the PMS and, in particular, in its control and risk management capabilities.

The mix and different types of alignment in service provision being applied by DMO and CSIG to the needs of the capability outcome groups are often not congruent with the PMS. Coordination arrangements between DMO and CSIG and the outcome groups should be reviewed to take account of the different forms of supply delivered, and to determine whether their services are properly coordinated internally in each enabling group as well as being accessible to the outcome groups.

The translation of the capability outcome groups' preparedness management needs into concepts and measurement systems, that correspond to the operations of the materiel and supply 'worlds' in which DMO and CSIG must operate, is ineffective in some areas, or at least incomplete. On the other hand, some areas have done substantial work on these matters that could be studied for its relevance to other support areas. Without progress in achieving a better translation, the 'enablement' of preparedness will be not be fully effective. As a result, inaccurate management information may produce distortions in the preparedness picture.

Governance systems in place across Defence in the materiel and logistic fields leave gaps which do not allow adequate performance controls. No accountable point of responsibility beneath the head of the DMO has overall control of logistic support for 'capability', as against logistic support for 'operations'. The coordinating entities located, or based, in DMO have consultative functions only. The contribution of DMO to whole-of-Defence preparedness management processes could be enhanced through better governance arrangements. The Defence Committee (DC) does not possess mechanisms to enable it to take a holistic view of the related strategic, tactical and operational 'enablement' services that are directly relevant to preparedness, especially in regard to longer lead time preparedness planning.

DMO, in consultation with Headquarters Australian Theatre, the Service Headquarters and Policy Guidance and Analysis Division, needs to provide comprehensive and integrated materiel preparedness assessments to the capability managers.

Performance Management of Preparedness

Preparedness performance management is centred in each of the Services, but is aligned with Defence-wide strategic planning and management arrangements. A wide range of information-collection processes and systems is in use across the ADF, with some measurement systems being more robust than others. A central feature is the On-Occurrence Preparedness Report (OOPR) system controlled by Commander Australian Theatre (COMAST). This deficiency reporting system enables a reasonable measure of quality control. As well, enhancements to it are planned. The OOPR system has imparted an element of coherence and consistency to performance management in the PMS. It allows timely decision-making in those areas of preparedness relating to shorter warning time contingencies, though less so for contingencies in the post-365 day period.

The ANAO found that the PMS enables Defence to instigate corrective action for deficiencies in the range of shorter warning time contingency tasks, within the limitations of the current capability costing systems. It also permits Defence to manage the risks entailed in the gap between funded levels of capability and the levels that would be considered appropriate in an unconstrained environment. In this way, senior Defence management are broadly able to assure themselves that preparedness types and levels required by current Government guidance are delivered. However, the management process does not provide Defence with the ability to consider alternative preparedness levels on the basis of detailed relative costs. As a decision support tool, the PMS relies on the development of whole-of-Defence financial systems, in particular the implementation of full capability costing mechanisms. Until such systems are available, the PMS will not fulfil its potential.

The ANAO considers that the reporting framework could be developed by introducing more focussed consideration of preparedness for contingencies in the post 365 day warning time band at the whole-of-ADF level. The effectiveness of the PMS should be made subject to formal review processes by the DC. This could be done in the context of the role and relevance of the PMS as tested in other Defence portfolio review activity. These other activities may throw light on the operation of the PMS.

In external reporting to Parliament, the different capability outcome groups present preparedness information in varying ways. With the exception of Navy, external reporting comprises primarily qualitative information, and the quantitative information related specifically to the PMS uses input metrics such as flying hours and aircraft numbers. This has meant that the development of PMS mechanisms in Defence over the last two years has not been well reflected in public reporting of capability on an ADF-wide basis. Navy's introduction of new indicators in the 2003–04 Portfolio Budget Statements for Defence was based on PMS metrics, reflecting some of the latter's dynamic features. This suggests that scope exists to improve external reporting, while not compromising national security information requirements.

Overall Audit Conclusion

The Defence PMS supports risk management decisions on the preparedness levels of ADF capabilities. The ANAO found that the PMS is essentially a sound framework with a cascade of linkages between Government strategic guidance and the Service outputs. This enables Defence management to generate preparedness types and levels required by current Government guidance. Improvements could be made to the design of the system so as to strengthen the linkages with strategic review processes. The PMS has a heavy reliance on subjective and professional military judgements in preparedness management processes, and on methodologies that vary between outputs. Scope exists for Defence to enhance the quality of preparedness measures and supporting systems for greater effectiveness and accountability for performance.

A significant weakness in the PMS is the relatively low level of development of the sustainment dimension of preparedness: in particular, the level of policy guidance, the ability to assess sustainment requirements and sustainment deficiency reporting. Strains have also been placed on the PMS as a result of the recent high operational requirement, in particular in regard to its flexibility to respond to system stresses associated with expeditionary deployments, and the changing strategic environment.

The relationships between capability outcomes and enabling inputs, while subject to continuing scrutiny and development, have not reached the point where they fully support preparedness management requirements. Governance issues in regard to the management of logistics and materiel that need to be better addressed impede the full development of the PMS. Management of these areas is characterised by complex networks of liaison, information and supply chain management, without adequate visibility at all relevant points of accountability. In particular, the DMO performance reporting processes in regard to its preparedness contribution need to be developed, so as to enable the DC to play a more comprehensive role in regard to sustainment matters.

Although there are security sensitivities that need to be recognised in the public exposure of any preparedness deficiencies, scope exists for enhanced and more consistent public performance reporting.

The openness of the PMS to continuing reform and development is crucial if the above issues are to be appropriately addressed by Defence. The role and relevance of the PMS need to be assessed on a regular basis.

Response to the Report

The ANAO made seven recommendations on the management, governance, coordination and reporting of Defence Force preparedness. Defence provided the following overview paragraph. Defence agrees with all of the seven recommendations and is pleased to see the acknowledgment on page 12 paragraph six stating: The ANAO found that the PMS provides a sound framework for preparedness planning down to the unit level. A number of linkages exist between Government strategic guidance, Defence operational planning and Service outputs. However, improvements could be made to the design of the system so as to strengthen and make more effective these linkages, which should result in better outcomes.

DEFENCE PREPAREDNESS MANAGEMENT FRAMEWORK

The Defence PMS is positioned within an analytical framework connecting strategic-level guidance at the top, provided by the Government, to operational level activity across the ADF. Senior Defence leaders characterise the development of the PMS as a dynamic system: as a work-in-progress project, with amendments being made to it on an ongoing basis in both its broad design and to specific elements of the system.

It is unrealistic, given apparent resource constraints, for a defence force to be equally prepared for every contingency. In addition, some tasks will have a higher priority than others. Also, a force element cannot be continuously maintained at its highest level of capability (for example, skills that have been built up decay, and equipment deterioration requires it to be taken out of service for maintenance). Financial costs of preparedness increase rapidly at higher preparedness levels. In an environment of constrained public spending, levels of preparedness will be chosen in accordance with resources the Government makes available. By the same token, maintaining preparedness at lower levels than those needed could mean that the ADF may be adversely placed to respond appropriately to tasking contingencies that the Government needs it to perform. Defence preparedness is, therefore, one of the main risk management programs in Government administration.

Over time, Defence has employed various means of applying resources to produce military capability. In the last decade, command instruments such as 'capability directives' from the single Service Chiefs or joint force commanders have been used to set preparedness levels of forces under their control. The need for a consistent approach to preparedness management across the ADF has been identified in Defence as a core deliverable, requiring a separate focus in planning, ongoing management and reporting at all levels of the Defence organisation. As a consequence, Defence has progressively developed the PMS and incorporated it into formal statements of Defence 'doctrine'.

The PMS attaches preparedness to the condition of specified forces, especially their proficiency and equipment. It thus focuses down to unit level and individual weapon platforms. Preparedness levels are determined with reference to specific mission, or war fighting, scenarios and the time at which they might be needed for such tasking. Finally, the preparedness of a force is driven by a sound appreciation of the period for which a force may need to be engaged and therefore sustained. As sustainment involves a wide range of inputs, including even industrial capability outside the area of direct Defence responsibilities, the management issues involved are highly complex.

The PMS has come to form a major part of the wider spectrum of management of Defence portfolio affairs. However, military preparedness does not itself comprise an outcome or output. Notwithstanding that, its targets and indicators form an important element in the operations of the Defence business model, which creates the framework for Defence's resource allocation and monitoring systems. It also contributes to the forming of the rationale of the structure connecting the various elements of the business model in their respective contributions to the achievement of the Defence mission.

The ADF is comprised of a series of specific capabilities, all drawing on range of human, physical and technological assets. The force elements that directly deliver these capabilities are spread across the Services and the joint operational command capabilities centred on the Chief of the Defence Force (CDF) and COMAST.

The different elements of capability—force elements and support elements —have to interact to produce military force that can be put to use. The various levels at which the force elements are readied and resourced to do so, and targets for them to be sustained to do so, are identified by the PMS. The PMS is designed to balance military planning requirements and resource flows to all the elements of Defence capability delivery (including the support groups), in such a way that the Government has as wide a range of options for the use of the Defence Force as possible, within the financial allocations made to Defence. A properly operating military preparedness system will thus enable the resourcing of capability to be logically and effectively related to planned levels of military activity.

The PMS provides for Defence resourcing of capability of the force-in-being to take place at two levels. The first level is a 'steady-state', operating on an annual cycle relating to the Budget timetable, where actual levels of activity—mainly in the form of exercises in the Program of Major Services Activities—match planned levels. This steady-state level would enable tasks to be changed and re-prioritised in response to developments in the strategic environment, but to a level falling short of a requirement for budget supplementation. The second level is the one where, as a result of specific tasking by Government, preparedness is actually 'used' beyond that provided for at the beginning of the budget cycle, and added resources are needed to support the performance of this tasking over and beyond the funding required to maintain the preparedness steady-state.

The Defence PMS is accordingly designed to be a whole-of-Defence model, with two equally important and interdependent aims:

- allowing the portfolio to generate measurable preparedness benchmarks and indicators for ADF force elements; and
- creating a matrix applicable to all Defence groups to enable control of the resources to be directed to the different capability outcomes and outputs produced by the ADF.
- A resourcing matrix for preparedness.

The PMS is intended to make visible the financial constraints imposed on preferred preparedness levels. These constraints arise out of the actual resourcing levels made available in the annual budgetary cycle. The annual sequencing of the steps needed to achieve this visibility, based on the actual Budget estimates, is being implemented and refined.

Through this cycle, the PMS closely links preparedness levels across all ADF units and supporting groups with Defence portfolio planning, and in particular with the DMFP. The linkage of the PMS to the matrix arrangements applicable to all Defence groups to control the resources to be directed to the different capability outcomes and outputs produced by the ADF, was a specific intended deliverable for the introduction of the system. The linkage expressly acknowledges the fact that preparedness levels require financial resources and that an appropriate management model will facilitate the ongoing balancing of expenditure on current and future capability, on a risk-managed basis.

Effectively, the PMS incorporates a major structural tension as a deliberate design feature of the system. A military capability assessment process presents an annual statement of an aspiration for capability: that is, the ASTOPR. This aspiration represents what military commanders would wish to see being provided to meet contingencies foreseen in strategic guidance, if resources were 'unconstrained'. Ongoing strategic monitoring by the Theatre Commanders Group and the Chiefs of Service Committee (COSC) keep the ASTOPR under regular review.

Side by side with this aspirational document, a system of financial allocations is linked to Directed Levels of Capability for each of the responsible outcome executives. These are incorporated as part of the annual OPAs, and present the 'real' capabilities—the ones that are authorised and to be paid for. The gap between the 'aspiration' and the 'real' must be risk-managed by the outcome managers, both within their groups' management processes and with corporate oversight of the DC.

Audit Approach

The ANAO conducted a performance audit preliminary study on the management of ADF preparedness in 1996. At that time, Defence was undertaking a range of initiatives to develop its preparedness planning methodology. Given the significant impact the developments were likely to have on preparedness management, the ANAO decided not to proceed with a full performance audit at that time. Audit Report No.17 1995–96, Management of Australian Defence Force Preparedness, was tabled in the Parliament on 2 April 1996. More recently, the ANAO conducted a performance audit on Navy Operational Readiness. Audit Report No.39 2002–03, Navy Operational Readiness, was tabled in the Parliament on 17 April 2003.

The objective of the current audit was to provide assurance to Parliament concerning the adequacy of Defence preparedness management systems and to identify possible areas for improvement. The audit focused on the systems and processes that Defence uses to manage preparedness but did not review the preparedness levels of specific capabilities. It included coverage of:

- the preparedness system architecture;
- the control and direction of preparedness;
- coordination among contributors to preparedness; and
- performance management of preparedness.

Audit fieldwork was conducted substantively in the period from July to October 2003. The audit covered a wide range of activities within Defence and involved extensive discussions and review of documents. Matters were discussed with relevant areas of Defence throughout the audit and the audit findings were responded to in a positive manner. The findings from the audit was provided to Defence in November 2003. An exit interview was held on 11 December 2003.

A consultant, Mr Christopher Conybeare AO, was engaged to provide expert advice to the audit team on Defence organisational constructs, corporate governance arrangements and performance management systems. The audit was conducted in conformance with ANAO auditing standards and cost $435 000.

MANAGEMENT OF DEFENCE FORCE PREPAREDNESS

This chapter considers the major elements of Defence preparedness management, as well as the readiness and sustainability planning frameworks.

Capability Measures

Defence defines specific 'levels' of capability that comprise measures of the force development processes or stages reached in 'work-up' cycles of force elements. These levels are a mix of benchmarks of capability that are in the nature of standards (that is, prescriptive or 'pass-mark-like' measures); and levels that reflect objective or normative measures of capability (that is, measures that are determined by empirical considerations or which are not primarily for evaluative purposes).

These measures of capability play a central role in the PMS. As the means of calibrating capability, they enable visibility of the readiness levels of the ADF's units, as assessed for the different purposes being served by the PMS, and for capability management in operating levels of the Services. They form the basis of the 'traffic light' system for documenting performance.

The capability measures are:

- standards measures: Directed Level of Capability; and Operational Level of Capability (OLOC); and
- objective measure: Minimum Level of Capability.

Minimum Level of Capability

MLOC is a level of capability that a force element is objectively required to have, in order for it to be able to progress to OLOC within the Readiness Notice period. The concept was considered for phasing out at the Management of Defence Force Preparedness time of introduction of the PMS in 2001, with DLOC replacing it. It is not prominent in current PMS doctrine. The DLOC documentation does not provide for any regular statement of MLOC status.

The MLOC concept varies widely in its perceived importance to capability managers across the ADF. For some, it is not regarded as important, and is not used. However, the MLOC concept is especially important to managers of some capability areas, to help ensure that their force elements do not degrade below a level that would permit them to achieve their OLOC within readiness notice and warning times. Having an MLOC in place that is clearly visible should therefore assist in maintaining directed levels of capability and clearly signal when difficulties may be emerging.

In some Operational Preparedness Objectives (OPO), under the present year's settings, DLOC requirements may be at a lower level for some Force Elements than the relevant MLOC. This further underlines the importance of the MLOC concept as it would clearly signal areas of concern for the actual preparedness condition of forces, especially in regard to proficiencies and/or equipment condition where significant time might be required for work-up. This would impede the capability of the ADF to be able to respond to Government directions that may not have been fully anticipated in the structure and/or elements of OPOs as defined, and associated warning times and Readiness Notice.

MLOC can therefore be used by the Services to assess the long-term health of their capabilities. Where DLOC standards are set below MLOC for any OPO, this should be marked for the attention of senior Defence management and command.

ELEMENTS OF THE PREPAREDNESS ARCHITECTURE

In the specific form in which it has been developed, the preparedness construct draws on a number of long-standing force planning concepts such as strategic warning time. It combines these in a management framework having a number of functional characteristics and inter-relationships.

Examination of PMS reports to the Defence Executive indicates that this management framework captures the three main dimensions of preparedness that can be particularised, assessed against standards, and documented:

- task—preparedness to do what;
- time—preparedness for action at some point into the future and required on task for a particular period of time; and
- unit—preparedness of what force element(s) to undertake the task.

The PMS does not presently identify further variables, such as geographic or climatic environment, for possible ADF deployments as standard dimensions of the preparedness construct (that is, preparedness to engage forces in what environment). Such variables are regarded as being included in the three specified parameters. The ANAO was informed of a number of instances where force elements have faced specific difficulties that were not envisaged and for which they were unprepared during deployments in recent years. These included harsh conditions of operation (such as sand storms), with resultant adverse impacts on mechanical endurance of equipment and long turn-around times for maintenance.

In examining overseas examples of preparedness management, the ANAO learned that some other countries' systems take such parameters explicitly into account. Given the expeditionary deployment of ADF forces in recent years and the possible role of the ADF in remote locations in wider coalition operations, it would seem desirable for Defence to consider whether the PMS should capture environmental aspects in its preparedness concept. This might be of particular value in increasing visibility of all relevant cost supplementation requirements (that is, costs arising beyond the 'steady state' of preparedness set forth in the PMS) resulting from deployments in particular environments. Such a variable would take into account the differences in the preparedness arrangements that would be relevant to planning for the deployed force, arising out of particularities in the theatre environment.

Task Preparedness

The definition of the nature of the military task for which forces need to be prepared is the starting point for preparedness planning in the PMS. The nature of the task determines a wide range of military planning matters such as what combination of force elements is required to perform the task, what proficiencies are needed in the skill sets in which a designated force element is trained, and what specialised equipment and stocks (for example, ammunition), are required. A Peacetime National Task (such as maritime support) requires much less sophisticated and more narrowly based military capability than anti-submarine warfare; as well, amphibious operations are joint force activities requiring a mix of units from more than one Service.

MANAGEMENT OF DEFENCE FORCE PREPAREDNESS

Preparing Task Lists

Identifying the nature of possible military tasks involves contingency planning at all levels: strategic, operational and tactical. At the strategic level, Defence is the main, but not the only, Government agency involved in the assessments that precede such planning. Operational and tactical levels are almost exclusively the domains of Defence. Although the early, strategic, stages of this process are public, later stages move into a strictly classified environment. At present, the PMS review cycle is integrated with the annual Defence budgeting process, with the result that it is reviewed on a twelve-monthly cycle.

In the PMS, Defence has not formally progressed the listing of tasks below very broad categories, called 'objectives' or 'outcomes'. Using the cascade of guidance from Government, Defence has promulgated 24 Operational Preparedness Objectives. Their derivation is the end-point of an extensive assessment process. Although the OPOs do not of themselves comprise 'tasks', they provide the basis for capability managers and commanders to define the precise format of tasks for which training should be undertaken, and that should be performed to achieve the relevant objective. While work has been done to develop Australian Joint Essential Tasks, promulgation of tactical and operational level tasks across the ADF has been a matter for each of the Services to this point.

The process of defining the OPOs starts with Government guidance in the form of the Defence White Paper and annual Defence Updates. These documents, along with the Australian Military Strategy—a classified development within Defence of the public documents—identify four major generic 'national tasks' for the ADF. OPOs reflect some 103 MROs which have been grouped for ease of understanding into 24 Aggregated Military Response Options. They are defined in the ASTOPR, which is derived from the Australian Military Strategy and which provides guidance on warning times for deployment to operations.

Apart from the White Paper, all these documents are (notionally) revised on an annual basis. The CPD document, as a series, has existed for many years. The OPOs from the ASTOPR were included in it from 2002. It is now the strategic cornerstone of preparedness planning in the PMS.

Concurrency Standards

The range of forces available will always be a constraint on the number of tasks that can be performed at the same time. The PMS lays down 'concurrency' requirements. These are, standards indicating what multiple or combination of tasks may be required to be performed simultaneously by aggregate forces. The ASTOPR provides guidance for concurrency. The CDF resolves outstanding concurrency issues based on military-strategic circumstances at the time, and Government guidance.

Periodicity of Task Listing

Actual 'tasks', in the form of new operations, may arise outside the planned cycles as the geo-political situation evolves throughout the year. Operational-level military planning takes place on a much more frequent basis, driven by daily strategic monitoring and military appreciations undertaken on a continuing basis.

This immediate strategic monitoring and response planning activity takes place independently of the PMS. However, the CPD mandates that linkages be maintained between them through COMAST (which covers both and which is required to keep the ASTOPR under review).

Defence has experienced considerable taskings that have resulted from assessments taking place outside the cycle in recent years (that is, since the INTERFET operation in East Timor in 1999). The experience of such assessments, and the consequential raised operational tempo, have raised questions in Defence about whether the task identification procedure in the PMS has enough flexibility to take proper account of timeliness requirements in Government tasking of the ADF. This concern relates both to the periodicity of the task identification process and the attendant preparedness settings linked to these tasks. Defence produces a formal Quarterly Strategic Review (QSR). The carriage of this rolling review process is undertaken to support quarterly review of the ASTOPR. The QSR is intended to facilitate and keep under review immediate or operational planning. The QSR does not purport to provide analysis or commentary on settings made in the PMS. The QSR is considered through Defence processes which involve principally military commanders, and which are separate to the mixed civilian/military committee processes which oversight the PMS (chiefly the DC).

The lack of congruence between the annually determined PMS framework and the more frequent QSR exercise has led to concerns about the linkage between the two. It would seem that the gap per se would not matter if developments on the strategic assessment plane were less volatile and ADF responsiveness was not so closely tied to that volatility. But the QSR is regarded by numerous command elements as a benchmark appreciation process that could be used for more 'fine-grained' preparedness planning. In one of the Services, it was considered that the QSR should be used formally to test the need for adjustments to be made in PMS settings for preparedness of force elements. It was pointed out that the QSR, as distinct from the monitoring of the PMS in the DC, provides a much more timely scan of the politico/strategic environment and contains much clearer indications of trends that may result in the ADF being tasked to use its capabilities in some way.

Although changes have occurred in formal PMS preparedness arrangements on an ad hoc basis between the annual cycle of changes to the PMS's settings, no formal nexus exists between the QSR and the PMS. The impact of the ongoing review process and the QSR influences the content of COMAST's contribution to monthly performance reporting. But this is through processes that are effectively invisible to the Services. The result is that two preparedness management arrangements are in simultaneous operation, one with the system working through the military operational command system, the other through the structured PMS. The PMS's periodicity is driven by the OPAs between the Secretary/CDF and the output executives. By its nature, this is an annual process. However, while the DC has the opportunity to consider any specific outturn from the COSC and QSR process (through the COMAST's contribution to the Defence Monthly Performance Summary, and the input made to the QSR process by the Preparedness Branch), the PMS would benefit from a more formal link being made to channel the results of the QSR process into the PMS process.

The Definition of Specific Tasks

The OPOs stand at the head of a planning process that cascades effectively from Government guidance to the unit level across the Services. They were observed to be directly and extensively used as the basis for task definition across all the commands, FEGs and formations that were reviewed by the ANAO. They are used as the framework for preparedness and operations management systems used in the single Services. The OPOs, both in concept and in detail (including the more specific guidance set out in the MROs), are well established in analysis and policy development in the enabling groups. Understanding them is important to enable these groups to effect the translation of preparedness concepts to supply and logistics concepts.

Though there were differences of view among various planning groups, the OPOs were regarded as forming a reasonable basis for the development of specific task requirements at subordinate levels in the Services. It was noted in several areas of the single Services that changes to the OPOs have the potential to have far-reaching implications. These include: long lead time planning being undertaken at operational levels for training; equipment; maintenance; demand for capability-supporting logistics (for example, rotable inventory); and the timing of usage/upkeep cycles for major assets.

Commanders in the single Services generally considered that the OPOs, as formulated, provided any necessary latitude while also creating the appropriate central disciplines in the preparedness management context. In some planning areas in the Services. concerns were expressed that the OPOs provide insufficient 'granularity' in defining what is required, leaving planning groups to develop the OPOs into forms useable in their operating units. The capability of the OPOs to provide a basis for Service-specific task development and downstream proficiency development is well demonstrated in the Army's capability management framework.

In its Force Preparedness Directive (issued by Land Command), Army has identified some 90 sub-tasks, which it uses to plan against and then conduct all its tactical level training down to unit level. All 90 of the sub-tasks are drawn from the OPOs and can be tracked to them. Army planners characterised the translation of the OPOs into Army-relevant tasks as relatively seamless. Fully integrated into the Army Capability Management System, it allows Army the flexibility to modify the tasks to which it trains independently from the ASTOPR revision process, but in a way that is fully aligned with the ASTOPR requirements.

There has been some adjustment to the listed items of the OPOs in the last year. The OPOs are only summary groupings of a much larger number of Military Response Options, which are comprehensively listed in the Strategic Response Options Table annexed to the CPD. Planners with access to the Defence Secret Network have full access to this listing to obtain any needed clarification of what they entail. Broad-based concerns exist about whether the OPOs form an adequate basis for conducting the dialogue on capability planning with Government. Should future capability review considerations result in changes to the definition of the tasks that form the basis of the DLOC system, it would have a major impact on the PMS and careful consideration will need to be given to the ramifications of changing this fundamental building block. For the present, however, there appear to be no moves to change it fundamentally. Sound planning suggests the need for minimum changes to basic parameters such as OPO definition.

Australian Joint Essential Tasks

In the joint environment, however, there are concerns to expedite the processes of articulating a more rigorous and comprehensive identification of detailed military tasks employed in the joint theatre of operations. Headquarters Australian Theatre (HQAST) would wish to see a firmer basis for appropriate cross-Service competency and skill development of forces assigned to theatre operations than exists at present. HQAST would wish to use ASJETs, originally commissioned to facilitate evaluation of results of ADF exercises, to achieve this purpose.

The development phase of the ASJET project is now completed. ASJET sets out a consolidated directory of essential tasks that need to be performed in the operation of joint forces in various types of combat and operations. ASJET has built on models developed in similar defence forces overseas (US, UK and Canada), but has adapted them to the Australian environment and the circumstances of the ADF. They are derived from doctrine, historical records of operations, Australian Military Strategy and single Service task lists. The ASJET listing has strategic, operational and tactical 'layers' of tasks. It is intended to provide linkage between Australian and international doctrine and so would, if applied across the single Services, facilitate interoperability of ADF units with foreign defence services.

Although ASJET has been approved by COSC, its future use is uncertain. HQAST hopes to see it used to lay the basis for common competency-based training that would be used in single Service force preparation, as well as for joint training.

The ANAO noted that Mission Essential Task Lists and Joint Mission Essential Tasks, defined to similar degrees of 'granularity', are used in the US and the UK and that these lists form important parts of their preparedness management systems. It is understood that the ADF Joint Warfare Centre has under review the value of the ASJET in designing training programs.

Adoption of ASJET would also create an important link between Australian proficiency development and that pursued in other countries' defence forces with which Australian forces could be involved in future combined operational deployments. This would facilitate interoperability with such coalition forces, a quality that is not specifically developed in the current OPO definitions.

The ANAO considers that there would be value in Defence exploring how the ASJET might be developed for use in the Australian PMS, as it would lend more coherence and rigour to the military skills proficiency building process and enhance the effectiveness of joint ADF capability.

TIME DIMENSION OF PREPAREDNESS

The time dimension of preparedness relates to readiness and to sustainability. Strategic analysis needs to be applied on a continuing basis, to identify possible defence-related contingencies, and to determine the likely implications for military preparations and operations. Setting indicative warning times and sustainment periods is a crucial component of risk management in the PMS.

The Defence PMS identifies time dimensions in preparedness and in the application of military power, in the following three major ways:

- Strategic warning time categorises contingencies by grouping the Aggregated Military Response Options into four 'bands' of warning time frames. The fourth band, with warning times in excess of one year, is designed to capture the range of less likely but possible contingencies with a long lead time, necessitating the maintenance of core war-fighting skills and organisational arrangements.
- Readiness Notice specifies the time assessed as realistic and appropriate to position a force element to the point where it will be 'operationally capable' for a designated task or mission. Readiness Notice is the period during which a force element can 'work up' to become fully

proficient in the skills needed for the mission, through collective training, and in which it can assemble all the necessary equipment and materiel resources for the Operational Viability Period.

- Sustainment period is the time planned for the force element to be able to be deployed for a designated mission or task, after the Operational Viability Period. Capability managers and theatre commanders need to plan so that they can sustain a force in theatre for the prescribed sustainment period: that is, if necessary, by rotation of force elements.

Sustainability entails the management of the very extensive range of logistic inputs a force needs to operate, such as fuel, ammunition, rations, health services and equipment spares. Sustainment also has to take account of concurrency requirements. Sustainability issues present significant challenges to Defence in implementation of the PMS and in broader budgetary management.

Another PMS time-related concept is the Notice to Move. Notice to Move has major relevance at the operational level as it is the time specified when all force resources, readied to an operationally capable level, have to be available to move from a base or a forward deployed point. A short Notice to Move places heavy strains on people and resources as it severely limits the scope for other tasking of units and for staff to utilise entitlements such as leave. In some units on continuing short Notice to Move, it can cause significant staff retention problems.

The ANAO found that the meanings of some of these terms were not consistently understood across various commands and FEGs in the Services. In particular, the difference between Readiness Notice and Notice to Move caused confusion: some groups effectively considered that there was no difference in the meaning of the terms. Various organisational elements understood that it was open to them to interpret the meanings of the terms in ways suiting their circumstances. Although the operational circumstances of different force elements and groups are very different, and management issues are frequently very complex, this variation in understanding could clearly lead to cross-Service distortions and inaccurate pictures of readiness at higher levels of command. The ANAO considers that the descriptors and meanings of the time parameters, as set out in Defence doctrine documents, could be reconsidered with a view to making them clearer and more widely understood.

Unit Preparedness

The third dimension of the preparedness model used in Defence disaggregates the ADF into its constituent weapons systems, down to force element level. It enables specification of what particular assets will be held at what level of readiness, and in what numbers.

The ANAO found that the precise numbers of assets so specified in the documentation are subject to some flexibility of interpretation at lower levels of capability management (for example, at FEG level). Some FEG executives, for example, considered that the numerical specification of actual platforms to be at particular Readiness Notice, did not reflect operational realities related to equipment/crewing ratios and rotational requirements etc. It was felt that, as budgetary limits were maintained by the actual arrangements put in place, the gap between what was documented and what was being done on the ground was not considered to be of any significance for preparedness management.

The ANAO considered that there were some risks in this view because the composite picture made visible at higher command levels may lead to overestimation of the number of assets available for tasking, especially in situations of possible concurrency of requirements.

Sustainability

Broadly, sustainability is the ability of a force to continue to conduct operations once committed and deployed, until completion of assigned tasks. It also encompasses the generation of additional forces and support outside the 'area of operations'.

The sustainment component of preparedness exposes the effectiveness of the PMS to the activities of numerous functional areas of the Defence Organisation outside the outcome groups. Sustainment is determined by the supporting infrastructure, both physical and technical, that is available, and how well that infrastructure may be able to perform in the future. Under the Defence business model, Defence delivers infrastructure through portfolio-wide functionally organised groups. The management systems employed for the delivery of services within and between these groups, and the resourcing decisions made in these groups, are quite separate from the management systems in the capability outcome groups.

Because of this, the sustainability of force elements in the Defence business model is heavily dependent on output executives being able to count on the full benefits of high quality service delivery by the enabling groups. At the same time, output executives are not without major responsibilities in making sustainment arrangements in their own realms. This is required by the CPD and Output Executive Preparedness Directives and the requirement to apply the Fundamental Inputs to Capability (FIC) in assessing the OLOC/DLOC status of their forces. COMAST has particular logistic supply responsibilities in operations.

The FICs list a number of inputs that involve infrastructure. Three of the eight FICs do so explicitly. Supply chain management, stockholding arrangements for the full spectrum of support elements that are used in the operation of current capability (ranging from spare parts to ammunition, fuel and food), are day-to-day variables that will strongly influence the degree to which forces can sustain operations over a period of time. Reserve stockholdings will be relevant to planning for higher-level contingencies. Less obvious among the sustainability tasks, but among the most challenging of support arrangements, are those embedded in other FICs such as the Command and Management FIC. This includes such issues as the consideration of funding 'not readily attributable to any other FIC element (for example, discretionary funding) and [this] encompasses the processes to ensure the correct and adequate allocation of resources to meet demands'.

Sustainment clearly needs to be an integral part of preparedness planning. The CPD stipulates that the requirement includes planning for reserve stockholding, a quite sophisticated and protracted process involving extensive technical, industry, and economic knowledge. However, the sustainment dimension of preparedness has received significantly less attention in development of the present preparedness model, and in development of appropriate procedures, than the operational readiness dimensions. Defence preparedness documentation acknowledges this lag.

Defence is currently seeking to redress this situation. The DC has initiated a number of related studies. It is understood that lack of resolution of sustainment requirements issues has been partly due to the complexity and perceived intractable nature of many of the issues that bear on sustainment. Significant resources are involved for Defence: according to a recent study, some $4.9 billion per annum is spent in non-personnel operating costs, a component of the Defence Budget which, with personnel costs, is growing at a faster rate than was projected in the most recent White Paper in 2000.

ASSESSMENT OF SUSTAINABILITY REQUIREMENTS

Outcome executives assess the requirements for sustainability and determine associated priorities. Requirements are driven by estimates of activity levels and usage rates (determined largely by activity levels) and by possible concurrency of tasks and use of force elements. As with the readiness component of preparedness, decisions on how much sustainability resources should be acquired require risk-managed judgements on what those activity levels will be.

Framework guidance for these judgements takes the form of defined 'concepts of operations' to meet roles and tasks, assessments of possible concurrency of tasks, the relative tempo and intensity of operations, the conditions under which operations will be conducted and the level of performance required. The judgements within this framework are essentially military ones, requiring intimate operational knowledge as well as understanding of logistical interfaces. These judgements involve the making of assumptions about what contingencies will be considered as well as about activity levels within those contingencies.

The ANAO observed that a collaborative process takes place between the capability outcome managers and the enabling groups to pursue the definition of these requirements. At this stage, it is a largely informal process, complicated by complex and difficult planning structures.

The issues involved, however, are key ones for Defence. In the resourcing decisions made by Defence, the costs of investment in sustainability need to be made in competition with other capability options. In conditions of high operational activity, it would seem that the trade-off between sustainment investment and new capability investment might naturally tilt towards sustainment. The converse may be the case in peacetime.

The policy guidance currently articulated in Defence is limited in its scope at this time. In managing the risks of supply, the CPD provides for force elements held at short notice to be given priority in full resourcing (that is, readiness and sustainability resourcing). Priorities for other force elements are similarly determined for the rest of the force-in-being in order of Readiness Notice requirements. While directives require that the requirements of the longer warning time Band 4 OPOs (greater than 365 days) should be properly considered in this framework, the guidance to do so appears to be expressed in very general terms.

A specific concern is that, while outcome and output capability elements can and do submit OOPRs on deficiencies originating in supply and logistics/sustainability issues, they have no guidance on the presentation of OOPRs on logistics (that is, sustainment) issues for Band 4 OPOs. Extant directives do provide for upward referral of concerns about preparedness originating in longer-term support and sustainment from capability managers. However, no effective guidance on procedures has been issued in this area.

Associated with this apparent gap is the consideration that COMAST monitoring focuses on shorter warning time preparedness. The current format of reporting on preparedness performance by COMAST to the DC against the ASTOPR does not provide for reporting preparedness against longer warning time Band 4 MROs. Defence could consider developing the PMS framework, to formalise the inclusion of a disciplined assessment procedure that would substantially capture sustainability issues in regard to contingencies beyond the 365 days time frame.

CONTROL AND DIRECTION OF PREPAREDNESS

This chapter outlines the various preparedness control environments across the ADF, identifies the different governance systems within them and assesses how preparedness control arrangements extend into ADF operating areas such as military training programs and support.

Preparedness Control Infrastructure

In order to produce an ADF-wide picture of aggregate capability, the military capabilities of the Services are brought together into a coordinated ADF-wide composite 'whole' by central Defence areas, in particular the Policy Guidance and Analysis Division (under Deputy Secretary Strategic Policy) and the Chief Finance Officer (CFO). Both the results of the individual Services' separate corporate processes and the analytical capability and financial reports generated by central Defence organisations, are provided to the DC. The resulting documents also have visibility at Ministerial level.

The DC brings together all the military and civilian executives under the Secretary (for civilian functions) and the CDF (for military functions). The DC's prominent role in the PMS (a role which has been increasing in recent years) as the point to which the preparedness control system reports, imparts great authority to the PMS. Reporting systems and processes in regard to preparedness, endorsed or decided by the DC on advice from the Policy Guidance and Analysis Division and CFO staff, have the authority of the portfolio's military and civilian Chief Executive Officers. Preparedness control has a single point of accountability in Defence. DC decisions, based on the PMS reporting, are implemented by the output groups.

In addition to the capability generated by the single Services, the capability overseen and/or generated by COMAST is brought into the preparedness picture submitted to the DC. COMAST produces military capability for operations and COMAST assessments of capability across the whole of the ADF have come to assume some prominence in the formal DC preparedness monitoring processes.

Underpinning the PMS is a formal cascade of directives and performance agreements that spread from the centre out to the Services and groups, and have two interlocking and mutually supporting streams. The first of the two streams, anchored in the CPD, tasks the military capability outcome managers (the three Service Chiefs and COMAST) to maintain levels of preparedness determined by detailed military planning set out in the ASTOPR.

The second stream commits all of the Defence outcome executives— that is, the military outcome managers and the other Defence outcome managers—to deliver funded levels of capability determined in the annual budget process. The instruments by which this is articulated are OPAs between the Secretary/CDF (as a joint authority) and the outcome executives. The OPAs allocate to outcomes their share of aggregate resources for the portfolio, agreed in the annual DMFP. These outcome allocations are made against judgments as to the military preparedness levels that can actually be afforded with the resources available. These are set out in DLOC schedules (issued as part of the OPAs) to the outcome executives. The DLOCs are, in turn, broken down into output-level preparedness standards.

The main link between the two streams is via the CDF directing subordinates through the CPD, in order to deliver the capability determined in the OPAs. This linkage flows down through the Outcome Executive Preparedness Directives, to the outcome executive subordinate units and divisions. Thus the Army, Navy and Air Force Chiefs and COMAST produce these directives that dictate the capability standards intended for each of the military capabilities within each respective outcome area.

With the two directive streams emanating from the civilian and military figures who preside over the DC, the DC functions in a corporate way to ensure that Government strategic, policy and consequential Defence contingency planning, and Government budgetary policy for Defence, are aligned.

The coordination as well as planning of these processes at staff level is performed by the Preparedness Branch within Policy Guidance & Analysis Division. It is the primary service point for the DC's preparedness interests. In performing this role it works very closely with COMAST and the Service Headquarters. The Director General of this Branch chairs a consultative forum, the Preparedness Working Group, which oversights the implementation and further development of the PMS on a whole-of-Defence basis. The Preparedness Working Group includes representation from the two enabling groups, DMO and CSIG. Figure 3.1 depicts this preparedness control infrastructure in graphic form.

The chief measure and analytical tool used in the capability resource control environment is the establishment, monitoring and reporting of the DLOC standard, and the exceptions report system of OOPRs attached to it.

The DLOCs specify at FEG or output level, and according to OPO serial numbers, what force elements will be held at what Readiness Notice and Notice to Move, for what Operational Viability Period and what sustainment period.

Though proposals for the content of DLOCs (in the form of draft DLOCs) are made from lower levels in the Services, the Service Chiefs and the Service Headquarters are the major participants in the annual processes of negotiating the content of the DLOC agreements.

The ANAO noted that a highly centralised environment creates the final DLOC 'products'. One bi-product of this is that it can, on occasion, produce results that do not align well with what capability planners at lowerlevels perceive to be realities of operational management of capability.

Governance at the Service Level

Consistent with guidance provided by the Defence business model, each of the Army, Navy and Air Force utilise planning systems and corporate structures in their headquarters operations to combine and integrate the two streams of directives.

The Army uses the Army Strategy Map to guide its planning and performance management framework. The Navy has developed two plans: Plan Green, a short-range plan (1–5 years outlook) and Plan Blue, for the further outlook. Air Force has developed the Air Force Plan. All these plans are subject to annual review.

Each Service Chief maintains a strategic advisory committee, comprising the heads of Headquarters departments and Service Commands. The strategic advisory committees all have representation from the relevant environmental division in DMO, that is, the Land Systems, Maritime Systems and Aerospace Systems Divisions—an important link between each Service to this further control environment in Defence.

Below the level of the strategic advisory mechanisms reporting to the Service Chiefs, structures that are very similar have been set up across the Services for the management and coordination of preparedness at the Service level. These mechanisms are all located in the respective Service Headquarters.

The Deputy Chief of each of the Services has oversight of the headquarters planning and management functions pertaining to capability issues, including preparedness. Functional specialisations are dealt with in the Services by different groupings of corporate committee arrangements located below these 'strategic' level committees. All Services have one committee dealing principally with capability management issues. These committees maintain provision for participation by representatives of DMO and/or CSIG. In the command chains from the Service Chief through the Deputy Chief, all the Services maintain a directorate of staff whose key function is preparedness planning and management, usually as part of a 'planning and policy' mandate. These positions are senior, generally at 'colonel level' rank.

Staff work in each Service on the higher level or strategic preparedness matters is done in these directorates or branches. The work includes the production of all the PMS documentation such as draft OPAs, draft Outcome Executive Preparedness Directives and draft DLOCs. These branches coordinate and produce all performance reporting to the Service Chief (reviewed by the strategic advisory committees, using the Balanced Scorecards formats for each Service) and the preparation of each Service's contribution to the Defence-wide Balanced Scorecard performance reports considered monthly by the DC. This material is a selection of the material that is considered by the Service-specific processes.

The imperatives of time cycles for the production of the monthly processes in the Services and that for the central Defence report, mean that the Service contributions are typically incorporated in the central reporting documents that go to the DC, before the respective Service Chiefs and their strategic advisory committee can review them. The advisory committees and the Service Chiefs look at the reporting after it is submitted, but before the DC meeting that considers the combined report. The phasing is regarded as imperfect but inevitable. The Service Chiefs are able to brief the DC personally on any developments of concern to them, including any elements of their Service's documentation with which they disagree. No concerns were raised by any of the Service Chiefs about the operation of this system.

The Service Headquarters Level

Management of the directives' requirements below the headquarters level in each of the Services varies widely. The Service Chief, or Deputy Chief, typically addresses directives to subordinate units responsible for delivering the outputs that contribute to the respective outcomes. Directives may also be, and typically are, issued to commands that are not directly responsible for an output. For example, a directive has been issued by Chief of Air Force to Air Force's Training Command.

VARIATION IN ARRANGEMENTS ACROSS THE SERVICES

The major variation across the Services is between different organisational arrangements chosen to deliver outputs. The Navy and Air Force have developed the FEG managerial concept to be accountable for delivery of their outputs within their outcomes. The Army has pursued a matrix management approach and considers this to be non-negotiable because its structure and roles in war fighting are different to those in the other Services.

Broadly, the Navy and Air Force capability outcomes are divided into outputs that align with group-based management structures. Each group has a specified commander and staff. Each of these structures groups together a cluster of weapon systems, functions or capabilities. Some of these weapons systems may be actual force elements. For example: the Navy's Surface Combatant FEG is the grouping of guided missile frigates; and the Air Force Air Lift Group is a FEG which groups the Hercules, Caribou and special purpose aircraft that perform the ADF aerial lift function. Other groups may be formed around systems, such as radar and surveillance (in the Air Force), or hydrographic functions (in the Navy).

In the Navy and Air Force, the commanders of these FEGs are the means by which accountability of the respective Service Chiefs for the 'raise-train-sustain' responsibilities are actually delivered, as each FEG commander has clearly-established delivery tasks defined in the directive cascade.

In the Army, the Chief of Army maintains a much more centralised responsibility for land force capability management as a whole. There is less devolution of responsibility for capability delivery and generally no equivalent FEG construct. Army's capability management system involves the definition of functional outputs, such as Mechanised Operations and Motorised Infantry Operations, to cover all Army deliverables. These are horizontal functionalities and the many brigades, regiments and units are the force elements in the Army.

The result in Army is that, although the Army's control environment is simpler and its business planning processes more coherent (in that Chief of Army, and therefore Army Headquarters, is clearly the central authority for preparedness raise-train-sustain outcomes), it is also less transparent in the way in which accountability for specific preparedness deliverables is mapped to individual decision-makers within the organisation. In this environment, Army's Land Command plays the major role in structuring the way the Army outputs manage and report their preparedness performance.

Despite the inter-Service differences, in this control environment the FEGs in the Navy and Air Force and the capability groups (or outputs) in Army are clearly designed to be the principal building templates for capability management, especially preparedness. They typically include a Staff Officer-Capability in their staffing to prepare material relating to preparedness. The FEG headquarters have the closest relationship with the Systems Program Offices (SPO) in DMO, which provide extensive support services for the delivery of outputs. The SPOs are frequently physically co-located with the counterpart FEG. In Navy and Air Force the material relating to preparedness management is channelled through the environmental command headquarters to the Service headquarters. In the case of the Army, it is Land Command which actually generates this material.

A further variation across the Services is the different ways chosen to group support functions, or 'inputs' to capability. Army and Air Force group training into separate Commands, directly reporting to the Service Chief. Navy incorporates training functions in a broader Systems Command and a separate training function for collective training in Maritime Command. Air Force groups functions around aircraft test and evaluation with combat-related electronic systems (which supports all three Services on a joint basis) in a FEG-like structure that is not a cost centre or output. It would appear that the single Services are moving towards the use of a DLOC-like tasking device to link subordinate commands and groups to the Service-specific DLOCs.

THE ROLES OF THE ENVIRONMENTAL COMMANDS

The Maritime, Land and Air Commands are assuming increasing responsibility for coordination of capability management among their respective outputs. Land Command is obliged to do so because of the absence of FEG groupings. Maritime and Air Commands are increasingly being driven by the Services' need to impose control over capability management taking place at lower levels.

The rise in environmental command roles in capability management is also linked to the PMS's relationship with the outcome structure. The FEGs' reporting systems have to be responsive to HQAST's as well as the respective Service Headquarters' needs. At the level of day-to-day accountability, many FEGs consider that they have a two-fold reporting line of command: to HQAST in regard to 'command of operations' issues (where the standard of most concern is OLOC) and to Service Headquarters as the Service-specific outcome manager (where the main standard of concern is the DLOC measure).

Diversity of Reporting Sources

Service headquarters and environmental command headquarters staff in all three Services emphasised the relative weight of subjective judgments in the generation of analysis in the reporting material. This originated in the FEGs but often with significant modifications or additions from the environmental commands, and the relative sparseness of quantitative information used at all levels of reporting.

The ANAO considers that the prominence of subjective factors and the varied location of sources of reporting, underline the importance of maintaining consistent and well-understood business rules for the PMS across the broad range of FEG organisational units and among the environmental commands. Such consistency of understanding was not, however, always shown, with officers in FEGs and commands offering often quite different accounts of meanings and definitions of important PMS concepts. Information technology systems are not consistently used. Arrangements for managing operational resource control vary widely between the Services.

A specific concern that was noted in this regard was that, across the three Services, no particular pattern or direction appears to have been determined for enabling the FEG commanders and their managers to workshop issues in capability management on a combined basis, so that individual best practice ideas may be diffused among the FEGs. Practice varies between such mechanisms as periodic conferences and attendance at various forums.

Service Output Groups

In the main preparedness control environment, the FEGs and the Army outputs are the cost centres for the ADF, as well as being the deliverers of the outputs in the Defence outcomes/outputs framework.

To obtain a full understanding of how the FEGs support the PMS in Defence, the ANAO conducted detailed fieldwork at this level. The ANAO had extensive discussions with all of the Air Force FEGs, a broad cross-section of the formations and units performing Army output functions; and, through the previous ANAO audit of Navy operational readiness, all of the Navy FEGs.

This broad-based process of inquiry revealed that at the FEG or capability output level, Defence has in place a wide variety of constructs for creating accountability for capability generation, and consequently preparedness management and control, across the ADF, and within each of the Services.

The ANAO 2002–03 audit of Navy operational readiness found that the seven Navy FEGs are very diverse in their organisational purposes and are formed around both functional inputs and outputs (for example, the Hydrography FEG) as well as weapons-system or platform type (for example, the Surface Combatants FEG). The ANAO found that there was a mismatch between the accountability given to these groups and the resources, including command and authority, to actually fulfil this accountability. Navy has since moved to align accountability levels with control and resourcing in a review of FEGs in 2002. Navy has done this by taking the accountability level 'upstream', to the Maritime Command, which has been positioned to play a front-end role in FEG operational coordination and resource management.

This same variety of type and organisation was found to characterise the Air Force's FEG structure: for example, the Air Force's Surveillance Control FEG is based on a combat capability; its Combat Support FEG is a provider of services. The Army's capability outputs also differ very widely. The form of one of Army's capability outputs, that of Army aviation operations, is almost the same as an Air Force or Navy FEG, and in fact provides all of one Army output. But, as indicated above, most of Army's capability outputs are not matched with discrete management structures as they are in Navy and Air Force. The division of capabilities into the present set of outputs follows closely Army's combat doctrine.

All the FEGs and Army capability outputs have in common one attribute: that of not being the organisational elements that are used in operations. In the words of one Service officer, 'we do not fight in FEGs' and this comment is applicable to all Services. The ANAO noted that Air Force does endow the FEG Commanders with a command role in regard to operational activities, and the directives from the Chief of the Air Force require the commanders to maintain certain operational proficiencies. On the other hand, Navy now quite explicitly excludes the FEG commanders from roles in the military chain of command. Navy's FEGs are overtly held at the status of being 'coordinators' and advocates on behalf of the force elements attributed to them. The ANAO found that the adoption of the FEG/output arrangements across the ADF has been characterised by extensive experimentation and exploration of different approaches, which have included both development of organisational forms (for example, Army Aviation, Air Force Combat Support Group, Navy Amphibious and Afloat Support) and determination of accountabilities. The following specific characteristics relevant to preparedness management were noted:

- FEGs are involved in very uneven ways in determining the preparedness settings leading to those set out in the DLOC agreements. The respective Environment Commands (Maritime, Land and Air) have, or are moving towards having, major roles in these matters.
- FEGs and lower level units originate some of the material that eventually goes into monthly reporting of preparedness to Service Chiefs and beyond. Numerous assessments are frequently made further up the command chain, based on military judgment of experienced officers on a subjective basis.
- In Army, because organisational units do not match specific capabilities (except for Army Aviation), the preparedness assessment functions need to be made by combat area specialists in Land Command, drawing from routine situation reporting from brigade, formation and even unit levels that does not appear to be generated from fully consistent and clear tasking patterns.
- FEGs have a very uneven understanding of the status of some preparedness settings: on key deficiency status issues, for example, some are intimately familiar with extant OOPRs, some have patchy knowledge.
- Little use is made of systematic information systems to generate preparedness information (as distinct from the use of such systems to manage ongoing programs such as training and operational resource allocations).

The ANAO considers that, while the diversity of template arrangements in which to invest 'capability outputs' across the ADF reflected the very widely different circumstances and roles of the different Services and relevant organisational units, and was probably appropriate from the point of view of command imperatives, this diversity is not consistent with robust preparedness assessment methodologies. It is accepted that military judgement will always, and quite appropriately, be paramount in assessing capability issues. However, the spread of practices across the Services means there is a high risk that aggregated information (especially when information is further collated and aggregated in summarised form) may not be robust in all areas.

The ANAO noted that staff officers in COMAST and in the central areas of Defence, who need to deal with preparedness management, have a reasonably sound appreciation of the systemic aspects of the diversity in shape and form of the FEGs, and accept that data quality in the flow of information needs to be improved as the PMS is developed. There is less appreciation of the degree to which the capability templates are different in their approaches to preparedness and in their governance arrangements. A major reason for this is that current procedures mean that these officers need to regularly communicate only with the Service Headquarters and/or environmental commands, not with FEG-level staff.

The ANAO found that, for Defence as a whole, these aspects of operational resource control are relatively weak. It considers that the task of achieving greater standardisation of the templates, and the measurement systems applied by, or to, them, across the ADF, should be given higher priority than appears to be contemplated at present. Given that the underlying trend appears to be for the environmental Commands to take on increasing responsibilities in this area, this task might best be performed by Maritime, Land and Air Commands, each responding to strategic direction from the Service Chiefs.

The Preparedness Role of COMAST

COMAST is the manager of one of Defence's capability outcomes, Command of Operations, and 'negotiates' an OPA with Secretary/CDF. COMAST is also required by the CPD to issue a capability directive to the relevant Service hierarchies in HQAST, to implement the requirements of the CPD.

These arrangements are in line with the theory that it is the Service Chiefs who generate the elements of military capability, and COMAST (on behalf of CDF) who uses them in operations. Thus COMAST's principal focus in preparedness is formally the OLOC standard, as that is the standard that force elements will be required to have if they are committed to an operation.

In actual practice, the dividing line is not as clear between capability generation and management, and operational use of military forces, for three main identifiable reasons. COMAST's assessment of ADF joint capability is the principal vehicle for bringing the preparedness of the ADF to notice at DC level. COMAST is the principal whole-of-ADF preparedness assessor for the DC and carries the burden of ongoing holistic reporting of capability and deficiencies in it. COMAST's assessments are based partly on the separate single Service streams of performance reporting against their DLOCs and, because COMAST controls the gateway to the OOPR database, the OOPRs across the ADF are a single dataset. COMAST draws on a range of other data and its own military assessments of preparedness and these can diverge from those of the Services.

Second, COMAST has significant training obligations, in particular for collective training and joint training of forces. COMAST has strong interests in achieving the critical OLOC level of capability of forces and, though the situation varies in degree between situations, frequently plays a major part in ensuring that that level of capability is reached by force elements assigned to COMAST tasking and command. The Joint Task Force Commanders, who are assigned to particular missions, are under COMAST and these posts have major de facto 'train and sustain' interests and functions. COMAST has the pivotal role to play in delivering, as well as assessing, the preparedness of the ADF when it comes to joint activity.

Third, in both immediate planning for, and in conduct of, operations, COMAST has significant formal sustainment functions for the forces used in operations and maintains a substantial logistic capability to do so. It is beyond question that COMAST has a significant role in the 'sustain' part of the 'raise-train-sustain' continuum.

Many aspects of these three roles derive from the fact that COMAST, on behalf of the Chiefs of Service Committee, is the manager of the ASTOPR, which is the key military planning document of the ADF. COMAST's planning staff are, furthermore, major players in the design and development of the PMS as a control structure across the ADF. Some of the main conceptual features of the PMS have their origin in COMAST planning studies. The staff perform these functions in close cooperation with Preparedness Branch in the Policy Guidance and Analysis Division.

THE OPERATIONAL CONTROL ENVIRONMENT

COMAST's preparedness role as discussed in the foregoing section forms a part of the operational dimensions of ADF command and control and is integrated fully into it. The preparedness of the ADF is not managed separately to other aspects of portfolio management. Thus an important part of its value is that it is integrated into most management areas of the Defence organisation. As a portfolio that has to run a military organisation, military functional and organisational concepts play an important role in forming the control environment.

The CDF commands the armed forces and delivers military capability for purposes determined by the Government. A cascade of command and control elements supports the CDF in this role. Immediate planning for operations takes place in this cascade. This activity ultimately includes coordination of operations once they have commenced. Key strategic governance elements in this operational control framework, under the CDF, are the COSC, the COMAST and the Strategic Planning Group. Under COMAST's command come the Commanders' Planning Group, Theatre Planning Group and the Theatre Administrative Planning Group.

A background planning process is the Joint Military Appreciation Process, which involves consultative activity between joint staff, component staff and specialist advisers. The injection of intelligence and strategic information take place in the cascade at all the governance levels. It is also provided, at frequencies matching operating requirements, to the subordinated planning groups such as Campaign Planning Group, both before operations and during them. The Strategic Operations Division provides staff support to the CDF and liaises with the political environment's stakeholders extensively, including the Office of the Minister for Defence. The theatre planning takes place in all these elements of governance and direction. They have ultimate accountability to the CDF rather than to the Secretary/CDF. They are not subject to processes that include the DC in its corporate governance role.

The PMS is involved in this operational control environment through a number of working relationships in Defence, and in the way in which military capability is actually managed in the field, on a day-to-day basis. These linkages are formed by:

- the ongoing operational management of capability at FEG or unit (force element) level impinging on the ability to maintain PMS settings;
- the 'two-hatted' roles of the Component Commanders (for Sea, Land and Air) in HQAST; and
- the role of Strategic Operations Division in initial planning of operations as part of its liaison role with Government.

The role of the branches of the Policy Guidance and Analysis Division in managing the QSR process provides a documented corporate linkage between the immediate planning plane and preparedness management. The QSR is considered by the COSC and goes no higher in Defence's governance system. In addition, COMAST uses the OOPR data to inform its role in the immediate planning processes.

The enabling groups have roles to play in these processes, and in the case of DMO, mainly through Commander Joint

Logistics (CJLOG). The situation with CSIG is complex and COMAST and CSIG are seeking to formalise their relations in this area in the latest Customer/Supplier Agreement between COMAST and Deputy Secretary Corporate Services in charge of CSIG.

STRATEGIC OPERATIONS DIVISION AND PREPAREDNESS

The Strategic Operations Division is a major contributor in the operational control environment. This division is headed by an officer at the two star level and, although its functions are in formal terms limited to being a staff headquarters to the CDF, the division's activities inevitably make it appear to be an authority separate in the chain of command. The role of the division should create an entry point for preparedness management issues to play a role in operations. This is because of the strategic position it occupies, on behalf of the CDF, in relation to the operations sphere and the preparedness sphere.

The Strategic Operations Division, in conjunction with the Service Chiefs, participates actively in immediate planning across the full spectrum of military tasks and interfaces on a day-to-day basis with the Government and the Parliament. It has the position, on behalf of CDF, of leading the small teams of officers that develop proposals to Government for actual military operations, prior to Government resource decisions being taken. Because of the public sensitivity of these issues, it is necessary to keep to a minimum, on a 'need to know' basis, the group of officers involved in preparing capability estimates and costs, and introducing force composition proposals and resource quantums, such as personnel caps on the size of joint forces.

In conducting these tasks, the Strategic Operations Division does not take information in the PMS fully into account. This would suggest that, the point at which preparedness management transitions to operations planning is neither under the control of the preparedness management arrangements, nor is informed by them. The ANAO learned from various field areas that sub-optimum arrangements frequently ensue from this procedure.

A particular improvement that could be made would be to involve COMAST more closely in the development of force deployment proposals being prepared for Government. This would lay a basis for preparedness information to be used more effectively in force deployment plans and decisions. COMAST could be used as the main source of advice on force deployment and costing proposals being developed for Government consideration and be given accountability for this role in Defence governance arrangements.

The ANAO considers that there would be benefits in Defence identifying ways in which to bring these two different Defence control systems into closer alignment. The interface between the PMS and the operations control system would seem to present an opportunity to measure and evaluate the ongoing performance of the PMS.

PREPAREDNESS PLANNING LINKAGES TO TRAINING AND SUPPORT

An effective preparedness management system needs to include strong functional linkages between the settings determined within the PMS and the operational programs needed to meet them. These programs fall into the two broad categories of training and supplies—the two FICs which bear most closely on preparedness. Ensuring that units have appropriately trained manpower, and that groups receive the necessary collective training to specified proficiency levels, requires extensive management and coordination of numerous inputs from Service entities. The planning and implementation of necessary logistic and materiel supply arrangements involves a wide range of different planning and management systems, and close working interfaces with other enabling organisations in Defence. These linkages would include appropriate gateways to resource management systems and controls in each of the capability outcomes. The three Services have made substantial progress in building systems to create these linkages, though they are at different stages of development. At the joint Service level, COMAST has been seeking to develop evaluation tools to measure progress in achieving joint training outcomes. In the logistic and materiel supply domain, some progress has been made in DMO's Maritime Systems Division to meet Navy's needs. In association with other initiatives being pursued in the Management Information Systems Division of DMO, these have the potential to be applied more widely across the ADF.

The ANAO noted that the three Services and COMAST are cognisant of the need to progress the initiatives that have been taken to date, which would have the effect of linking the PMS to programs in the training and skills development fields.

Service-specific Linkages to Training

The main mechanisms being used in the Services are their specific capability management systems, which align with the PMS. Most do not at this stage have electronic gateways into preparedness management reporting. In the Army the main system is the Army Capability Management System (ACMS), in Air Force the Capability Evaluation and Reporting Tool (CERT) and in Navy, Management of Naval Integrated Capability Assessment Reports (MONICAR).

The ACMS, launched during the period of audit fieldwork, has wide functionality in supporting the Army's need to be able flexibly to re-package and re-group different units to create combat capability for each combat or exercise task. ACMS incorporates a system of Training Activity and Resource Plans to track training status and requirements of units so as to enable the Army to link its training programs to individual OPOs.

The Air Force's CERT program had not yet been fully launched during the period of audit fieldwork. Unlike the ACMS, this system is not designed to support the detail of the training requirements and systems across the various highly skilled disciplines in Air Force. Reflecting the traditional autonomy of some of the Wings, CERT will exist alongside specialist training control systems that are in use, for some time to come. An Air

Force audit has been commissioned by CAF to ensure that the flow-through of CERT principles to the Wing level is effective. It is hoped that CERT will be able to present a comprehensive capability reporting system for Air Command once it is properly established.

Navy's fleet readiness measurement tool, MONICAR has been developed through two major revisions since it was introduced in 1999. MONICAR compiles 'Full Mission Capable' days from ships' weekly reports system, to capture linkages to the Maritime Command system of sea training and work-up. It captures training and equipment condition levels. In line with findings in the ANAO's audit of Navy Operational Readiness in 2003, MONICAR has been developed to generate data that more directly reflects Navy's achievement of preparedness management standards—the concept of 'Unit Ready Days' for a platform. This data is also designed to be used in external reporting.

Joint Force Training

COMAST is applying fresh emphasis to the development of the collective training agenda for joint forces. COMAST and the Service commands are working on plans to enhance the effectiveness of activities in this area. At the time of audit fieldwork, the ASJET list was to be applied as an evaluation tool for the first time at Exercise Crocodile in September 2003. ASJETs have a close linkage with the PMS.

Logistic and Material Support

Less progress has been achieved across the Services and COMAST in associating the PMS settings with supply chain requirements in logistic and material support. Development work has been undertaken in parts of DMO to support specific Service requirements. The Maritime Systems Division in DMO has worked to Navy Headquarters requirements to produce a system based reporting framework for monthly monitoring of material support requirements for all of Navy's platforms against the OPOs. These relate sustainment needs, based on consumption modelling across various capability classes, tracked to current inventory stock levels. This study had completed pre-release testing at the end of the period of audit fieldwork but had not been fully introduced.

Potential exists for this work in Maritime Systems Division to be integrated into the much wider Defence 'data warehouse' initiative being conducted in DMO. The Defence data warehouse proposal will provide a web-based single source of combat support information, supporting multiple perspectives and drawing on legacy Defence systems.

4

Conceptualizing Forces for Change

One of the seminal influences on thought about alternatives to the neoliberal order—Karl Polanyi's *The Great Transformation,* first published in 1944—offers a perspective on the nineteenth-century liberal order and its breakdown that remains highly relevant. For Polanyi the most radical and socially disruptive nineteenth-century innovation was not industrialization but the attempt to create a self-regulating market, to which society and government would be subordinated. The idea of the economy and the market constituting a separate sphere, as against society and government that would be constrained by the working of its laws, was new and was essentially a political and ideological project, one that might be tolerable in exceptional circumstances "such as exist-ed in North America," but elsewhere, "the conflict between the market and the elementary requirements of an organized social life provided the century with its dynamics and produced the typical strains and stresses which ultimately destroyed that society" (1957, 249).

Poianyi's image of this dynamic is the "double movement": first, the move by strong states to establish, coercively, the rules of the self-regulating market ("laissez faire was planned"); and second, spontaneous reactions by many diverse elements in society to protect themselves—their livelihood, their communal ties, their culture—from the ravages of unregulated market forces. He depicts two phases of this reaction. First, in the later nineteenth century there was the movement among the industrialized states not only to regulate the conditions of economic life but also to introduce wide-ranging social legislation—the collectivist or social-liberal trend. Second, in reaction to the attempt in the 1920s to restore the international liberal order based on the gold standard, there were the far more radical or violent reactions that accompanied the collapse of that order in the Great Depression—protectionism and the formation of trading blocs, fascism, and militarism. The last-mentioned went far beyond Polanyi's image of spontaneous self-protective reactions from society, yet the initial acceptance of fascism owed much to the disorder and destitution that accompanied the attempt to reconstruct the liberal order.

From this point of view the current period can be seen as the next move to reconstruct the self-regulating market on a global scale and to subordinate all societies to its "laws." And a recurrence of the double movement is to be expected: that is to say, attempts from within societies to secure protection against the disruptive impact of unrestrained market forces. If so, the central world-order question is whether such social protection can be secured peacefully, through the normal working of existing political institutions, as in late-nineteenth-century Europe, or whether it can be achieved only through violence and the overthrow of political regimes, as in many countries in the 1930s. And as during that time, the return of internal violence and authoritarian rule would spell the end of those liberal expectations.

The present situation appears to resemble the interwar period more than the late nineteenth century, insofar as measures of self-protection against the unregulated market cannot be taken by governments acting independently but require a high degree of international collaboration, whether to maintain the system and manage its recurring crises or to reform it—tasks beyond the reach or even imagining of policymakers in the 1930s, which could be undertaken only in the aftermath of World War II. It is true that liberal democracies are far more securely established in the West than in the 1930s, as are welfare safety nets, albeit under stress, and support for extremist movements in the West remains limited. But the volatility of the international money markets in the late 1990s and the fragility of the financial system of so significant a country as Japan revived fears of system-wide financial or economic crises with unpredictable social costs and repercussions.

Some authors have sought to find clues in Polanyi for identifying contemporary forces for change, that is to say, to discern the nature of the double movement at the present time. This may be asking too much; even in 1944 he left it to others to propose concrete reforms, and attempts to link his analysis to the role of today's radical social movements do not advance the discussion very far. More interesting, Robert Latham finds in Polanyi a normative commitment to "democratic provisionism," a view that not only maintains that economic institutions should serve social and cultural purposes but also asserts the importance of what Polanyi termed *habitat,* which can be taken to foreshadow environmental sustainability. Polanyi is usually associated with the socialist, not the liberal tradition , yet his rejection of marxism and the "paramount importance" he ascribes to the classical liberal freedoms suggest an affinity with social liberalism. Polanyi, then, anticipates today's concerns but should not be read for specific insights into forces and directions of change. His contribution is his diagnosis of the incompatibility between the dynamics of the self-regulating market and the conditions for maintaining a viable social order. This provides a framework for thinking about alternatives and enhances the sense of urgency. Unless there is as strong a resolve as that of Keynes and his generation to constrain the raw power of market forces in the interests of a broadly acceptable social philosophy, the stresses imposed by the unregulated global market are likely to provoke massive countermovements. Neoliberal ideology, by seeking to exclude such reforms from the agenda, exacerbates social tensions, making for confrontations with the disaffected and risking a 1930s-style systemic breakdown.

CONTESTING THE FORCES SUSTAINING NEOLIBERAUSM

Although the formation of a counterhegemonic coalition of radical social movements is not likely to prove sufficient to challenge the dominance of the neoliberal coalition, these movements could form part of a broader inclusive liberal coalition, to which they would bring a high level of political commitment.

What are some of the conditions that might favor such a coalition? What are its potential assets? Prima facie, given that the neoliberal coalition consists of relatively narrow elites, the greatest asset for social liberalism is the power of numbers: voters. This, however, is subject to the major qualification that the electorate has become ambivalent toward the social-liberal agenda. That is to say, although surveys frequently suggest there is majority support for effective social programs, sometimes even at higher cost, in practice electorates are averse to tax increases and to perceived inequities in the taxation system and may not trust governments to allocate increased revenue to the programs voters prefer. Moreover, to the extent that governments of social-liberal inclination are constrained to reduce costs for all the reasons noted earlier, their policies may be perceived as differing only marginally from those of their neoliberal counterparts.

A second, more specific asset is the solid support for existing welfare systems, which represents an important obstacle to the full realization of the neoliberal program. Neoliberal governments, too, are subject to constraints and cannot avoid taking on some social-liberal coloring. The welfare constituency may provide secure support for social liberalism only where programs are popular and broadly based.

A third element favoring social liberalism is the scope for variation in the level and nature of public provision. The market tends to take existing programs as given ; it does not punish the more high-spending welfare states unless their economies experience difficulties for other reasons, nor does it reward states with relatively low public-sector spending, it is even possible for a state to introduce a major new welfare program, such as the Australian Medicare, provided the overall economic policy selling does not create alarm.

Fourth, some impending structural changes are likely to require a greater, not lesser degree of state regulatory capacity. The most obvious of these are in the environmental domain. A responsible policy approach to global warming is still some ways off, but it is difficult to suppose that the major governments will be able to defer indefinitely the kind of hard decisions that would never be taken by market actors alone. And there are more immediate problems relating to waste disposal, the conservation of scarce resources, and biodiversity, for example, that already involve considerable intergovernmental cooperation. It is a secondary issue whether and to what extent this complex of issues is better addressed by market mechanisms as against direct regulation. But there is a prima facie case that effective international measures may require more of the latter. For example, financial incentives and disincentives may be an effective way of regulating pollution within a state's jurisdiction (though nonetheless requiring a strong capacity to monitor and to implement penalties), but the international trading of greenhouse emission rights may be little more than a means of permitting wealthy industrialized states to avoid internal adjustments, by taking advantage of unused "quotas" of states that for a variety of reasons are unable to reach the level of emissions assigned to them.

Finally, a major potential asset of social liberalism in the longer run is its normative richness, in comparison with the ambivalence of neoliberalism—between the appeal to expertise or necessity on one hand, and the assertion of a narrowly defined individualism on the other. In a world in which political legitimacy has come to depend increasingly on democracy, however imperfect its actual institutions, neoliberalism's normative deficit is a major weakness and this in turn constitutes a standing invitation to social-liberal thinkers to address more vigorously the task of translating their values into practical policies capable of winning broad support. Nonetheless, despite these potential assets and the electoral success of the left in the 1990s, there remains a sense of a lack of alternatives to neoliberalism. In spite of attempts to define one, there is no generally recognized social-liberal position, globally or nationally. The drastic weakening and loss of confidence in the old social-liberal coalition and the inchoate nature of support for a successor, then, represent major obstacles to the revival of an effective social-liberal project. These tendencies are furthest advanced in the Anglo-Saxon neoliberal states and least in the continental democracies, but the forces of neoliberalism are pressing their agenda in the latter with no less determination.

Whether for this or for other reasons, the governments of the left have singularly failed to devise any strategy for countering the power of transational capital. Nothing has been heard of the long-standing idea of the Tobin tax, a modest charge on all international currency movements intended to serve as a disincentive to speculation. Since this would require the agreement of all the significant financial centres, such an innovation would not be easy to implement. But it does not appear to disadvantage governments, and thus the silence on the issue is noteworthy. The absence of taxation on international financial transactions is a striking instance of the power of international financial interests.

American Preponderance

The second pillar of support for neoliberalism, it was suggested, is the preponderance of American power, the securing of which has been seen as the most fundamental goal of U.S. foreign policy since the onset of the Cold War. From this perspective American stale officials, conscious of having at their disposal resources that far outweigh those of any potential rival, have consistently acted as classical realist theory would predict. Whether in the name of maintaining the balance of power, projecting Western values and norms, or constructing a liberal order, these officials have resolutely insisted on America's right to exercise this preponderant power—

essentially, to reshape the world in the American image. Over the decades, U.S. officialdom has developed habits of leadership that have never been seriously questioned and are infrequently commented on. More surprising, despite the rhetoric of partnership, occasional disputes, and France's more frequent dissent, the other major Western states have consistently deferred to American leadership. A preponderance of power resources has been successfully translated into an accepted leadership role.

Inevitably, this influence has been exercised in accordance with the values most deeply embedded in the American political culture this embodies the virtues and limitations of classical Lockean liberalism. While not excluding pragmatic concessions to social liberalism, the vision that inspires U.S. officialdom seeks to reproduce not so much the contemporary American reality as the idealized image of liberal America, in a world where states have a diminishing role as the removal of economic and financial barriers opens the way to the liberal utopia. Those suffering acute deprivation enter into such a vision no more than the underclass whose presence in U.S. cities in no way disturbs the country's rulers. Among the manifestations of this influence have been the U.S. role in introducing the regime of unrestricted capital mobility, the promotion of the Washington consensus on economic management and development, and America's controlling position in the IMF and the World Bank, where the habits of deference appear to be particularly well entrenched.

One of the few works tnat addresses the question of countering this pillar of support for neoliberalism in any detail is the study of globalization by German journalists Hans-Peter Martin and Harald Schumann (1997, 218-226, 235-240). In accordance with structural realist logic – only an equal power can restrain or challenge the hegemon—they see the formation of the European currency union, with a potential market of 400 million consumers creating an economic power equal to the United States, as a prerequisite for countering neoliberalism's global offensive. Assuming that the European Union was committed to social liberalism, it would have the economic and political weight to render its social model viable. It would be strong enough to determine the conditions for investment within the EU, rather than yielding to the preferences of the money markets.

The crucial assumption is that a united Europe would have such a commitment to social-liberal values. Is this likely? It is true that the political cultures of most states in continental Europe are more deeply influenced by variants of social liberalism (social democracy and Christian-social philosophies) than the Anglo-Saxon democracies and that classical economic liberalism never gained a strong hold there. Neoliberalism, however, is now far more strongly promoted than social liberalism has ever been in the United States, not only in Britain but by well-placed elites throughout Europe. Traditional political culture is important over the long run, but there can be periods when policy is shaped by different values. Far from being a social-liberal bastion, the European Union is a major arena for the struggle between neo- and social liberalism. The provisions of the Maastricht agreement read as a neoliberal design for Europe (Gill 1998), and Martin and Schumann note that policy in the existing Brussels institutions is made by bureaucrats in consultation with corporate interests, with little input from other social groupings —precisely Cox's neoliberal pattern. They place their hopes in a massive upsurge of democratic politics in the EU's decisionmaking processes, but like others who have lamented the EU's "democratic deficit," they are more convincing in drawing attention to the extent of unrepresentative, elitist decisionmaking than in showing how an infusion of democracy might be brought about.

A second question raised by the idea of a European counterweight to the United States is whether the EU is likely to be sufficiently united and cohesive to play such a role. The outcome is as uncertain as the question of the social philosophy Europe may adopt, but the projected expansion in the number of members reduces the chances of cohesion. For some, the logic of the common currency requires the formation of central governmental institutions to formulate economic policy for the union as a whole. So momentous a constitutional development would, needless to say, be highly controversial. Short of this, others call for a harmonization of policies, for which the conditions required for membership of the common currency union provide a precedent; yet to some critics such conditions introduce rigidities that may make the system unworkable in the long run. Britain's place in Europe raises further divisive issues, both in terms of institutional structure and economic policy orientation.

The problems likely to be experienced in the next phase of Europe's expansion and institutional development, then, place a question mark over the thesis of Europe as a social-liberal counterweight to the neoliberal United States. Moreover, these preoccupations will probably leave little room for Europe to address the needs of the globally disadvantaged. Whereas a social-liberal philosophy would accord their needs the highest priority, it is unlikely Europe's elites will focus on those most neglected in the neoliberal perception of globalization.

Thus far we have followed the structural logic that sees the formation of a second economic power equal to the United States as a prerequisite for modifying the neoliberal global project. But is this necessarily correct? This kind of structural logic has proved unpersuasive in other contexts. For example, Robert Keohane has made a strong case against the claim of hegemonic stability theory that international cooperative regimes require the support of a hegemonic power. Similarly, it may be argued that normative changes within a regime do not necessarily require the support of a state actor as powerful as the supporter of the existing norms. Change might be brought about, for example, by a transnational coalition of governmental and nongovernmental actors committed to a different ideology.

Favorable conditions would also be required, and unfortunately, the most plausible of these would be an economic crisis sufficiently serious to shake the hold of the neoliberal orthodoxy. The Asian financial crisis prompted some questioning of the orthodoxy in official circles, but not for long. Short of a far more serious international crisis, the development perhaps most likely to transform the psychological climate of world politics would be a major setback to the U.S. economy. The appeal of the American model in the 1990s owed much to spectacular economic success, in contrast to the sluggishness of the other major economies, so recently perceived as dangerous rivals. A serious setback, for which there was no lack of warning signals, would undermine the American model, just as economic stagnation following the collapse of the "bubble economy" discredited the Japanese model. Contextual developments of this kind may well be more significant than presumed structural prerequisites as conditions favoring normative change.

The Economic Discourse

Before considering how the dominance of neoliberal economic discourse might be challenged, it may be instructive to observe how an earlier intellectual hegemony was challenged and eventually undermined. The perception of a lack of alternatives to neoliberalism had its parallel in the preceding period, when attempts to challenge the Keynesian mixed economy and welfare state similarly lacked credibility. The structural changes working against it did not automatically create the neoliberal ascendancy. This had to be constructed; elite coalitions had to be formed in various states, taking advantage of the favorable transnational environment, but the nature, extent, and timing of the transition to neoliberalism depended on the particular circumstances of each case. A constant factor in these developments, however, was the intellectual movement inspired by Hayek's uncompromising, hard-edged economic liberalism, which gained momentum over time.

Hayek's identifying of social liberalism with totalitarianism may indeed have rested on a profound misreading of the twentieth-century experience, but it was deeply felt and serves to explain the strength of his commitment and that of some of his followers. Others were inspired by a more simplistic identification with the American classical liberal tradition or by libertarian philosophies. Whatever their motivation, the neoliberal organic intellectuals were notable for the dogged persistence with which they argued their case, both in general terms and in relation to specific issues, despite the lack of public resonance of their appeal in the early postwar decades.

Their eventual success in the Anglo-Saxon world, and in influencing the agenda more generally, can be attributed partly to their success in exploiting specific weaknesses in certain economies and partly to the appeal of their general message to well-placed transnational elites. In Britain, for example, successive governments' ineffectiveness in relation to foreign exchange crises, inflation, sluggish growth, and trade union militancy (widely referred to as the "English sickness") opened the way to a government promising a radically different approach, and the neoliberals were at hand with a ready-made paradigm. In the United States, where a similar but less acute economic malaise coincided with a rather more salient sense of a weakening of America's geopolitical position, the Reagan administration's neoliberal rhetoric was matched by a patchy and opportunistic implementation of the doctrine as it sought to rationalize its combination of tax reductions with increased military expenditure. In each case, then, neoliberal policymakers can be seen as exploiting a failure in a specific policy area or areas to introduce a broad agenda of fundamental economic change, an agenda well understood within certain elite circles but not by the public at large.

One lesson from the success of the Hayekians is the importance of persistent argument. This alone is not sufficient, but without the intellectual preparation—the winning of support for a particular vision of the alternative—favorable circumstances are unlikely to lead to the replacement of an established doctrine." There is a major difference, however, between the neoliberal challenge and that of its social-liberal adversaries. The former had the polemical advantages of simplicity and universalism: whatever the specific economic and social ailments, the remedy was the same. The apostles of change were a close-knit band with a common training and mind-set and a message that was appealing to well-placed elites. The social-liberal challenge to the new orthodoxy is diffuse, like its political constituency, drawn from varied intellectual traditions and by and large opposed to universalism and committed to the principle that solutions need to be tailored to particular circumstances. Such diversity, a source of intellectual richness, is disadvantageous in political debate.

The economics profession has a unique place in the challenge to neoliberalism. Only economists—whose expert knowledge and technical skills enable them to address the issues in the same language as the neoliberal "authorities"—can critically examine policies in their own terms. The arguments of professional economists cannot be dismissed, like those of other critics of orthodoxy, as lacking in expertise. What they lack, however, is political appeal. So long as the contentions of social-liberally inclined economists are perceived as no more than a technical argument among experts, the incumbent elites can adopt the strategy of ignoring them. Politically, social-liberal economists need powerful allies, but there is no ready-made constituency for their views.

The economists' contribution needs to be supplemented intellectually as well as politically. Some of the reasons have been touched on earlier. Much of the debate among economists focuses on policy instruments; it tends to be assumed that these are politically neutral, which is seldom the case, and that the goals of policy are agreed upon, when what may be needed is clarification of the tension among goals or of the appropriateness of favored instruments to the multiple goals. Shared biases within the discipline lead to the downplaying of noneconomic considerations. To the extent that the economic discourse dominates public policy, issues are acknowledged only insofar as they can be reformulated in the language of the contemporary economics discipline.

As a first step toward reorienting the public discourse, the normative assumptions behind economic analyses and proposals need to be made explicit. This general norm of social science has special force when important decisions are taken on grounds that purport to be solely matters of technical expertise but that necessarily presuppose value judgments. As we have seen, the point is conceded by most economists when the issue is actually raised, yet the policy discourse relies heavily on the perception of neutral expertise, or "science." Normative explicitness would make clear whose interests were being served or sacrificed, and which broader social values were being upheld or abandoned.

Normative discussion, however, should go much further than bringing hidden principles into the open. The reassertion of the normative over the technical would entail a change in the political culture; leaders increasingly comfortable in the role of manager would be expected to serve as representatives of definite social values. Policies would be driven by social goals, not the supposed imperatives of the market. Needless to say, the economy imposes constraints on goals that can be pursued at any given time, but these should be subject to constant review, as should trade-offs among them. A perverse situation arises if the only actors in a position to influence economic developments constitute a narrow elite, while the great majority are comprehensively constrained. At a time when technology enables the economy to satisfy basic needs and to provide an unprecedented range of other desired goods for all, the way in which it is organized elevates a few to positions of untold wealth and power while imposing harsh personal and social penalties on others, all quite capriciously. A value-oriented liberalism could begin by seeking to determine what goals society might expect so bountiful an economic machine to serve, and how its various mechanisms might be regulated to those ends.

Liberalism would thus recover the normative emphasis that characterized it for most of its history. Just as the original liberals insisted on the rights and freedoms of individuals against arbitrary powers of government, so would social liberals assert the equal rights and opportunities of individuals against the arbitrary power of the untamed market. The former were not so impressed by the power of absolutist monarchs as to refrain from challenging it; neither must social liberals assume that the power of market forces is beyond reform.

A revival of a more radical liberalism along these lines, however, would confront a further, less evident obstacle: the role of the social sciences in the contemporary culture. The priority they accord to empirical research and the slighting of the normative—indeed, its demotion to the subjective expression of value judgments—serves as a subtle reinforcement of existing realities and power relationships. The nineteenth-century social liberals wrote in an intellectual environment that was more hospitable to normative concerns. Contemporaries need to confront explicitly the empiricist (or positivist) bias of the prevailing intellectual culture.

Once again, the easy part of this agenda is to expose the normative assumptions and silences that underlie particular arguments. Far more demanding is the construction of normative projects, not simply as abstract principles but as they relate to salient contemporary social realities. Such endeavors are sometimes undertaken through collaboration between philosophers and social scientists (e.g., Braithwaite and Pettit 1990). Normative theorizing has seen a revival in international relations even though, as we have seen, it has had little impact on the mainstream of the discipline, at least in the United States. Economics is even more resistant to constructive normative theory, yet arguably it is here that it is most needed, given the influence of the economics profession at the present time. A rare exception among professional economists is the work of Amartya Sen, but for the most part, the exploration of normative economic ideas is left to authors with a background in economics but experience as commentators on public affairs, such as Hutton (1995) and Ormerod (1994).

The normative deficit in contemporary social science has its counterpart in the political culture, with its uncritical attitude to scientific and technical expertise and its readiness to discount normative claims as merely standard political rhetoric or the special pleading of interested parties. This cynicism is doubtless often well founded, and indeed, the manipulative character of political discourse has never been so prominent as at the present time. The shallowness of contemporary political "debate" no doubt owes something to the medium—television—in which it reaches the public, but this is a symptom rather than the cause of the malaise. The fashion for the slick image and the sound bite could not survive if viewers were offered an alternative: leaders who engaged in serious normative reasoning, for example, as a way of broadening the vision of what is acceptable and legitimate. This would also require a more assertive and critical democratic culture, a move beyond the elitism of Schumpeterian democracy, which so neatly complements the elitism of economic globalization. While a high degree of political activism on the part of the populace as a whole is unlikely, it is reasonable to seek ways electorates might become more competent and informed and genuine debate might be encouraged. In general, the present situation reflects a vicious circle in which a number of factors converge to perpetuate a low intensity democratic culture: the lack of perceived alternatives, the perception of economic issues as beyond the competence of the great majority, the preferences of media proprietors. But proprietors would accept lively political debate if it were clear this is what readers and viewers demanded and if there were a perception of significant choices to be made.

The Neo-Gramscian Approach

Scholars inspired by Gramsci's thought take the next step, identifying radical alternatives to the emerging order and the forces that might promote them. The basic Gramscian image of historical change focuses on the idea of the historic bloc that seeks to secure its rule through hegemony rather than coercion—that is to say, primarily through consent achieved by controlling the institutions of civil society, distributing benefits widely and propounding an ideology that legitimizes the ensuing constellation of power. To the extent the disadvantaged can gain control over potential resources of power, they may seek to challenge the hegemonic order, but to do so effectively in a modern slate with a well-developed civil society, they need to conduct a "war of position" in order to gain control of important institutions of that society in the name of a new ideology. In formulating such an ideology and in mobilizing a potential counterhegemonic coalition, "organic intellectuals" play a crucial role. Gramsci's conception of historical change affirms agency.

Contemporary scholars, well aware of the problem of translating a theory originally formulated in the context of class conflict within particular states into the present global setting, employ these ideas heuristically. For Cox it is by no means certain that the ascendant neoliberal forces can achieve a stable hegemony. He draws attention to structural tensions in the present political-economic order and to the potential for a counterhegemonic bloc, but only in general terms. A number of other authors suggest that the potential for a counter hegemonic coalition is to be found in the multiplicity of radical social movements working for goals that are marginalized by, or in direct opposition to, the priorities of neoliberal governments: community groups, indigenous peoples, women's groups, land reformers, environmental NGOs, labour and religious groups, and so forth. While most such groups are local, they are increasingly drawn into regional or global networks. For some this points to an optimistic assessment of their capacity to challenge the neoliberal pattern of globalization. But the weight of argument appears to be with those who hold that radical social movements are too diverse and fragmented, lacking the cohesion and command of resources to mount an effective challenge to neoliberal globalization—notwithstanding certain local successes and the fundamental social changes that some of them, the feminist movement in particular, have brought about.

Neo-Gramscian analyses present two further problems. First, they are embedded in revolutionary socialist thought and are thus inclined to perceive the goal in terms that, in light of the experience of the ex-Soviet world, lack credibility: the overthrow of global capitalism. Second, while this flawed Utopia remains in the background, the foreground is well depicted in the title of a recent symposium, "Globalisation and the Politics of Resistance". The focus of the contributions (several of them inspired by the Gramscian approach) is resistance to the present hegemonial order, not an alternative conception of the order that might be constructed. Perhaps for this reason, one of the theorists who has contributed most to the development of neo-Gramscian international relations theory, Stephen Gill, has moved a long way toward social liberalism in his thinking on alternatives to "disciplinary neoliberalism" (Gill 1998). In relation to Europe, he opposes "the arid financial vision" of the Maastricht agreement, looking to "an alternative form of state" that would be "more democratic, green and social". He urges the left to formulate more concrete policies for both the short and the long term: for example, on the sustainability of the tax base, structural unemployment, the consequences of aging populations, the logic of our present lifestyles, and associated patterns of consumption. Just as there was formerly a great deal of overlap between the practical proposals of social liberals and social democrats, Gill's agenda suggests a similar convergence between a Gramscianism modified along reformist lines and current social-liberal approaches.

CONSTRUCTING ALTERNATIVES

The most prominent attempts to update the social liberal vision cluster around the image of the third way, associated with the policy orientation of the Clinton administration and the government of Tony Blair. The policies are not entirely new; some were adopted earlier by parties of the left in Western Europe and Australia. Practice preceded doctrine. As Anthony Giddens expresses it:

> Theory lags behind practice. Bereft of the old certainties, governments claiming to represent the left are creating policy on the hoof. Theoretical flesh needs to be put on the skeleton of their policy-making—not just to endorse what they are doing, but to provide polities with a greater sense of direction and purpose.

Giddens undertakes this task in *The Third Way,* defining a position that, he claims, "transcends both old-style social democracy and neoliberalism," adapted to a world "which has changed fundamentally in the past two or three decades". Globalization has opened up societies as well as economies; the communications revolution has brought about a "transformation of time and space in our lives". There have been fundamental changes in the nature of the family and the position of women; lifestyles have become far more diversified. Accelerating technological change is transforming not only the workplace but also the nature of work, undermining the norm of long-term, stable employment; the labour market is fragmented and differentiated. All this makes for a new individualism, not in the sense that individuals are more self-regarding, but that far more aspects of life are becoming matters of choice, no longer regulated by the norms of family, class, or tradition. "New" issues such as drugs and crime are high on the political agenda, along with "old" issues such as economic management and welfare and a long-suppressed issue, the environmental consequences of "old" industrialization.

Third-way theorists see a need to rethink the role of the state, in particular the welfare state, not just because its tax base is under threat while the demands for its services are increasing, but also because it must meet new needs that require new kinds of response. These include "lifelong learning"—training programs to keep the workforce abreast of the constantly changing demands of the labour market and to prevent the long-term unemployed from becoming unemployable. They also include programs to promote the inclusion in the society of disadvantaged persons and groups whose special needs must be addressed if they are to have reasonable access to education and work. In other words. something more is required than the allocation of benefits to passive recipients. This is variously expressed as active or positive welfare, or Giddens's "social investment state," and there are suggestions that the old services should be redesigned along similar lines. The individual has responsibilities as well as rights—an idea that is less of a departure in social-democratic (and social-liberal) thinking than is claimed.

The Internal

We may now turn to a closer examination of the proposed alternative to neoliberalism, first in the internal context. The discussion focuses on three of the many potential sources: Tony Blair, the political leader most strongly identified with the third way; Will Hutton, author of an influential critique of the practical consequences of Thatcherism; and an Australian, Mark Latham, for his comprehensive formulation of third-way policies. Latham writes in a different political and institutional context from the others (Australia has not experienced the full-blooded neoliberalism of Thatcher's Britain), but his viewpoint is remarkably close to Giddens. Hutton's is somewhat different; his work thus serves to illustrate the range of variations among those seeking to update social liberalism.

Third-way writers invoke the social-liberal tradition along with the social democratic. For Blair, it is the values espoused by the early ethical socialists that give substance to the notion of a community, and in words that echo T. H. Green, he affirms "the need for society to act together to achieve what the individual cannot do alone," and "the use of the power of society to protect and advance the individual". Latham, invoking the theme of "mutuality," seeks to *recast* social democratic ideology such that it draws from the most attractive aspects of liberalism and socialism: liberal in the sense of selectively pursuing state powers for the creation of social and economic freedoms: socialist in the sense of wanting to foster a dense web of social responsibility and respect for the common good. (1998, 326)

Unemployment is recognized as posing the most urgent challenge—indeed, as the litmus test of the credibility of the social-liberal alternative. Hutton voices a shared theme: "the fulcrum around which the good society turns is an equitable distribution of work and income". "Equitable" implies a rejection of the perceived American model. The deregulation of the labour market does not necessarily achieve high employment, and the improvement it does achieve may come at a high price: reduced living standards for those already impoverished, not only materially but in terms of opportunity for self and family. The starting point is the familiar idea of the need for a highly trained, technically skilled workforce, capable of producing the high-quality goods and services that can compete in the global marketplace, and for retraining programs (lifelong learning) such that the economy can cope with the onrush of technological change. The priority, as Blair is frequently quoted, is "education, education, education."

But clearly this is not sufficient. Not all can have the skills sought by firms competing in the global market, and an increasing share of employment is in "in-person services". It is recognized that specific programs are required to address the needs of particular groups, such as the young with little or no work experience and the long-term unemployed. Here, it is argued, there may be a need for subsidies to employers to offer work to those who would otherwise be passed over. The rationale for such programs is not to increase aggregate employment, which must be sought by other means , but to avoid the formation of a permanent underclass excluded from work and marginalized in society.

Both Hutton and Latham pay particular attention to the regional concentration of unemployment, not only between different parts of the country but also between suburban clusters in large cities, that renders the problem of structural unemployment so intractable. The stimulation of the economy may create full employment and inflationary pressures in prosperous areas, while leaving disadvantaged areas little affected, Hutton looks to political devolution as a response to this problem: if genuine power and resources are transferred to the local level, elected community leaders will have every incentive to fund projects calculated to attract investment, breaking out of the vicious circle that otherwise leads to further stagnation (1997, 74-77). Latham proposes different measures, which take account of Australia's vast distances and sparse population. These include regional infrastructure programs aimed at increasing the productivity of local investment; the location of public sector services in disadvantaged areas; and public funding to support employment in community services that would strengthen the "social capital" and address some of the unmet needs of the disadvantaged. If unemployment is the most pressing immediate concern, the over-riding long-term issue for social liberalism is the adaptation of the welfare state to the changing needs and circumstances noted earlier. There are major differences in the scope of welfare services and in institutional structures and practices across Western societies, but they are experiencing certain common problems. The aging of the population increases the cost of state-supported pensions and the demand for health services, which are also rendered more costly through technological change. Higher levels of education and training and special programs for the disadvantaged impose further costs, as do high levels of long-term unemployment, which were not envisaged in the original design of unemployment relief.

The third way has no simple blueprint to set against the neoliberal drive to privatize as many of the services as possible. "Active welfare," "social investment," and "responsibility" are open to a range of interpretations. It envisages a mix of public and private provision and funding of services, maintaining that considerations of equity, social balance, and also efficiency require that public welfare programs be maintained and revitalized. Both Giddens and Latham offer radical suggestions that indicate the potential for achieving social goals through novel means. Giddens, while insisting on "an adequate level of state-provided pension," would abolish age retirement and the right to a pension at any given age. The old would not be in a retirement ghetto but would be part of the normal society, linked to younger generations through their involvement in work and the community.

Latham goes into greater detail in developing an ambitious conception of a system that would enhance the individual's social capabilities through the customized delivery of services for lifelong learning and income support. Instead of a multiplicity of separately administered schemes for which persons might seek to qualify, they would have a single social security account, into which they would pay contributions and from which they would be entitled to draw support in a range of circumstances. Modern technology makes it possible to administer such customized individual programs, allowing for different phases in the lifelong experience of employment, parental responsibilities, and aging.

Other aspects of the new thinking may be noted more briefly. "Big, centralized government is out. Devolution and decentralization are in". This is not only a reaction against the extreme centralization of power under the Thatcher government but against centralized administration more generally. Accountability is to be increased by bringing government close to the people and by fostering public-private collaboration at the local level. Latham argues along similar lines but with greater emphasis on the need for a sophisticated central administration capable of monitoring local variations. It is part of the third-way philosophy that the associations of civil society, valued in themselves for promoting a sense of community, should be involved in the delivery of services.

There are formidable problems, however, in implementing the program, which lead to a slippage between theory and practice such that to many, and not only radical critics, it becomes difficult to distinguish the third way from the neoliberalism it opposes. Privileged elites are strongly placed to resist state initiatives; as Gill (1998) and others have pointed out, determined efforts have been made to lock in the neoliberal measures and institutions, such that their reversal becomes extremely difficult. If governments have surrendered many of their powers to the market, it is not easy to recover them. Fears of this kind are frequently expressed concerning the Blair government (Jones 1996, 154-157). Furthermore, it is difficult to establish firm political support for the new approach; third-way rhetoric alienates the old left, while the heterogeneous new middle remains ambivalent.

Taxation presents a particular challenge to third-way governments. Hutton argues convincingly that repair of the welfare services most damaged by neoliberal cutbacks would require an increase in taxation that Britain, near the lower end of OECD comparisons in this respect, could well afford. However, whether for electoral reasons or from conviction, Blair presented New Labour as a party of low taxation, severely constraining welfare improvements. Increased expenditure on the notoriously rundown National Health Service, for example, was delayed until, in the winter 1999-2000 public anger over its inability to cope with seasonal demands forced the government's hand. More generally, if social liberalism is claimed to be without cost to taxpayers, it is likely to remain at the level of aspiration and will soon lose credibility. It is ironic that parties of the right appear more willing to risk unpopular tax measures than the new reformists.

We may conclude that in the internal context third-way thinkers have devised an intellectually appealing approach to updating social liberalism in the light of far-reaching changes in Western societies. They highlight diversification and individual initiative and also provide for the inclusion of the disadvantaged. The balance they seek to strike between public and private is fragile, however, and in seeming to position themselves midway between social democracy and neoliberalism, they place themselves under constant pressure to yield ground to the single-minded neoliberals, which they are ill equipped to resist.

The External

The limitations of third-way thinking are even more serious in the international domain. Here, to a disappointing extent, its perspective is inward-looking. Blair's speeches on the "new world order" do not look beyond Europe and the relationship with the United States. Button argues for a more active British role in the European Union and devotes a few pages to the international financial system, but he makes no specific reference to the non-Western world.

Giddens does indeed acknowledge the "daunting" problems of poverty, world inequality, exclusion, and ecological risk ; however, as we have noted, he considers only one way of addressing them, viz. institutional change—"progress towards greater global governance." He endorses the views of theorists of cosmopolitan democracy, who would redress the limitations of contemporary democracies through democratizing international institutions, for example, through reform of the UN Security Council to give a significant voice to the third world and the creation of a directly elected representative assembly as a new UN institution. However, it has thus far proved impossible to reach agreement on more modest reforms in the UN, nor is there sufficient reason to suppose that, even if they could be achieved, such changes could in themselves bring about a new approach to the issues of inequality and development. Giddens does not address these issues directly; in effect, his perspective is little less Eurocentric than that of other exponents of the third way.

The problems confronting societies in an early phase of the development process are quite different from those of the information age societies with which third-way theorizing is concerned. There is a presumption in favor of theories of development that take account of different phases and permit policies to vary in accordance with specific conditions in different societies, and that the universalism of the development orthodoxies of international financial institutions is a major obstacle to the success of their policies.

Third-way writers have thus far not addressed these issues, but a promising alternative approach is set out in the reports of the United Nations Development Programme. Its concept of human development—noted earlier as "both the *process* of widening people's choices and the *level* of their achieved well-being"—is not limited to the economic. In 1990 the UNDP put forward the Human Development Index (HDI) as a more satisfactory means for assessing development than indices based on per capita income alone. The components of the HDI are life expectancy, education—measured in terms of literacy and years of schooling—and income adjusted for purchasing power parity. It is acknowledged that these are crude measures, and subsequent reports take account of other criteria, notably gender, where the data are available. Even the crude indices, however, show that although there is often a close correlation between income and level of development, exceptions are not infrequent in either direction. To take extreme examples: in 1997 Kuwait ranked 6 in per capita income but 53 in human development, while Costa Rica ranked 33 in human development but 60 in per capita income.

In principle, members of the UNDP and like-minded specialists could be recruited to the World Bank. But it is difficult for large institutions to change course; it is likely this would lead merely to a watering down of existing policies. A better option would be to upgrade the UNDP as a separate institution. The UNDP should be given access to a new source of revenue. One that would be singularly appropriate would be the long-canvassed tax. on international financial transfers, the Tobin tax. Taxes on gambling sometimes raise ethical concerns, but currency speculation is an unavoidable byproduct of a system unreservedly supported by the major governments. Its adverse consequences would be mitigated if it were taxed in the interest of the globally disadvantaged. A clear use for the tax would assist toward overcoming the lack of governmental motivation that is one of the practical obstacles to its introduction, not lack of feasibility. But governments would have to come under strong public pressure in order to overcome other disincentives: the success of NGOs in doing so on a range of issues, notably on debt relief, shows that this is not impossible. It is thus conceivable that the most urgent global issue could be addressed even without a change in the prevailing ideology.

This chapter has sought to identify conditions that could make for a successful social-liberal challenge to neoliberalism. They include mobilizing the extensive but fragmented support for a genuine inclusive-liberal alternative, the creation of an effective counter to the deep-seated American aversion to social liberalism, and a normative shift in the intellectual and political culture of Western societies. Short of a major crisis—the most likely catalyst of change—these developments appear to be some ways off. Nonetheless, Hayek's followers have shown that persistent argument can shake the hold of a dominant ideology. Historical analogies are never straightforward, but social liberals can take encouragement from that experience. In the first instance it is necessary to update the social-liberal program in light of the movement of ideas from social to inclusive liberalism as well as the social and economic changes that receive greater attention in policy discussions. In other words, there is a need for a credible and generally recognized alternative.

Two partial alternatives have been considered. The strength of the third way is its sensitivity to social and economic change in Western societies, but its weaknesses are all too evident. In seeking to strike a subtle balance between the old and the new, it concedes too much to neoliberalism—in practice, if not in principle—and at this stage it does not address the issue of the globally disadvantaged. The global perspective is present in the ideas of the UN Development Programme, not a doctrine but a practical application of inclusive-liberal values. Although the UNDP lacks the resources to undertake major development projects, it is conceivable that governments could be brought to make funding available, even without a change in the ruling ideology. It would not be the first time that changes in practice have preceded a change of doctrine.

STATE DEFENSE FORCE IN THE 21ST CENTURY

For the most part the horse cavalry has passed into the history books. Once such an integral part of the forces of every army, they have been consigned to the elucidations of authors and the visual panorama of artists and film makers. Those World War Two soldiers for whom "taps" has not yet been sounded may still remember the day in the United States Army, when thousands of horse soldiers, dressed in khaki breeches and brown campaign hats, passed in review to the triumphant sounds of the military band.

This article is concerned with briefly discussing the role of cavalry in the armies of the 18 -21centuries, and then making a connection with the modern day military emphasizing missions that can be successfully accomplished by the State Defense Force (SDF). Given the lack of equine expertise of most officers possess, the SDF might present a way for keeping the cavalry tradition alive. These activities, though not regularly sanctioned, may be authorized given the appropriate situation. This article is not directly concerned with the author's modern day unit, Cavalry Troop A of the Maryland Defense Force (MDDF). However, it is the intention of this article that other SDF units will see the benefit to be derived from constituting a horse formation and will emulate what has been done in the State of Maryland.

HISTORICAL OVERVIEW OF THE ROLE OF CAVALRY 1750-1854

As Napoleon stated so well, "Cavalry is useful before, during and after a battle". The armies of the 18 and 19 centuries could not wage war successfully were it not for a proficient cavalry arm, and bold and courageous cavalry leaders. The armies of this time had many uses for cavalry, and some of these uses were paramount to winning not only a battle, but a campaign.

Reconnaissance

Where is the enemy? In what strength is he? Where are his weak points? What will the terrain be like that our army will have to traverse? These and a myriad of other questions will need to be answered by the leader of a cavalry troop that is scouting in advance of the army, gaining vital information to be transmitted to the commander.

Line of Supply Protection

Although armies of this time period occasionally"lived off the land," which they passed through, an army's line of supply and communications must be protected, as not all supplies are obtainable "on the spot."

Flank and Rear protection

While some commanders of the period were not as concerned with protecting their flanks, cavalry functioned as a mobile force that can be rapidly moved wherever there is a weakness.

To Fall on the Enemy when he is Wavering

An astute commander knew exactly the right time to employ his cavalry in a massed charge to break the enemy's squares or line of battle. During the Napoleonic Wars in particular, massed cavalry charges influenced or decided the outcome of many battles. At the battle of Eylau in Poland in 1807, Napoleon ordered Marshal Joachim Murat to deliver such a charge when the French centre was threatened. He charged the Russians at the head of 11,000 cavalrymen to stabilize the lines and preserve a sanguinary victory.

Pursuit of a beaten Enemy

Cavalry is useful to follow up a victory by moving with swiftness, to capture demoralized prisoners and much needed supplies, often turning a defeat into a major rout. This period, 1750-1854, was the height of the mounted cavalryman, where the charge with drawn saber would play a decisive role in the outcome of a battle and where the paucity of cavalry could lead to an army's quick demise. There would be few times again where the cavalry would be utilized as the arm of decision, and could impact the outcome of the day of battle so decisively.

1854-1914

It began with one of the most celebrated and criticized actions in history, the Charge of the Light Cavalry Brigade at Balaclava in the Crimea, in 1854. Some of the finest light cavalry in the world charged into a valley bristling with Russian artillery and were subsequently decimated. French Marshal Pierre Bosquet, an eyewitness, commented "It is magnificent, but it is not war" (Woodham-Smith, 1953). Most of the British cavalrymen who participated in that action understood the recklessness of their charge, and many paid with their lives for the folly of the decision. It would not be the last time however, that cavalry would be used in a situation where the tactics were lagging behind the technology. With the advent of advanced weaponry (rifled artillery and small arms), with a greater range and rate of fire, the cavalry charge was a decidedly risky tactic that had to be used wisely, and at exactly the right moment.

The cavalry at this time period is characterized by and significant for the creation of the mounted infantryman, a highly mobile soldier with mounted skills, who can dismount and fight on foot. While there were some isolated charges during this period such as during the American Civil War and British Wars of Colonization, the cavalry charge was for the most part over. The armies of this period used their cavalry for screening and foraging operations and for scouting and raiding the enemy's rear areas and line of supply such as General J.E.B Stuart's famous raid around the Federal Army of General George McClellan in 1862.

1914-1945

The invention of the machine gun and the static trench warfare that developed in World War One heralded the beginning of the true demise of the cavalry on the modern battlefield. Barbed wire and quick firing artillery and rifles meant that the cavalry could only function in those theatres of war that had more open space, such as the desert or the vast expanses of Russia. By 1918 most of the European armies has dismounted their cavalry and used the vitally needed manpower as infantrymen. A notable exception was the four mile mounted charge of the 4th Australian Light Horse Brigade at Beersheba in Palestine in 1917 where they captured the town and routed the Turkish forces there. The 800 cavalrymen took 38 officers and 700 other ranks prisoner as well as four field guns. In the two regiments, only 31 men were killed and 36 men wounded (Bou, 2006). On the Western Front, the birth of the tank meant that a highly mobile and survivable force capable of breaking through the enemy line and causing havoc was now available to the commander who saw its worth. The cavalry's historical role was passed on to the armoured force.

In World War Two, many nations still saw the value in having mounted troops. Contrary to popular conception, most of the supplies and artillery of the armies of the world in 1941 were in fact horse drawn. Many countries in Europe continued to use horse cavalry, including Germany, Russia, Italy and Poland. A popular myth is that Polish cavalry armed with lances charged German tanks during the September 1939 campaign. This arose from misreporting of a single clash on 1 September near Krojanty, when two squadrons of the Polish

18th Lancers armed with sabers scattered German infantry before being caught in the open by German armoured cars. Most countries by the end of the war had mechanized their cavalry. The United States began dismounting its cavalry in the 1930's and the last unit was reorganized in 1944. The last charge of the U.S. Cavalry took place by the 26th Cavalry (Philippine Scouts) on the Bataan Peninsula in 1942.

This period was characterized by the use of large masses of cavalry in a mounted infantry role in coordination with motorized units, most primarily on the Eastern Front. Those enterprising and adaptable commanders utilized the horse, especially when the extreme weather of the Russian winter rendered the panzers and other vehicles immobile. The horses showed that they could still get through.

1945-2007

In the post World War Two era to the present day, some "low intensity" conflicts have seen the use of cavalry in challenging terrain and where the logistical or cultural situation makes it advantageous to use mounted troops. Examples of these would be the Portuguese armyin Angola, Rhodesian cavalryand the Chinese army in Vietnam in the 1970's. U.S. special operations personnel deemed it efficient to use horses in Afghanistan, as the terrain is difficult and it made them better able to assimilate with the Afghan tribes. Apart from ceremonial units which exist in many nations, China and many Central and South American countries still have active cavalry units.

This period was characterized by the innovative and limited use of the horse to meet the needs of a certain tactical situation with success and the formation of ceremonial cavalry units to carry on the tradition of the time when cavalry played an integral part in every army. At the present time, with the ongoing technological innovations that have shaped the battlefield, it is important to see that anachronisms such as horse cavalry will have a place when the correct situation presents itself.

DEVELOPMENT OF MISSION IDEAS FOR THE STATE DEFENSE FORCE

Ceremonial

As previously mentioned, many countries currently have ceremonial formations of cavalry. Two of the most famous are England's Horse Guards (Life Guards and Blues and Royals) and France's Garde Republicaine. Sadly, the United States, with its rich heritage of horse mounted units, has no officially recognized cavalry regiment, other than a few small detachments at the unit level, most noticeably that of the 1st Cavalry Division at Fort Hood, Texas. The United States Army does have an infantry unit, the 3rd U.S. Infantry Regiment (The Old Guard), which carries on the traditions and heritage with ceremony utilizing horses. They are most visible as the guardians of the Tomb of the Unknown Soldier, as well as providing funeral duties for soldiers interred at Arlington National Cemetery. From 1921 until 1941, the 3 U.S. CavalryRegiment provided ceremonial functions at Arlington and for a time was under the command of Colonel George S. Patton, Jr.

It is advisable for any SDF unit that has an equestrian bent to begin by embracing a ceremonial mission. This is especially true of states with a pronounced military history or a large equine population. A ceremonial unit forges a link with tradition by continuing the history of a certain unit by maintaining the presence of it in the public eye. The SDF unit can have a spiritual connection to the original unit (difficult for a State Defense Force unit to prove) or can choose to honour the original unit by recreating the name, with or without the duplication of a historic uniform. It is recommended that the state begin by forming a ceremonial color guard. The advantages of forming a unit with a ceremonial mission are as follow:

Public Relations

It is generally accepted that horses are appreciated and respected by the general population. This fact serves to enhance and encourage interaction between the public and the military department in a friendly and non-threatening environment. This positive exposure will increase the unit's public visibility.

Work with Children

Children love animals and most have affection and interest for horses. Animals teach children responsibility and patience, as well as developing in them a work ethic. It is highly advisable that the unit engage in programs with children where the troopers model ethical behaviour while teaching a no tolerance for drugs policy and other initiatives.

Military Department Recruiting

A mounted unit is immediately recognizable. The advantage for recruiting is that this serves to put the soldiers in the public eye. It is desirable that the unit liaise with the National Guard (NG) and SDF recruiting personnel so that appropriate materials and correct contact information can be forwarded to those interested parties.

Working with the Governor and other VIP's

It is worthwhile that the SDF unit undertake missions for the Office of the Governor and other important personages. This will create goodwill and help to reinforce relations between the state administration and the military department. Recommended events include parades, ceremonies, historical activities, equestrian related competitions and exhibitions, school and summer camp programs, support for state military and political officials, and state and county fairs.

Rural Search and Rescue

Search and Rescue (SAR) is a humanitarian mission and can be immediately useful in those states which have terrain that is very rural, and where horses can be utilized to their best ability. In creating a Standard Operating Procedure, several important concepts come into focus. Firstly, it is suggested that certification for the members be pursued with a nationally accredited organization like the National Association for Search and Rescue (NASAR). Secondly, the training regimen should include emphasis on those essential skills that make up search and rescue. These include: These subjects should be constantly reinforced by continued training to insure that a high level of competence is established, and continues to be met. The highly specialized field of equine SAR requires that team members and their mounts are adept at negotiating difficult terrain on horseback. It is the complex terrain normally encountered in wilderness areas and state parks in which persons normally get lost. To perform this mission successfully, specialized equine equipment, such as lightweight saddlebags, collapsible water buckets, electrolytes, and tools to either pull or tighten a loose shoe while in the field is necessary.

Finally, team members should take classes in the National Incident Management System (NIMS) (National Incident Management System, n.d.) and Incident Command System (ICS) (Introduction to Incident Command System, n.d.), which will facilitate integration of the team with other state agencies and their command and control system. A manageable and trainable structure, such as 2-3 man teams with base camp logistical and communications and information technology (IT) support should be established. A realistic response time, such as rider and mount departing the farm one hour after receiving the deployment order, should be implemented. The suggested sustainability of the teams in the field is 24 hours.

Urban Crowd Control

Some cavalry units, most prominently the excellent cavalry unit from the State of Connecticut, the Governor's Horse Guards (The First Company Governor's Horse Guards, n.d.), do train for a mission of Urban Crowd Control. This is a mission that is most commonly utilized by federal, state and local law enforcement agencies that have mounted patrol units. It involves the control and manipulation of hostile crowds by forcing the horses in tight formations. This is obviously a mission that requires a great amount of training, both for the horses and troopers. Additionally, there is a risk to the safety and security of both in an intimidating environment. Some factors that must be considered are, first to train horses and riders in formation riding and then in special crowd control formations, as follow:

- Line
- Column
- Wedge
- Left and Right Diagonal
- Box
- Diamond
- Obliques
- Side Pass.

Next, it is important to use desensitization training to familiarize horses to the sight and sounds of the crowd; any horse that has been conditioned to be comfortable with a multitude of distractions and frightening circumstances will be easier to deal with, no matter what his job. Lastly, the command cadre must appreciate the need for specialized equipment to be able to carry out urban crowd control operations efficiently.

Remote Access Medical Team

The principal of the Remote Access Medical Team (RAMT) can be best utilized in a state that has a large amount of wilderness areas without easy access by improved roads. The RAMT would give a four-man medical team the ability to provide medical and logistical assistance to those persons in need at the time of a state emergency. The Team principle is copied from the U.S. Special Forces Team, and cross training of the team members is a necessity:

Team Leader: Responsible for decision making, expert at communications and land navigation, extremely competent equestrian

Assistant Team Leader: Best equestrian, responsible for the horses' welfare, trained as veterinary technician, handles pack animal

Physician: Responsible for medical care, trained as equestrian

Nurse or EMT: Assists Physician whenever needed, trained as equestrian, cross trained in communications.

A feasibility study was undertaken and it was determined should the need arise that it was possible to transport a four man RAMT team by airlift using a C-130E aircraft in the same way that sport horses are transported by passenger jet everyday around the world.

Security and Homeland Defense

With the current level of threats to America's homeland, it would behoove the military hierarchy to take full advantage of the SDF as a trained pool of manpower within each state that maintains a United States Code Title 32 authorized SDF unit. It is especially noteworthy that the NG currently comprises approximately 40% of the deployed military forces. With the NG's homeland mission being severely strained by these deployments, it is natural that the SDF within the state fill the void.

Specifically, a mounted unit could be used in a variety of ways: The unit could guard national and state monuments and historic sites; reinforce, at their request, the U.S. Park Police Horse Mounted Unit; guard sensitive sites where the visibility of a mounted patrol would be a deterrent; augment local and state police mounted patrols, at their request, to enhance those that have been stretched thin by budgetary constraints; augment, at their request, the NG and U.S. Border Patrol forces deployed during Operation Jump Start due to the rural nature of the terrain along the border with Mexico (and Canada as well).

Generally, SDF units are not armed and typicallyhave been given missions that support the NG's homeland security and disaster mitigation missions, which support this precept. The rules of engagement are so complex as to make the arming and training of these forces a prohibitive undertaking unless more means are made available, vis-à-vis, the State Defense Force Improvement Act H.R. 826 and there is support for this in the literature. One source of literature presenting the history of the SDF movement, SDF activities, plans, and thoughts for the future can be found in the State Defense Force Publication

Centre. One of those articles presents a guide to the many different homeland security activities for which a SDF unit might undertake in support of their NG unit.

Large Animal Rescue

During a state disaster, such as a hurricane, flood or tornado, that necessitates the evacuation of citizens homes, persons owning large animals (i.e., horses) would face the agonizing decision to abandon them. The other alternative is that they flout the local authorities' edict, in which case their lives are in danger. In the aftermath of Hurricane Katrina, the fine Army Reserve cavalry unit from Michigan, the Blue Devils Horse Platoon, undertook to rescue these animals. They performed admirably, thereby presenting a mission concept that highly specialized cavalry personnel could perform competently. Increased training in handling animals and a thorough equine first aid course would be appropriate.

Cavalry Troop A, Maryland Defense Force, An Example

The Maryland Defense Force is part of the Maryland Military Department. Cavalry Troop A currently consists of twenty officers, troopers and their mounts, and reports directly to the Chief of Staff. The Troop has two missions: (1) Function in a ceremonial role for the Maryland Military Department as an aid in recruiting and public relations; and (2) Partner with Maryland agencies as a rural terrain.

It is advisable that the commander of a cavalry unit vary the unit's training schedule so that mounts get exposed to different schooling opportunities. In this vein, MDDF Cavalry Troop A has developed a specialized and historical training program. The Troop is undergoing a saber qualification course based upon the 1926 U.S. Army course. This course has twenty targets and measures swordsmanship and horsemanship equally. Troop Deputy Commander Captain (MD) R. Hammond wrote "Troop A will never draw its M1913's in combat, real or simulated, since the Troop members are neither combat soldiers nor living historians. Nevertheless, the Troop requires confident riders and obedient, fit mounts for the missions we do have.

There is already a great deal of training in the Troop's annual cycle, but there are few things that match the saber qualification course for confidence building and unit pride.". Furthermore, the United States Cavalry Association annually hosts a National Cavalry Competition. This is an event where riders can improve their equitation and skill-at-arms on horseback by competing against like minded individuals.

WELL, WHAT IS THAT DANGER?

There is a significant probability of another catastrophic emergency in the near future, whether it is a terrorist attack or a natural disaster. I have spent a great amount of my time in the past five years analyzing these catastrophic emergencies. A catastrophic incident or emergency is defined in the National Response Plan as follows:

Any natural or manmade incident, including terrorism, that results in extraordinary levels of mass casualties, damage or disruption severely affecting the population, infrastructure, environment, economy, national morale, and/or government functions. A catastrophic event could result in sustained national impacts over a prolonged period of time; almost immediately exceeds resources normally available to State, local, tribal, and private-sector authorities in the impact area; and significantly interrupts government operations and emergency services to such an extent that national security would be threatened.

The Catastrophic Incident Supplement to the NRP says further that a catastrophic emergency will require immediate and proactive action by the Federal Government. I am going to discuss five potential catastrophic emergencies in brief. The scenarios I will mention are a nuclear attack, an influenza pandemic, the New Madrid Earthquake, a prolonged power outage in a metropolitan area, and prolonged disruption of electronic communications.

A Nuclear Detonation

The most serious threat is a nuclear attack on a major metropolitan area. This is Scenario Number one of the fifteen standard national planning scenarios issued by the Homeland Security Council to provide a common basis for national planning and preparedness.

The concept of operations for managing the consequences of a nuclear detonation calls for organizing the space around the point of detonation into three zones.

The Primary Zone will encompass the direct blast and thermal effects of the detonation and also the primary alpha, gamma, and beta radiation. During the response, this Primary Zone will be defined and sealed off with a cordon to prevent egress by untrained and unequipped persons and to receive and process survivors who can leave the primary zone. The Primary Zone will contain the bulk of the structural damage and the immediate fires from the thermal effects, although there may be secondary fires outside the Primary Zone. For a 10kt weapon, the Primary Zone will have a radius of about two miles. Depending on population density for a city and the time of detonation, about 200,000 people will be killed inside the Primary Zone. In effect, the idea is to lay siege to the Primary Zone and move the perimeter inward as the radiation decays.

The Fallout Zone will encompass the area affected by gamma radiation emanating from fallout particles borne aloft. The explosion will cause small particles to be borne by winds aloft downwind and deposited there. The radiation intensity is greatest near the point of detonation and decreases thereafter. There is no physical damage in the Fallout Zone. Again depending on population density, there could be about one million people or more who have to take shelter or evacuate the Fallout Zone. The major thrust of the entire response operation is to help these million people avoid a dangerous dose of ionizing radiation. That means that we have to be able to measure the intensity of radiation, predict the path of the fallout plume, and establish cordons around the Fallout Zone to prevent people from moving into the radiation and provide a means of processing, decontaminating, and treating people who evacuate the Fallout Zone. We advocate a mixed survival strategy for people in the Fallout Zone that includes both sheltering and evacuation in an orderly manner. This requires that we be able to communicate with the people and conduct a phased evacuation. For a 10kt weapon, the length of the Fallout Zone could be as great as 200 miles. The idea is to get as many people as possible out of the zone before they receive a dangerous dose of ionizing radiation.

There is also a Secondary Zone that will serve as a base area to support the response operation and to shelter the people who are evacuated from the Fallout Zone. This area will also be cordoned off to limit the movement of evacuees, who might be suffering from radiation illness from leaving the Secondary Zone and to prevent entry into the Secondary Zone of unauthorized persons who will increase workload in that zone and complicate the working of the response operation. The secondary zone population could be as much as six million people, who would have to be able to accommodate the one million refugees. The idea is to limit the effects of the explosion so that the rest of the Nation will not be impacted.

The parts of the United States outside the Secondary Zone will be in a state of increased alert and even panic. Authorities will anticipate a second attack and citizens will be afraid. This means that lateral reinforcement programs such as the Emergency Management Assistance Compact (EMAC) that draws forces from other states will not work.

Managing the response to this nuclear detonation will require 200,000 or more organized, trained, and disciplined responders, about half of whom would have to be armed to do their jobs. Armed personnel are needed to form and enforce the cordons around the Primary Zone, Fallout Zone, and Secondary Zone, to manage the evacuation, secure response personnel processing evacuees, protect shelters and camps for evacuees, and maintain law and order within the Secondary Zone. This demand can be met only by law enforcement officers, active duty and reserve military troops, National Guard troops, and armed members of State Defense Forces.

In the response to a nuclear detonation, the first few hours are of critical importance. The response operation will essentially be over after the first 48 hours. All who can be saved will have been saved by that time. The rest will die of injuries or exposure to radiation—sooner or later. This reality places a premium on rapid response. The first actions will be taken by the local responders. The initial reinforcements will be state resources, including nearby National Guard elements and SDF units. Federal resources will arrive on the scene as rapidly as they can. They cannot wait until asked for but must as proceed instantly and automatically as soon as the nuclear weapon detonates.

At present there are too few organized, trained, and disciplined responders available to meet the demand in the first 48 hours. There are not going to be enough armed troops available rapidly to provide an adequate response when they are needed most. Filling that gap in armed responders is the duty of the State Defense Forces. Local militia units organized, equipped, trained, and armed can provide what is essential for the first hours after a nuclear detonation. Acting on pre-scripted assignments, these units can help the local and state police set up the cordons, patrol the evacuation routes, respond to civil unrest, and secure key facilities. It might be possible also to enable the local SDF units to help in measuring radiation intensityand delivering emergency public information. This is the most demanding emergency the nation faces.

The Government is making a great effort to interdict nuclear weapons before they can get into the United States. However, let me tell you that it would be foolish to assume that dedicated terrorists would not try to do this. It would be doubly foolish to assume they cannot succeed. If they do detonate a nuclear weapon in the United States, and we have not prepared to minimize the effects of the explosion, we will have failed the nation.

I want to explore for a minute why we do not prepare for this emergency or for other catastrophic emergencies. It is a matter of attitude. Many people would rather deal with the known and familiar hazards and are reluctant to address the big ones. It was obvious for years that a Category Four Hurricane would strike New Orleans and that the levees were weak, but only a few hard core members of the Emergency Management Community took that possibility seriously.

I want to share with you're a story that illustrates the difficulty of getting people to support an armed SDF. In November 2005 I went to Columbus, Ohio at the request of Michael Moran, a member of the Ohio Military Reserve Association, to support the efforts of Moran and others to improve the Ohio Military Reserve. The occasion was a hearing of the Ohio Military Reserve and Homeland Security Study Commission. The objective of this exercise was to persuade the Ohio General Assembly to provide for modernizing the authorizing legislation for the Ohio Military Reserve and provide funding for expansion of the strength of that organization. My role was to testify before the Commission and advise them of the need for Ohio to have a strong SDF. The Commission included the Director of Homeland Security, the Adjutant General, Director of Public Safety, two Senators, and three Representatives.

I told the Commission that a strong, organized, disciplined, trained, and armed Ohio Military Reserve was essential in an age of terrorism. I spoke about the effects of a 10kt nuclear detonation in Chicago. I explained that the Fallout Zone for such an attack would extend eastward from Chicago across Northern Indiana and Ohio to Toledo, Ohio. Thousands of Hoosiers and Ohioans would be fleeing southward to escape the radiation threat. I had done my homework and pointed out that the combined resources available to the Governor of Ohio in the form of state police and National Guard would be inadequate to manage that situation. I said the Ohio needed a strong, armed SDF of tens of thousands of armed troops to deal with that kind of emergency. I also noted that such a volunteer force would be of great value to Ohio for lesser emergencies.

The efforts Mike Moran and his colleagues were to no avail. The leadership of Ohio would not support a strong SDF. All that Moran wanted was to achieve legitimacy and have a cadre force of about 1,500 unarmed members and a miniscule budget.

I had suggested an armed force of about 30,000. None of this was achieved. The Commission decided not to do anything for the Ohio Military Reserve. The greatest opponent of the enhanced SDF for Ohio was the Adjutant General, who said that he could do it all with the National Guard and did not need any help. I was distressed by this view. Upon reflection, I concluded that in addition to turf and money problems, the Adjutant General and most of the others did not believe there would ever be a nuclear attack in Chicago.

The problem is with attitude. Complacency is not a virtue for those charged with defending the United States. To be truly effective, responders have to believe that emergencies will truly occur.

Influenza Pandemic

An Influenza Pandemic with the Avian Flu H5N1 virus could be more devastating than even a nuclear detonation. We know the Avian Flu virus has infected a lot of birds and that it has already been transmitted from birds to other animals and in a few cases from birds and animals to humans. When that happens, it is possible for the Avian Flu to affect the entire country very quickly. The pandemic will spread in two waves. The first wave will last about three months and attack mostly healthy young adults. There will be an inter-pandemic period of about three months, and then the second wave will start and last about two months and attack mostly older adults. As it spreads, the virus will mutate and shift to new forms that cannot be predicted in advance but can be determined only by isolating and identifying each new strain. Depending on the number of patients that become infected, the effects will range from 90,000 to 210,000 dead, 300,000 to 700,000 hospitalizations, 18 million to 40 million outpatients, and total infections of from 38 million to 93 million people. Whether the workload is the upper limit or the lower limit or something in between depends on how the response is conducted.

The public health and health care delivery system cannot deal effectively with this kind of pandemic. Vaccinations will not stop the spread of the disease because the correct vaccine cannot be made until the exact virus is identified. Once the causal virus is isolated, it will take six to nine months to produce the appropriate vaccine. Even if an H5N1 vaccine is stockpiled in advance, it might not be effective. Even if it is effective, it will be impossible to vaccinate more than about 10% of the population.

The public health and health care delivery systems will be overwhelmed. The number of physicians, nurses, and other health care professionals is finite and cannot be expanded enough to cope with the workload. The number of hospital beds with supporting paraphernalia in the United States is also finite, and there will be too few beds to cope with the workload. There are only about one million hospital beds in the United States, and almost all of these are already occupied.

Medical professionals realize they cannot stop this pandemic. Their best advice is to wear a mask and wash your hands frequently. Even the palliative medicines, such as TamiFlu are inadequate to the task.

This means that a major emphasis has to be made on stopping the transmission of the virus and reducing the rates of infection at least to a manageable level and perhaps stopping the spread of the virus entirely. The experience with the Spanish Influenza Pandemic of 1918 suggests that quarantine or isolation works well in stopping the spread of the disease.

Present plans call for states to call for voluntary quarantines. I suspect that in the real event, the states will impose mandatory quarantines. When quarantine is imposed, the major problems are how to sustain the people after stocks of food are exhausted, how to distribute medicines, and how to perform vaccinations. Doing these things will be a major challenge for emergency managers and medical people.

The law enforcement community with the help of the National Guard and State Defense Forces will have to enforce the quarantines and maintain law and order. Foolish people will refuse to obey the rules of the quarantine and wander about carelessly spreading the virus. Desperate people will use force to obtain scarce vaccines and medicines. Hungry people will take it upon themselves to obtain food for themselves and their families. Angry people will take out their anger on medical and other people trying to help them. Criminals and street gangs will take advantage of the situation to enrich themselves.

During such a pandemic each governor will need a large number of organized, disciplined, trained, and armed troops to help law enforcement agencies enforce the quarantines and provide security for those who the spread of the disease and see that supplies of scarce commodities are distributed fairly to all. A strong SDF will be needed.

The New Madrid Earthquake

This is a very real possibility. If a magnitude 8.0 earthquake occurs along the central portion of the Mississippi River Valley, the consequences would be wide-ranging and serious. This has been a concern of emergency managers for years, and FEMA is now engaged in preparing a plan to deal with it.

The consequences will be severe. All the bridges across the Mississippi River from Cairo to St Louis will be down. Roads and bridges in seven states will be damaged. Pipelines and electrical cables will be down. Transportation will be at a standstill. Millions of people will be left without essential services. Thousands will be injured by collapsing structures, and many more will be left temporarily homeless. The damage and disruption will be great.

A good concept for managing this catastrophic emergency is to ask all residents to remain in their localities instead of trying to move outside of the affected area. Search and rescue operations will be conducted on a local basis, and localities will have to deal with casualties from the effects of the earthquake. Essential supplies and services and additional responders would be brought into the affected states from outside private sector and federal resources and private sector resources under Federal management. This will preclude having thousands of persons on the highways trying to leave and making it difficult for outside help to get to the survivors inside the affected states.

In this kind of situation, there will be numerous instances of violence. The local police will be overwhelmed, and the governors of the affected states will have to provide National Guard and SDF forces to assist in the immediate response tasks and in the subsequent delivery and distribution of essential goods and services. While Federal forces will be used, much of their effort will be on the logistics of providing support. Responsibility for maintaining law and order and securing the responders will fall on the governors. They will need to have strong SDF units with organized, disciplined, trained, and armed troops to augment the police and National Guard forces.

A Prolonged Power Outage

It would be relatively easy for a terrorist group to cause a widespread power outage either by physical means or by a cyber attack. If this occurs, there would be widespread disruption of essential services and distribution of essential goods. We all depend on electrical power for what we do. We cannot pump gas without power. We cannot work in offices, keep cool, or keep warm without power. We cannot communicate or do business without power.

It such an outage lasts for a few hours, it is a nuisance. If the outage lasts a few days, it is an irritant. If the outage lasts for a few weeks, it is an emergency. If the outage extends over a large region, those in the interior will not have recourse to support from areas with power. A few families and a few businesses will have backup generators. People living in houses with solar panels can get by. But the rest of us will have to do without.

Imagine if you will what your neighborhood would be like if the power were out for six weeks. Cars will run out of gas. Food would spoil. Neighbours could turn mean. Street gangs could rove the streets doing bad things. After food, water, and medicine, your most important need would be for security, which can be provided only by the police or troops.

The concept of the response operation for this catastrophic emergency is to provide essential survival goods—food, water, and medicine—to those without power. The policy will be to ask people to stay in their homes and wait for help to come to them. Large numbers of people will try to self-evacuate to areas with power, thus impeding the influx of supplies and workers and equipment to restore the power supply. So a major challenge for the authorities will be to enforce the stay in place policy, assure fair distribution of essential supplies, and maintain law and order. The police will be overwhelmed. Governors will have to deploy their National Guard and State Defense Forces to augment the police within their respective states.

A Prolonged Disruption of Electronic Communications

The final catastrophic emergency I will address is a prolonged disruption of electronic communications. This would be similar to the prolonged power outage but greater in scope and even more disastrous in its consequences. It is possible to survive for a time without power using the old fashioned way. Few of you can even envision what it would be like to live without the internet and cell phones for a long time.

We are very vulnerable to the failure of electronic devices. We have abandoned the old methods that were used before electronic devices appeared. Most of us have lost the skills necessary to function in a non-electronic world.

As a society we have become very dependent, perhaps overly dependent on the internet and electronic systems to manage data and to communicate. When those systems fail massively it would be a catastrophic emergency.

If our economy and society are suddenly deprived of electronic communications, the disruption of will provoke disorder and provide a fertile field for criminals and some normally law abiding citizens driven to rage by frustration. This condition on a regional or national basis will soon become too hard for the police, and troops will be needed to help maintain order and provide security while we reestablish systems and learn to cope with a world without the internet, cell phones, and electronic systems of all kinds. This is yet another situation for which the existing of a strong SDF with organized, disciplined, trained and armed troops would be very useful.

There are other catastrophic and lesser emergencies in which the SDF can play an important role. But in order to have an adequate SDF, some things have to be done.

WHAT NEEDS TO BE DONE

There certainly is a persuasive case for having a large number of SDF troops available to the Governors to deal with catastrophic emergencies as well as lesser emergencies. It is up to all of us to see that this case is made the basis for persuading the governors to sponsor and fund such a program. I will address three of the controversial issues that plague the SDF community. They are whether the SDF is to be armed or not; whether the SDF is to be a cadre or at full strength; and the overall strength of the SDF.

Arming the State Defense Forces

To Arm or not to Arm? That is the question that gets to the bottom of what the SDF is to be. Some TAGs want the SDF to be nothing more than a source of low-cost help to perform administrative work and provide support services. They perceive the proper role of the SDF is to do some low priority programs for the Guard such as taking care of the armories—sort of a supplementary caretaker group. That is not my image. An unarmed SDF cannot perform the security and response missions for which the SDF is needed and which is the sole basis for having the SDF in the first place. An unarmed militia is an oxymoron.

Except for the Naval Militia, which truly has the right idea on this issue, none of the numerous competing volunteer organizations envision arming their members. They resemble what we old soldiers would characterize as camp followers whose duties were to wash the clothes and cook the food for those in the ranks. Indeed, it may be a good idea to provide unarmed civilians to provide some of the support for the National Guard that DOD has failed to provide, but that is not the proper role of the State Defense Forces. The Nation has many law enforcement officers to enforce the law and maintain order. There are about a million sworn police officers in the United States. This number has remained stable for a decade despite increasing population and crime. There are also almost a million criminals and members of violent street gangs in the United States. The balance between the cops and the criminals is precarious even in normal times. When a catastrophic emergency occurs, the police will need help. That help can be provided only by military forces trained and armed to perform security duty. These military forces can come from Federal active duty and reserve units, from the National Guards of the several states, and from the State Defense forces—provided the SDF troops are trained and equipped with weapons appropriate for their role.

Numerous other volunteer organizations exist to provide specialized services for emergency response. The Red Cross is one. The Disaster Response Medical System is another. The Neighborhood Watch is still another. The Civil Air Patrol and the Coast Guard Auxiliary perform valuable services and can do so without being armed. The Citizen Corps sponsored by DHS offers willing Americans an opportunity to participate in Homeland Security programs by performing a variety of jobs—none of which require them to be armed. If an individual objects to serving in an armed force, he or she should join one of these civilian organizations.

Often, when I mention the need for armed SDF, someone says that you SDF members are not to be trusted with weapons. One retired regular major general said he doubted whether you SDF members would be capable or qualifying with your weapons on a range. Another senior person said that arming you would be a threat to the nation. Many members of the National Guard and some Adjutants General with SDF units oppose arming your troops.

Those who oppose arming the SDF also offer some practical objections. There is the additional burden of storing arms and ammunition, conducting weapons training, and assuring that weapons safety is maintained. Some fear consequences of accidents and the liability issues that could result from them. Some fear that armed militia men will go on a rampage in the woods and kill or wound civilians. These arguments appear to be excuses to avoid arming the SDF. These same objections apply to the National Guard itself. None of the objections are sufficient reason either to disarm the National Guard or deny weapons to the SDF.

All of these are excuses to avoid arming the SDF, but they are not good enough to offset the need for organized, disciplined, trained, and armed troops when they are Such arguments reflect badly on you. You have among your ranks veterans of active and reserve duty with many years of military service and experience. How do you feel about being labeled as either too incompetent or too untrustworthy or both to command and train your soldiers to bear arms in defense of the Nation?

The US is awash with handguns, rifles, and even some heavy weapons in the hands of gangs, illegal militias, and other unauthorized criminal groups. The bad guys will have arms, and experience indicates they will use them for their own advantage. Sworn law enforcement officers are responsible for maintaining law and order, but there will be too few of them to maintain law and order during and after a catastrophic emergency. National Guard troops will have arms, but they also will be too few to do it all during and after a catastrophic emergency. Federal troops will be armed, but they will arrive at the scene after a delay. The need is for more organized, disciplined, trained, and armed troops—and that is the role of the SDF.

I said before and I say again that sending unarmed SDF troops out to enforce cordons, secure critical assets, manage evacuations, provide security for firefighters and medical teams, and suppress civil disorders would amount to criminal negligence.

Finally, I ask that you ponder this proposition. It is far better to have arms and not need them than to need arms and not have them.

I note with sadness and disbelief that some states have adopted a policy of maintaining their SDF units at cadre strength with the expectation that they will be able to recruit, train, and bring their units to full strength in time to do some good. This will not work.

I can just picture it now. And I want you to think about it also. A nuclear weapon has just detonated in Washington DC. The chief of staff of the Virginia National Guard rushes into the AG's office and says breathlessly: General, Washington DC has just been attacked with a nuclear weapon. What do we do now? The AG then says, "Send out the recruiters to bring the Virginia Defense Force to full strength!" I think not.

It is the nature of catastrophic emergencies to be unforgiving of delayed responses. The attacks will occur without warning or with little warning. There may be warning of some disasters but too little advance notice to spend six to ten weeks bringing the State Defense Force to full strength.

The only pseudo-advantage of cadre units is to provide the illusion of readiness without the reality.

For catastrophic emergencies in particular and for lesser emergencies as well, it is absolutely necessary to be fully prepared in advance. That means that the SDF units must be at full strength, fully equipped, have access to stockpiled supplies, and trained and rehearsed on pre-scripted responses to catastrophic emergencies.

Strength of the SDF

Finally, there ought to be some strength goals to pursue. The present situation of 25 units sharing 20,000 active members is unsatisfactory. That amounts to an average of 800 active members per state. This is far too few members to provide adequate support for a response to a catastrophic emergency.

My own initial strength goal would be to have 300,000 armed active members of the SDF nationwide. This is an average of only about 6,000 per state. Surely that is a feasible goal.

The current small strength of the SDF is due to more to self-inflicted budgetary wounds and worries about administrative burden rather than difficulties of recruiting and retention. Recruiting will succeed if it is tried. Retention will succeed if the troops are given realistic training and important missions.

There are large numbers of trained veterans of the campaigns in Iraq and Afghanistan that have left active duty, do not want to join the National Guard or a Federal Reserve Component, but would like to help provide for the security of the United States in some way. These prior-service personnel could be integrated into SDF units, undergo some refresher training, and be ready to serve. Many of these people will be NCOs and junior officers, but the tables of organization can be modified to have a grade structure that could accommodate them.

The rationale for the initial goal of 300,000 active members is that this is about half of the strength of the Army and Air National Guards. The future employment of the National Guard on Federal active duty to support the conduct of the war on terror is not known, but the policy has been that each governor will have at least half of his or her National Guard available for Homeland Defense and Civil Support missions. We don't know the future, but it is prudent to assume that the National Guard will continue to contribute large numbers of units and individuals to the Army and Air Force respectively.

A strength of 300,000 active members will solve a lot of problems. The SDF will become a recognized and reputable contributor to Homeland Security instead of a little known, ineffective fringe group. The stigma attached by some to a force considered by some to consist mostly of self-styled generals and colonels will vanish. As the strength of the SDF increases, the value of this military force in lesser emergencies will be even more apparent. The National Guard may even recognize the value of their SDF units and accept the SDF soldiers as comrades.

In particular, the increased strength at low cost will be welcomed by Governors when they face emergencies beyond their capacity to manage. If Louisiana, Alabama, and Mississippi had large SDFs, the late arrival of Federal troops for the Katrina Emergency would not have been so damaging to the response. As it was, the use of 5,000 SDF personnel mostly from other states was very useful in the Katrina response operation.

A strong SDF would or should be welcomed by DOD. The increased capability of Governors to deal with attacks and disasters would allow the states to deal with more emergencies without needing federal help. When, as will be the case for catastrophic emergencies, Federal resources and troops will be needed immediately, the presence of strong SDF units in the incident area will fill the needs until the Federal troops arrive.

Another factor is that the ability and perhaps the intention of DOD to have the President federalize all of the National Guard elements in an affected state will strip the governors of any resources needed to support his or her own operations. In that event, the SDF will be the only military forces available to the Governors. If that occurs, a governor is certain to wish that he or she had done the right thing for the SDF before the emergency occurred. It is up to us to relieve governors from that prospect.

WHAT DOES THE FUTURE HOLD FOR THE SDF?

The SDF program is at a critical juncture. The State Guard Association has to take some action. You have to decide whether you are in business to advocate and lobby for a strong, armed militia or to continue to maintain an unsatisfactory status quo. Taking action for a strong SDF will not be an easy task. You have few allies. You need to develop champions for a strong SDF. There are individuals out there, some with great stature, that realize the importance of a strong SDF and will work with you to make that happen. You need to provide leadership and a focal point for all of individuals. In particular, you have the ability to influence the governors and the adjutants general who can make their SDFs valuable assets if they want to.

The title of this talk is The Role of the State Defense Forces in Homeland Security. In my view, that role is to provide large numbers of organized, disciplined, trained, and armed troops to augment the police, National Guard troops, and federal troops in anticipation of and in response to catastrophic emergencies. It is up to you members of the State Guard Association to assure that the State Defense Forces are adequate to perform this role.

FUNDAMENTAL INFORMATION FOR THE CITIZEN VOLUNTEER

The American public is besieged with the uncertainty of terrorism and the next terrorist attack. Is the reason economic, social, political, religious, or is there no reason at all for it? Steven Deitz, American playwright and dramatist suggests that "*A people who's primary aims are driving, shopping, and television are subject to terrorism at any time.*" Unfortunately, whatever the reason, there are global Salafist extremists who have already attacked America and are regularly threatening to continue their acts of terror. What's to be done, what's to be done?!?

Fortunately, the American public has an option for combating all forms of terrorism. It begins with learning about and understanding the terrorists' mode of organization, their motivation, where they congregate and recruit, and how they select their targets. Once equipped with this understanding, the citizen volunteer must learn how to observe and recognize possible terrorist activities and to differentiate between innocent members of the community and the truly potential terrorist activity. Finally, the citizen volunteer must know who to contact with this information and how to present that information (also known as intelligence) in a way that the proper authorities can make use of that intelligence.

Imagine three males of seemingly Mid-Eastern descent seen driving around locally in a late model van, stopping periodically for no apparent reason, or walking in the local mall or sporting event acting suspiciously. What to do? What should be done? These, and many other questions, have been asked by average citizens and students during lectures on terrorism, and its continued and ever increasing presence here in the United States. As local and state law enforcement agencies begin to train on identifying, preventing and reacting to the militant Islamic extremists, it is becoming more apparent that this newest threat to our homeland will require a tremendous amount of assistance from the average citizen. This much needed support from the citizens of the various communities can only come as a result of education in the identification phase of our homeland security measures.

Defining Terrorism

As this newest threat continues to penetrate our porous borders and the terrorist leaders assimilate themselves within the general public of our society, it becomes necessary to find a working definition of terrorism to have and use as an effective tool. It is this elusive definition that has had a direct and debilitating impact on the struggle to identify and defeat terrorist attacks thus far. At every level of government, there are multiple definitions for the act of terrorism leading to considerable confusion. Instead, it is possible to identify this new enemy through the application of terroristic-guerilla warfare, which is, "…the deliberate use of violence against a person or persons using guerilla warfare tactics in an effort to achieve political, ideological, or religious goals." With this working definition, it is possible to more readily identify the forms of terrorism facing this country and develop a proposal at the strategic and tactical levels to combat any terroristic operation within the U. S.

Operational Phases of Terroristic-Guerilla Warfare

Now, with a good starting point, it would serve to better understand a theoretical approach as to how terrorist cells penetrate a particular community and patiently plan and execute their future attacks. Terrorist cells within the U.S. operate under the following seven phases in preparation of executing their terroristic-guerilla warfare tactics (Note: All seven phases might not be used all the time and some of them might occur out of the order presented in this article.): Preparation – Terrorist groups look for a location from which to base their operations and begin recruiting. Community selection and socioeconomic structure are two critical factors in their choice of location. The socioeconomic structure of a community is crucial to a cell's intelligence preparation in a given area of operation. Understanding the sociological elements of a given city, along with its economical structure, is critical for terrorists attempting to exploit and undermine a social system while recruiting for their cause. People from every level of the social strata, from the educated to the unschooled and from the social elite to the criminal derelicts are potentially subject to the recruitment techniques of these local cells. Location is critical as they require an environment conducive to recruiting as well as privacy for planning their attacks.

Initial Contact – Over time, the organizational structure begins to take shape and positions within the cell are filled with recruits from the local community. In order to recruit locals to meet their specific needs, cell members set clandestine operations in motion to begin identifying those who meet the special needs within a particular cell. While looking for those individuals who might meet their strategic and tactical needs for future terrorist operations, cell members integrate themselves into the daily lives of their target population with absolute discretion, giving the appearance of the average U.S. citizen residing in "Anytown, USA." Once they have comfortably maneuvered themselves into the everyday events of their chosen community, then, and only then, will they begin their initial contact.

Infiltration – Infiltration is defined as complete submersion into a society. A critical factor for the development of the cell's structure in this stage is the process of isolating promising recruits in U.S. society who may harbor ill feelings toward either the current government or Christians and Jews. They begin to quietly spread their religious and political ideologies as a more acceptable alternative to the democratic governments in the evil empire of the Western world. Militant Islamic terrorist cells are building mosques and other infrastructures designed to quietly train U.S.-born Muslims and others throughout the

U.S. to engage in a continuing jihad (holy war) against the U.S. way of life in order to impose a worldwide Islamic rule.

Organization – Once the infiltration phase has been positively established in an area of operations deemed satisfactory to the needs of the newly formed insurgent group, the terrorist cell's organization begins to take shape. With decentralized cells working toward a common objective, those caught during the commission of an illegal act are unable to give any operational intelligence on other sections of their cell or on the existence of other cells. A terrorist cell evolves in both size and sophistication as new recruits enter their training and progress to any of the cell's three organizational forces: auxiliary, intelligence and operational. A cell's organizational structure can vary from this suggested configuration but will have similar characteristics, regardless of the structural framework.

Buildup – Although the name of this phase implies there is a massing or increase in size of the cell, the size will vary with each location (and sociological environment), organization and intended mission. Twenty-first century terrorist cells located within the U.S. are organized in small and illusive elements more suitable to meet their needs for conducting covert operations at every phase of their insurgency. Furthermore, recruits with special skills are also scrutinized more heavily when considered for recruitment, unlike the average guerrilla fighter in previous wars. Understanding this philosophy is critical for law enforcement agencies throughout the country that must identify and disrupt terrorist cells within their jurisdictions. On the basis of its beliefs, leadership, teachings, training, and geographical and social conditions, each organization will adapt to its natural surroundings and begin to take its own shape over time.

Combat Employment – Once a cell has determined that it is time to conduct combat operations, plans will become actions set into motion with finite precision, leaving little room for identification or interception by first responders. The asymmetric actions of typical guerilla warfare are a product of months of detailed planning, resourcing, organizing and rehearsing. Once this phase has begun, law enforcement agencies and other first responders enter a mode of emergency management, while the perpetrators -if not killed in the attack themselves - take measures to avoid capture or any lasting damage to the remaining terror network members.

Demobilization – Demobilization during guerrilla warfare is more likely to occur in the form of a dismembering of the operational cell responsible for the actual terrorist attacks - that is, if the members do not die for their cause (e.g., homicide bombings) or are caught during the commission of their criminal act. It could also be concluded that the parent cell itself could stand down and relocate to another area or region if the situation proved dangerous to its existence and execution of Usama bin Laden's second fatwa. The organization's decentralized operational control allows the separate cells to function independently, providing uninterrupted and continuous operations. To successfully terminate a local cell's operational status, a way must found to demobilize the actual base facilities (e.g., mosques, school and training camps) where they recruit, train, plan and project terror against their intended targets.

HOW TO IDENTIFY A POTENTIAL TERRORIST

During any of the beginning phases of a terrorist operation, there is a chance one or more of their cell members can be identified and apprehended as they move about freely. Most citizens might be convinced that a definitive profile would prove the easiest way to find and identify a terrorist, but a qualitative profile (e.g., male, of Muslim descent, between 21-40 years of age) is all but impossible to offer up to the general public without the fear of causing undo problems with those innocents living in the Muslim-American communities. While this type of profiling has worked in the past with serial rapists and killers, hostage takers and potential suicide victims, it is not advisable to rely on the same identifying factors for terrorists; thus, it is possible to profile terrorists and their organizations with quantitative data. Such numeric data does not necessarily provide law enforcement and other first responder agencies with enough information to definitively identify a potential attacker. Another concern in offering the general public a profile of a potential terrorist directly relates back to the "Red Scare" of the McCarthy era from 1950-1954. The thought that neighbours and fellow workers fall within the general profile of a terrorist is exactly what must be avoided. What should be determined is suspicious activity, things that look out of the ordinary from everyday occurrences. Situational awareness of the neighborhoods and new individuals seen around businesses and housing areas are a couple of examples of how the citizen volunteer could potentially identify terrorists living among the citizenry and studying their cultural and daily habits. By this time, the profile may sound exactly like the characteristics of a stalker, a rapist, or a serial murderer. The point is that while all criminals are not terrorists, all terrorists are in fact criminals and will display the very same discriminative qualities to the average citizen.

PROTECTING AGAINST BECOMING A VICTIM

On several occasions, the terms antiterrorism and counterterrorism have been used as exchangeable terms, but they are distinctly different. Antiterrorism is defensive and passive in nature and includes physical security measures such a lighting, fencing, alarms and security guards. Counterterrorism, on the other hand, is more offensive and active, almost aggressive. In protecting against becoming a victim, the citizen is enacting antiterrorism measures in his daily life and he should begin with his own domicile. Simple things such as protecting a home with alarm systems, living in gated communities with contracted security, increasing outdoor lighting at night or fencing in the yard will increase the odds against potential terrorist activity. While traveling away from home, try varying daily routes to work and school. Also consider changing times of travel. Pay attention to the surroundings and take note of anything out of the ordinary. Ensure that a cellular phone is readily available to call first responders if needed.

THE CITIZEN'S ROLE IN FIGHTING AGAINST TERRORISM

All of these suggestions might appear sophomoric at first glance, but the average citizen is not trained in these fundamental security and observation skills. Notice that everything suggested is preventative. The average citizen can assist local law enforcement agencies to collect intelligence that might prove valuable in a collective effort. Any information gathered and shared could lead to a potential investigation of a local terrorist cell. That average citizen, while possibly alert to his surroundings, is not trained to prevent a terrorist attack once an overt act has been initiated. It is during the prevention stage where the volunteer citizen can play a critical role in protecting neighborhoods and cities. By acting together, the volunteer citizens can become an impromptu community policing agency in direct support of the local law enforcement agency. In a collaborative effort to protect the infrastructure and citizens of a given community, these volunteers, with the proper training, can become an extension of any local law enforcement agency.

This particular effort directly relates to the ability of citizen leadership to properly train the citizen volunteer in the understanding of terrorism and its mujahiden warriors, and in how to identify, deter and subsequently defeat this national enemy. This training should include areas such as communications, threat identification, weapons proficiency and less than lethal courses of action. To better facilitate this training, police departments should welcome the opportunity to conduct joint operations in conjunction with these citizen volunteers and seek the appropriate state and/or local legislation affording the much needed directives to enable this inevitable blanket of protection.

Therein lies the problem. Unless such legislation is already in effect, the likelihood of being passed is low. What is needed is a recognized group of citizen volunteers already covered by such legislation. The State Defense Force (SDF), a United States Code Title 10 authorized volunteer military unit, which reports to the Governor through the State Adjutant General, meets that criteria.

THE STATE DEFENSE FORCE AS A SOURCE FOR COMBATING TERRORISM

Although the SDF would be an excellent choice for such an assignment, it is highly unlikely at the present time that such an assignment would be approved. There are already many National Guard and the state Emergency Management Agency needs for which the SDF can provide support. Most SDF units do not have sufficient personnel to perform these identified critical missions to permit this new concept of supporting local police departments in community based anti-terrorism activities.

There are some SDF units that do perform homeland defense missions; however, the literature only contains one article that describes the activities and performance of a homeland security mission. This article relates how the South Carolina State Guard's Homeland Defense Brigade determined the need for statewide support for public safety, public health and emergency preparedness. The result of their effort was the development of a database of community volunteers for police chiefs, sheriffs and emergency preparedness agencies across the state.

Volunteer Citizen Soldiers

Even though it is unlikely at the present time for a SDF unit to undertake an anti-terrorism effort, the demonstrated desire to support and protect the community and its citizens is a resource that should be considered. These citizen soldiers are all proven volunteers and have the discipline that allows them to accept and complete the mission.

State and/or municipal officials should consider forming a group of SDF personnel in their civilian capacity as a part of their local police department within one of the department's divisions, possibly entitled the Volunteer and Community Services. This group can then obtain the necessary training, prepare a community plan for observing and for reporting what may be critical intelligence.

Training the Citizen Volunteer in Anti-Terrorism

Training can come from the military to local police departments and to civilian contractors. While military training has proven the most viable form of preparation in overseas operations, it has had minimal, if any, impact in protecting against terrorism in the U.S. What has been validated thus far are the tactics used by law enforcement agencies. By taking their current techniques to identify and apprehend the average criminal and making the necessary adjustments to apply that template to terrorist operations, local police have identified the necessary steps to prevent the next attack through the use of community policing. The "X" factor in training to defeat terrorism is the civilian contractor. In the age of the September 12th terrorism expert, multiple agencies have opened for business with the intent of sharing their ideas of what a terrorist threat looks like and how this nation can prevent future attacks. Finding a company that has a thorough understanding of the psychological perspective of an Islamic extremist and the ultimate goals of an attack against innocent civilians is the key to successfully preparing your forces to protect porous U.S. borders. In preparing to successfully defend against terrorism, the following areas should be covered:

Application of the Training

This impromptu group of volunteer citizen soldiers should petition the local or regional police department to establish a Volunteers In Police Service (VIPS) Project in support of the local or regional homeland security effort. The expanded project effort could be referred to as the Volunteers In Police Service for Homeland Security and would be responsible for integrating all volunteer efforts in homeland security within the area. Once established, the police department leadership should enable the following activities, some of which are required under the VIPS grant (suggested activities are adapted from a proposal to the COPS Program)

- Appoint a police officer who will then register the program with the USA Freedom Corps.

- Identify a law enforcement officer familiar with tactical and strategic planning activities associated with homeland security to be assigned the additional duty of project Coordinator of Law Enforcement Activities. The Coordinator will arrange for a law enforcement response to observed potential threats to homeland security.
- Arrange for two senior project members to attend the mandatory COPS Office VIPS-related training.
- Identify suitable training sources in accordance with the seven (7) areas identified above for the citizen volunteers and appropriate police officers.
- Survey and integrate all volunteer homeland security activities within the police department.
- Determine events that may pose a homeland security danger within the local or regional area that can be readily identified and reported by the citizen volunteers.
- Identify and meet with community groups to explain the potential dangers to homeland security that certain events might pose and to solicit volunteers for the VIPS project.
- Develop a 311-style reporting system utilizing a web-site to report observations and a dedicated telephone line.
- Purchase off-the-shelf portable computer hardware, software and a projector to develop and maintain the reporting system, and to enable automated presentations for briefing and training.
- Train other volunteer groups to identify and report suspicious activity.
- Train the VIPS project personnel, including Reserve Officers and volunteers, on how to receive, review and report observed events to the project Coordinator.
- Obtain police department wind breakers and caps, appropriately marked with the letters VIPS in clearly recognizable color, to be worn by the citizen volunteers

when assisting law enforcement officers in homeland security activities.

- Make it veryclear that VIPS citizen volunteers will not represent themselves as law enforcement officers or carry a sidearm, nor will they commingle with law enforcement officers except when required to do so as part of their Project assignments.
- Develop statistical measures that will enable evaluation of the VIPS project's success.
- Prepare a final report documenting how the COPS funding directly enhanced the volunteer program and its overall benefit to the police department.
- Additional activities that citizen volunteers may undertake in support of the police department's homeland security activities are:
- Establish an advisory council of businessmen, educators, and retired military and public safety leadership to assist in the volunteer effort.
- Identify federal, state, municipal and business groups that provide security efforts within the county for possible volunteers.
- Inventory of all bridges, tunnels, highways, hospitals and public buildings within the local or regional police department's area of responsibility that could be damaged by terrorist action.
- Outline an in-depth, integrated information technology approach addressing intelligence, data search, cross-referencing and analysis of information, and recommend computer, system programming and data entry.

The success of the citizen volunteer project is dependant on four critical actions: Establishing an operational milieu between the citizen volunteers and the police department ! project coordinator to ensure that designated events and reported observations are meaningful and will be pursued by police officers. Identifying and recruiting community volunteer groups who appreciate the danger to the community from terrorists and who are willing to observe and report events that have been identified as critical to homeland security. They may include Explorer Scouts, secondary school Junior ROTC units, Civil Air Patrol, retired military and police groups, businessmen, community organizations, educators, and Neighborhood Watch groups. Developing and conducting meaningful training for the identified volunteer groups. Preparing a reporting system that properly collects and coordinates citizen volunteer observations, and reports the information to the project coordinator in a usable form. The police department must commit itself to implement the VIPS project in such a manner that these four critical actions will be fully and faithfully implemented as the damage that may occur from a failed program is totally and unequivocally unacceptable.

FINAL THOUGHTS

As the movement of global Salafist jihadi terrorism continues to emanate inside the United States and other Western countries, citizen volunteers must continue to educate and protect themselves to assist federal, state, and local law enforcement agencies identify and prevent against other attacks. While the citizen volunteers are not going to prevent all future terrorist attacks, they can strive to harden their particular homes, buildings, and cities to the extent that future terrorist cells are forced to move on to other, softer targets. The only question left to ponder is whether the community has chosen to become the tiger or remain the sheep?

Consider once again, for the moment, the SDF as the penultimate uniformed citizen volunteer. If the SDF unit's Commanding General might consider this anti-terrorism effort as a suitable activity and the state Adjutant General sees the value of such a mission supporting the goals of the military department, it becomes a suitable activity to undertake as a SDF project. The planning, organization, training and operational aspects are precisely what the SDF volunteer citizen soldier excels at.

5

Development of the Armed Forces

The rebirth of the Armed Forces of the Republic of Latvia is to be found shortly after the declaration of independence on 4 May 1990 or, phrased more accurately, as the consequence of the declaration of the independence. At the end of May 1990, after the attempted storming of the provisional government headquarters by students of the Russian military academy, volunteer units were formed to ensure uninterrupted functioning of the government. In June of that year, the chairman of the Highest Council's Defence and Interior commission, Mr. Talavs Jundzis, consults with Latvian officers retired from Soviet forces on the subject of defence and defence forces. The next month, on the initiative of another member of the commission, Mr. Odisejs Kostanda, a joint Baltic States Defence and Interior commission meeting on self defence is held in Ligatne, Latvia to which the former Soviet officers are invited. Over the next four months these meetings continue in Lithuania and Estonia. These same officers, among other, participate in organising barricades and in leading resistance against the OMON forces on13-23 January 1991.

Due to further Soviet political and military pressure, the Latvian Highest Council on 20 January 91 establishes a Department of Public Security with Mr. Janis Baskers and Mr. Auseklis Plavins as director and deputy director. The Highest Council additionally decrees essential defence tasks, places all territorial defence units under the Public Security Department and starts establishing border guard units. On 2 August 1991, the Cabinet of Ministers directs the Department of Public Security to organise self-defence units and alternative service units throughout Latvia and to establish an NCO training facility. The development of national defence forces gains momentum. On 23, August 1991, the Latvian Home Guard is established as a voluntary self-defence organisation. On 29 August the Cabinet of Ministers asks for volunteers for the formation of Border Guard, in October a Borderguard Training Centre is established in Malpils and a naval forces training centre in Liepaja. On 13 November the High Council establishes a Defence Ministry, on 13 December a department of Border Guard and seven border guard battalions with Mr. T. Jundzis as the Minister of Defence. In January 1992 Defence Forces staff and Naval Forces are established with National Defence Academy and Air Defence departments the next month. That same month, Col. Dainis Turlais, who has extensive combat experience in Afghanistan, is appointed commander of the Defence Forces. Understandably, he places priority on establishing, arming and training the Border Guard, eventually totalling some four thousand men, mostly conscripted.

NATIONAL ARMED FORCES

The next problem to be solved is that of a joint commander for the newly established National Armed Forces. In view of the incompatibility of the two existing structures, a consensus is reached in the government that the commander should be neither the Defence Forces commander nor the Chief of Staff of National Guard, but an officer with western military experience. The choice falls on Janis Kazocins, British army lieutenant colonel of Latvia descent at that time serving as Great Britain's military attaché in Latvia. However, the British government, obviously for political reason, can agree only in seconding him to the National Defence Forces as deputy commander and LTC Juris Dalbins, from the National Guard staff, is therefore nominated and appointed Commander of National Armed Forces on 5 October 1994. At this point several

National Guard officers assume key staff positions in the NAF staff but the National Guard itself remains somewhat in limbo since it has both military and police functions and its exact status could not be agreed upon and as a matter of fact it still remain unresolved.

Meanwhile, work begins on an orderly defence forces planning process – with the help of western experts, a National Risk Analysis and an Military Threat Analysis is conducted, followed by the National Security Concept and a Defence concept approved by the National Security Council and Cabinet in the spring of 95. Meanwhile Mr. Trapans, another western Latvian, had replaced Mr. Pavlovskis as Defence Minister. Unfortunately, in less than a year, because of policy disagreement with the Prime Minister, he is asked to resign, and the Prime Minister retains the defence portfolio for the rest of his term. The preparation of a Force Development Plan was required by the approved Defence Concept and this would have been the obvious domain of Col. Kazocins who eventually assumes the position of Deputy Chief of Staff. Unfortunately at this very time, Partnership for Peace Program come into being and for the duration of his tour Col. Kazocius time is taken up almost entirely with BALTBAT, NATO and PfP issues, with considerable success. This, however, leaves the inexperienced staff to struggle with the force development plan. The problem essentially narrows down to what we want versus what we need versus what we can afford. The problem is further aggravated by the retention by the Defence Ministry and National Armed Forces of far too many military objects taken over from the departing Russian forces. It is obvious the objects that will be required in the future can only be determined when we know what the defence forces structure will be in that future and that still, even today, remains to be settled.

The situation is further aggravated with the transfer of the border guard, with its full equipment and weapons to the National Armed Forces and the lure of commercial structures which pay considerably more for the skills possessed by some of the middle grade officers. The worst part is the fact that many of these officers have recently acquired these skills at overseas training centres as part of foreign military assistance. As enthusiasm is beginning to evaporate, especially after a series of conscript beatings, notwithstanding the fact that sociologists agree these were not problems created by the military but pre-existing conditions inherited by the military, retention of qualified officers becomes a problem. As a consequence of all this there existed and still exists some scepticism in the government how well increased defence revenues would be spent. On the other hand, it cannot be denied that the classified National Armed Forces 5-year development plan submitted to the Cabinet and accepted "for information" is not based on realistic or even possible budget allocations. Especially, since the first year (97) anticipated budget fell far short of that projected therefore rendering the entire document irrelevant. At the present time, by direction of the new minister, Mr. Girts Kristovskis, the military threat is being re-evaluated, the defence concept is under review and hopefully a defence plan and a more realistic and sustainable force development plan will be produced. Lack of an approved and funded long range force development plan impacts not only on selection of military objects to be retained, but also on weapons acquisition, training requirement forecast and supply base. No doctrinal publication on tactics, operations, training or logistics have been developed and approved although traditionally that should be the responsibility of National Defence Academy. Obviously, if NATO compatible doctrinal documents are developed and approved, they will be put in practice, taught to conscripts, NCOS and cadets and thus institutionalised to drive and compel interoperability not only with NATO forces but among the military forces of the Baltic States as well.

With almost non-stop foreign visits to the National Forces staff and return visits to foreign countries, force development and other planning becomes near to impossible and by 1997 it became obvious there needs to be a subdivision of international and national political responsibilities from tactical planning responsibilities. Since the Defence Concept specifies National

Guard based territorial defence and National Guard constitutes about 90% of the ground forces. In February of 1998 a reorganisation was promulgated essentially , placing all ground forces, including LATBAT and appropriate training centres, under National Guard – Territorial Defence Forces command.

Special Mission Unit, Military Police Battalion and Security Service remain directly under the commander, as indicated in the illustration. Currently, in the Defence and Interior Commission of the Saeima, the appropriateness of having the Presidential and Parliamentary Security Service directly subordinate to the NAF commander is being evaluated, since Interior Ministry is already responsible for the security of foreign embassies and the Cabinet of Ministers. Quite possibly it could revert to Defence or even Interior ministry's subordination with a wartime TO&E mission with the NAF. The SUV's military mission still needs to be defined which then will determine its numerical strength. Over the last years it has been constantly at only about 50% of required strength and under current law it can perform any anti terrorist missions only as backup, upon request, to Interior Ministry's anti terrorist unit. A logical military mission for this unit would be perhaps waterborne operations, similar to the US SEALS. The Military Police Battalion was formed for two purposes – guarding MoD and NAF facilities and providing provost Marshall type services to NAF training centres, to include criminal investigation services. The Military Counterintelligence Service is being downsized and reorganised since some of the investigations conducted by it previously are finally being transferred to the MoD Inspector General and military police.

DEFENCE FORCES AND NATIONAL GUARD

Early in 1993 Latvia finds itself with two different armies, each subordinate to different institutions-and with the Russian forces still occupying portions of Latvia's territory. The Home Guard, after exposure to US National Guard, renamed also National Guard, is headed by Col. Girts Kritovskis as Chief of Staff subordinate to the Chairman of the Highest Council, and subsequently to the newly elected President. The fledgling Defence Forces (DF), Naval Forces and Air Forces on the other hand, are subordinate to the Minister of Defence with the commander of these forces also being deputy Defence Minister.

It is understandable that the two structures are at odds with each other since National Guard are volunteer citizens, generally with no real prior military experience or training, and the Defence Forces are constituted from former Soviet officers who are slowly drifting back to their national homeland. While unquestionably their military experience is much more extensive than that of the National Guard leadership, most of them come from technical support branches rather than from combat arms. They also arrive with abbreviated, if may, military records to substantiate their expertise and many initial assignments therefore do not correspond to actual skills. Needless to say, many of them, after 20 or more years in the Soviet system, can think only in terms of that system and therefore tend to envision the evolving Latvian defence forces. So to say "in the face and likeness" of the heavy, inflexible, massive Soviet forces they are familiar with. On the other hand, the National Guard leadership although nationalistic and well intentioned lacks the discipline, experience and managerial skills needed to effectively organise and lead large military units. Nevertheless, the National Guard leadership recognises these shortcomings and when Great Britain offers tactical training to the Defence Forces and they decline, the National Guard takes up the offer with enthusiasm.

The problems encountered by both of the evolving forces are significant; lack of consensus on doctrine, lack of consensus how the defence forces should be organised, armed and equipped. Not the least of the problems is foreign humanitarian assistance – the defence ministry tends to accept anything that is offered for free without a clear understanding how it would be used and soon the warehouses are bulging. We must remember that the Baltic States at that time are considered potential flash points and only non lethal military assistance is therefore available. As a result of this, the Defence Forces can be seen attired in the uniforms of a dozen donor countries while the National Guard, not being entitled even to these hand me downs, have mostly only civilian clothing. Although there is a mobile infantry brigade, a combat engineer battalion, a chemical company and some others units, these exit mostly on paper.

There are many issues that are not resolved, and even more not even addressed. There is no military threat analysis, no defence concept, no defence plan and therefore obviously no justified armed forces end strength or development plan. The Defence Ministry and Defence Forces lack experience with cost estimates, budgetary process, and force planning – consequently the realm of what is possible for a small country's defence forces financially has not been determined. The former armour officers dream of tank battalions, the artillery officers of field artillery battalions, the air forces of jet fighter squadrons and antiaircraft missiles and the naval forces of real warship. The organisational charts (TO & E) of combat battalions, of course are based on the Soviet model with overabundance of officers in battalion staff with a tailor, cobbler and tinmaker thrown in for good measure.

In May of 93, under the MIL to MIL Program, a military liaison team led by Colonel Ower Moon, Michigan National Guard is established in Latvia. This not only demonstrates tangible western support for the fledgling Latvian Defence Forces, but also sends a clear international political signal. We must remember that at this time the Russian army occupies parts of Latvian territory and their departure is still uncertain. Through the MLT program a partnership is established not only between US Department of Defence and the Latvian Ministry of Defence but also between the entities of Michigan and Latvia as well. Although the program was originally intended only for about a year, it proves so beneficial in exposing Latvian Defence Forces and National Guard to the US military way of doing thing, that Colonel Koppa, Colonel Emery, Colonel Allen and now Colonel Jajick follow Colonel Moon. The Adjutant General of Michigan, General Gordon Stump, is personally involved in this project and has established a wide range of contacts not only among the Defence Forces and the National Guard but among Latvian politicians and businessmen as well. The arrival of the team is significant because it introduces an alternative, western way of looking at military planning, force structures and leadership. Appointment of Mr. Valdis Pavlovskis, a former US marine, as defence minister, reinforces this trend. Above all, it becomes clear that to ensure democratic control over the military, the Defence Forces and National Guard need to be brought under single command in the Ministry of Defence. Col Juris Eihmanis, who at that time is the Chief of Staff of the National Guard, realises this to be nevitable. From this point on, I can speak from personal experience – in the true tradition of shuttle diplomacy on one day I remember conducting close to 10 trips between the two parties before both Defence Forces and the National Guard consented to sign the agreement.

NATIONAL ARMED FORCES MISSIONS

We believe the defence forces of Latvia, as well as those of Lithuania and Estonia, have four basic missions, further subdivided in specific tasks, for the accomplishment of which they must develop appropriate structures. These missions are:

- Ensuring compliance with applicable international conventions
- Attainment of political goal – NATO membership
- Real defence capability attainment
- National administrative and disaster relief missions.

Budgetary Consideration

Within realistic defence budget constrains the Latvian defence forces must accomplish all these missions simultaneously or in some order of priority. At this time, as previously indicated, there is no approved force development plan; because cost of proposals submitted to the government far exceeded resources that could be made available for defence. The situation is hampered by absence of accurate base line cost data-obviously we must first know how much things cost, before we can determine what we can afford. Clearly as well, we cannot create military structures, which we cannot subsequently maintain within a 1-15% GNP budget. A further complication is the fact that defence allocations have not been broken down in an acquisition budget and maintenance budget. We have so far tended to maintain forces too large to permit acquisition of weapons and equipement – in affect we have been paying conscript salaries for performing duties for the performance of which we have neither equipped nor trained them. Additionally, previously mentioned excessive military objects have proven to be a drain not only on resources, but on manpower to guard them from vandalism as well. This problem has been considerably alleviated, by Mr. Jundzis, the previous Defence Minister and the current defence minister is continuing this process of devastation.

Unfortunately, politicians and even some military planners have so far not succeeded in making the government and parliamentary decision-makers aware of the fact that NATO forces already have all their equipment. Therefore the 1% comparison with NATO 3% average is totally misleading – if NATO, like the Baltic States, had to simultaneously acquire their equipment and weapons then individual country budgets for several years would have to be at least 25% of GNP until the accusation bell curve levels out. In short, the dilemma of Latvian armed forces development is lack of knowledge what they can realistically afford.

Attainment of NATO Membership

The second mission is political attainment of NATO membership through participation to the maximum extent possible, in PfP and peacekeeping activities. To this end, the organisational structure of a Latvian peace keeping battalion (LATBAT) has been approved on the existing base of the so-called Suýi battalion. The structure and authorised strength of this battalion is indicated in illustration NR 1. Individual weapons (M-16's, 15's) for this battalion have already been provided by USA as well as individual equipment and some EDA vehicles. A full battalions communications set is on order through Warsaw Initiative funding as well as additional organisational equipment. The additional funding available through the IMET Program has been used for specialised unit officer training in USA training centres. While I feel the establishment of BALTBAT was at that time politically important and useful; its current status must be re-evaluated since without a defence agreement among the Baltic States, within any Baltic state it will never be used in its entirety for real defence purposes. That is a political reality. There also appears to be a problem with its employment when it is not required to be on mission. Perhaps it could be transformed into a Baltic States basic training centre as an extension of BATDEFCOL. Since the battalion, as such, can be used only *outside* the Baltic States, it would appear to make sense to retain a small BALTBAT command element thus ensuring its political continuity. But to disperse its companies to national battalions where during non-mission times they would train with the parent unit and perform national missions. Should a mission be offered, then each country would provide, in rotational order, one company out of their battalions thus eventually ensuring thus entire battalions interoperability and combat readiness. A country then could provide the whole battalion independently or, if required or so desired, each country could provide a battalion to participate with a Baltic Peace Keeping Brigade or BALTBDE.

In short, to ensure the attainment of the political goals, Latvia needs one fully NATO interoperable battalion which in a national emergency also serves as a rapid deployment military reserve force or participate, with other government agencies in national disaster resolution. Latvia can *afford* only one such battalion but it also *needs* deployment of military reserve force or participate, with other government agencies in national disaster resolution. Latvia can *afford* only one such battalion but it also needs only one such battalion. Its real defence must rest on mobilizable reserves and the National Guard.

International Conventions

The first of the four missions in ensuring as a minimum,

sea border security, land border security, air space and rescue. If the accomplishment of these missions contribute to national defence all the better. We already have the BALTRON and regional Air Space projects and are, therefore, committed to a Regional Airspace Centre a National Centre and a joint naval squadron structure. Three previous governments have discussed the search and rescue project but no decision has been reached primarily because of uncertainty about the most suitable helicopter. It would appear the aircraft could be bought for money that foreign shopping pay to the communication ministry for search and rescue service while in Latvian territorial waters. A 3-6 helicopter detachment was envisioned which would be operated by the air force in support of search and rescue, natural disaster, border control and national defence. I believe the new government will again take up this issue.

Development of Self Defence Capability

This is the third and perhaps the most important mission. The five-year-old military threat analysis is currently being re-evaluated and should provide adjusted end strength for the accomplishment of this mission. The defence concept is also being re-evaluated – the planning process is depicted in the figure.

To attain required end strength for full self defence capability, current law needs to be modified to allow conscription of all able bodied citizens subject to draft, putting them through a 2-months basic training course, retaining a small number on active duty, with the rest being offered a choice of either voluntarily joining the National Guard or joining reserve battalions, collocated with National Guard units throughout the country. The available annual number of conscripts has not been accurately established but varies somewhere between 10 000 and 15 000.

The reservists would serve to a specific age, calculated by computing the conscript pool against required end strength. However, the annual costs of basic training first need to be established and budgeted for in advance and it makes no sense to do basic training unless each conscript upon completion of the training is issued at least a uniform and individual weapon. To this end, the Ministry of Defence is planning to request an additional 30 000 M-14 rifles from the US (10 000 have been previously requested and received) to ensure standardisation of individual weapons as well as spare parts. Additionally, reserves require not only weapons but refresher training as well and the cost this needs to be computed as well.

The current defence concept mandates small unit territorial defence, light infantry weapons and portable anti air and anti tank weapons. The recent reorganisation has announced the intent to formally place all ground forces, including the LATBAT and corresponding training centre under National Guard headquarters but the question reasons how long it will take the National Guard to fully implement this decision.

The 16 000 strong National Guard, which as stated previously comprises close to 90% of the National Armed Forces and is the mainstay of territorial defence is currently at a crossroads. The early enthusiasm is slowly dissipating, willingness to sign up for a 3 year term is becoming a problem, some of the law and order duties are being assumed by trained police and there are still no governmental compensation for the time put in, no retirement plan and in some cases even a long wait for a uniform. Only when the state assumes full responsibility for the National Guard cap it legally mandate obligatory service in a time of crises – currently reporting for such duty is up to individual conscience and patriotism. It is hoped that the new law " On National Guard " will address these problems and more reciprocal accommodation is reached between the state and the National Guard; without that territorial defence is impossible.

With this arrangement, the National Armed Forces Commander essentially commands the three traditional components and some small special units. Figure no.1 provides the possible force structures with the unshaded units already being in existence. The exact numerical strength of the territorial defence forces will be determined by the threat analysis-available resources compromise.

NATIONAL ADMINISTRATIVE AND DISASTER RELIEF MISSIONS

The last of the four missions consists of national administrative responsibilities; staff functions and maintaining in peacetime infrastructures needed to support the previous 3 missions. To execute these structures these missions consist of the Armed forces Staff, staff battalion (honour guard company, band, motor pool etc.) military hospital, athletic club, logistics facilities Adazi and other training centres. High on the list is National Armed Forces support for relief of disasters. Needles to say these supporting structures need to be reduced to the minimum to ensure that sufficient funds are available for the execution of the three priority missions.

On the legislative side that portion of the law that pertains to theNational Armed Forces has already been extracted from the law " On State Defence " and now the law "On National Security" will incorporate the rest of that law. Because many questions dealing with security have not been resolved. Exact role of State President in defence, what happens when Cabinet, Saeima or president cannot carry out their responsibilities in emergency and may even require changes in constitution, it will be discussed at National Security Council prior to second in Saeima. The law on National Armed Forces should be passed within a month or two – the sticking point of the exact status of the National Guard volunteers, as indicated previously, will be addressed separately in a law "On National Guard".

Much ado is made over the disparity of the Baltic States defence budgets, expressed as percentage of GNP. Clearly, the expenditures are for foreign relations, not defence, but these are national computations and I'm not sure how they would compare when reduced to required NATO budget guidance. I believe, however, that once the progress that is finally under way in the defence area is recognised by the government, the additional funding to bring the expenditures to a full percent of GDP will be found before the end of the year. And next year will see additional promised increases.

Finally, looking at defence at the regional level, it is obvious that Latvian defence establishment needs to determine where they see their future – Lithuania, no doubt, will have the sponsorship of NATO member Poland while Estonia will have NATO sponsorship of Finland. The military threat to Finland has changed significantly, other northern countries are reducing their defence forces and I feel it is only a question of time before Finland will ask for and receive NATO membership. I feel with the reduced threat, the voters in Finland will not accede in the future supporting enormous defence costs when the same can be achieved for considerably less with the NATO insurance policy.

GUNDARS ZALKALNS graduated from Boston university in 1963 as ROTC Distinguished Military Graduate and was awarded regular US Army commission. Subsequent to that, he has served in different branches, mostly in plans and operations positions in US, Germany and Korea. His assignments include a combat tour in Vietnam 1967-68 with the 4th Infantry Division. His last assignments were at HQ 6th US Army, V Corpus HQ in Germany and as advisor to California National Guard. His 18 decorations include Vietnam Service Medal with 4 Campaign stars, Bronze Star, Legion of Merit and FRG Cross of Honour (Ehrenkreutz). He retired from service as a lieutenant colonel and since 1993 has been a consultant at the Latvian Ministry of Defence, Presidential Defence Advisor and since January 1995 National Security Adviser to the President and Secretary, National Security Council of Latvia.

MODERNISING THE INDIAN ARMY

For over a decade the Indian Army's efforts to modernise have been thwarted due to political neglect and lack of adequate budgetary support. The defence budget for Financial Year 2008-09 increased 10 per cent in nominal terms, barely adequate to keep up with inflation and the fall in the value of the rupee against the US dollar, but decreased to less than 2.0 per cent of India's projected GDP. A sum of US $12 billion was provided for capital acquisitions (US $9 billion for the army), but of this

US $0.6 billion (Rs 3,000 crore) is expected to be surrendered as unspent. Nothing exemplified the army's lack of preparedness for war more than the fact that 155 mm ammunition for the Bofors howitzer had to be imported from South Africa during the Kargil conflict in 1999. Had the conflict not been confined to the 150 km frontage of the Kargil sector, T-72 and 130mm medium gun ammunition too may have run short and it would have been politically embarrassing for the government as well as the army.

Not only that, in the plains the army would have had to fight with obsolete Vijayant tanks and several other vintage equipment that were unsuitable for combat. Even though A.K. Antony, the Defence Minister, has said, 'We need to cut down on the unnecessary procedures, bottlenecks and red tape in our procurement mechanism,' the Ministry of Defence has been unable to give modernisation of the armed forces the priority that it deserves. The Army Chief's modernisation vision is to 'adapt to high-end technology, improve night-fighting capability... (and) information technology, information warfare and network centric warfare.' The indigenously designed Arjun main battle tank (MBT) has been in the pipeline for over two decades. Though the tank has many good features, it has consistently failed to meet the army's GSQR for an MBT and orders have been placed for only 124 tanks to be manufactured. The lack of progress on the Arjun MBT has significantly slowed down the pace of armour modernisation. In the year 2000 India signed a deal with Russia to acquire 310 T-90S tanks. Subsequently, India began to assemble these tanks at Avadi. It has recently been reported that in addition to these, India has decided to acquire another 347 T-90S tanks and assemble them within the country.

The first Indian assembled T-90S (Bhishma) rolled off the production line on 8 January 2004. Meanwhile, a large number of T-72M1 (Ajeya) tanks are still awaiting modernisation. The lack of a suitable fire control system and night fighting capability are major handicaps. In a future conventional war that will be fought under the nuclear shadow, manoeuvre will be extremely limited. This restriction will lead to much greater emphasis being placed on firepower to achieve the laid down military aim. Hence, it is imperative that artillery modernisation is undertaken with alacrity so as to generate firepower asymmetries on the future battlefield. The last major acquisition of towed gun-howitzers was that of about 400 pieces of 39-calibre 155mm FH-77B howitzers from Bofors of Sweden in the mid-1980s. This gun had proved its mettle in the Kargil conflict. Just when a contract for 120 tracked and 180 wheeled self-propelled (SP) 155mm guns was about to be concluded after years of protracted trials, South African arms manufacturer Denel, a leading contender for the contract, was alleged to have been involved in a corruption scam in an earlier deal for anti-material rifles (AMRs).

Since January 2008, the Ministry of Defence (MoD) has issued three global tenders for 155mm guns and howitzers for the mountains, the plains and self-propelled guns for the deserts. Summer and winter trials were expected to be held in 2009-10, but so far the bids received are still being evaluated. The artillery modernisation programme is bound to see further delays.

The probability of the next conventional war breaking out in the mountains is far higher than that of a war in the plains. With this in view, the artillery recently conceptualised a requirement for a lightweight towed howitzer of 155mm calibre for employment in the mountains. Neither the present Bofors howitzer nor its 52-calibre replacement will be capable of effective operations in the mountains. A lightweight 45-calibre 155mm howitzer weighing less than 5,000 kg, with a light but adequately powered prime mover, is ideal for the mountains. In January 2008, the MoD floated a Request for Proposal (RfP) for 140 pieces of ultra-light 39 calibre 155mm towed howitzers for use by the Indian Army's mountain formations. Presumably, these will also be employed by its rapid reaction divisions – as and when they are raised – as the howitzers will be easy to transport by air. India has floated a global tender for the purchase of 400 52-calibre 155mm towed artillery guns for the army, to be followed by indigenous manufacture of another 1,100 howitzers. An RfP has also been issued for 180 wheeled self-propelled guns for around Rs 4,700 crore for employment by mechanised forces in the plains and semi-desert sectors. Approximately 180 pieces of 130mm M46 Russian medium guns have been successfully 'up-gunned' to 155mm calibre with ordnance supplied by Soltam of Israel. The new barrel length of 45 calibres has enhanced the range of the gun to about 40 km with extended range ammunition.

A contract for the acquisition of two regiments of the 12-tube, 300mm Smerch multi-barrel rocket launcher (MBRL) system with 90 km range was signed with Russia's Rosoboron-export in early 2006. This will be a major boost for the long-range firepower capabilities of the army. Extended range (ER) rockets are being introduced for the 122 mm Grad MBRL that has been in service for over three decades. The ER rockets will enhance the weapon system's range from 22 to about 40 km. A Rs 5,000 crore (US $1billion) contract has also been signed for the serial production of the Pinaka MBRL weapon system, another DRDO project plagued by time delays and completed with help from Larsen and Toubro and the Tatas.

Since the Bofors 155mm Howitzer was introduced into service, the indigenously designed and manufactured 105 mm Indian Field Gun (IFG) and its (not so) light version, the Light Field Gun (LFG), have joined the 75/24 Indian Mountain Gun, the 100mm Russian field gun and the 122mm Russian howitzer on the obsolescence list.

Counter-bombardment (US term counter-fire) capability is also being upgraded, but at a slow pace. At least about 40 to 50 weapon locating radars (WLRs) are required for effective counter-bombardment, especially in the plains, and only a dozen have been procured so far. In addition to the 12 AN-TPQ 37 Firefinder WLRs acquired from Raytheon, USA, under a 2002 contract worth US $200 million, Bharat Electronics Limited is reported to be assembling 28 WLRs. These radars will be based on both indigenous and imported components and have been approved for introduction into service after extensive tests.

The radar is expected to match the capabilities of the Firefinder system and will have a detection range of about 40 kilometre.

The BrahMos supersonic cruise missile , with a precision strike capability, very high kill energy and range of 290 km, was inducted into the army in July 2007. It is a versatile missile that can be launched from TATRA mobile launchers and silos on land, aircraft and ships and, perhaps in future, also from submarines. 50 BrahMos missiles are expected to be produced every year. Efforts are underway to further increase its strike range. BrahMos Aerospace has orders worth Rs 3,500 crore (US $0.65 billion) from the army and the navy, which has opted for the anti-ship as well as the land attack cruise missile (LACM) versions. These terrain hugging missiles are virtually immune to counter measures due to their high speed and very low radar cross section and are far superior to subsonic cruise missiles like Pakistan's Babur.

Despite its large-scale employment on border management and extensive commitments in IS and CI operations, infantry modernisation had been languishing for several decades when the Ministry of Defence (MoD) finally cleared a visionary plan to modernise the army's infantry battalions by according 'in principle' approval in the form of Modification 4B to the war establishment (WE) of a standard infantry battalion in 1998. However, no funds were specially sanctioned for this purpose till the NDA government approved the expenditure of Rs 3,500 crore (US $0.6 billion) in September 2003. The army has initiated a project for a Future Infantry Soldier as a System (F-INSAS). 'F-INSAS basically aims at "converting an infantryman into a fully-networked all-terrain, all-weather, weapons platform with enhanced lethality, survivability, sustainability, mobility and situational awareness" for the digitised battlefield of the future.'

While 250 Kornet-E anti-tank guided missiles (ATGMs) with thermal imaging sights have substantially increased the anti-tank capability of infantry battalions, most efforts to modernise the equipment held by infantry and Rashtriya Rifles (RR) units are aimed at enhancing their capability for surveillance and target acquisition at night and boosting their firepower for precise retaliation against infiltrating columns and terrorists holed up in built-up areas. 200 hand-held BFSRs with practical ranges up to seven to eight km where clear line of sight is available, 2,000 hand-held thermal imaging devices (HHTIs) with ranges up to 2,000 metres for observation at night and stand-alone infrared, seismic and acoustic sensors with varying capabilities have enabled infantrymen to dominate the Line of Control so completely that infiltration has come down to almost a trickle.

The newly acquired weapons, which complement these surveillance and observation devices, include: 1,500x 84 mm rocket launchers, including some disposable ones; 1,000 AMRs (anti-material rifles); 8,000 UBGLs (under-barrel grenade launchers); 4,000 new generation carbines; 300 bullet proof vehicles; and, several hundred accurate sniper rifles. However, the numbers acquired and the ammunition stocks are still inadequate and need to be made up more rapidly. While the INSAS 5.56 mm assault rifles have now been in service for almost 10 years and proved to be effective, the light machine gun (LNG) version is still facing teething problems and the carbine version for close quarter battle has not found favour with the army. New 5.56 mm assault rifles of bull-pup design with an integrated laser range finder and grenade launcher are under development. Efforts are also being made to provide infantry platoons and sections with integrated GPS-based navigation system, secure lightweight walkie-talkie radio sets and better protective gear with a helmet that incorporates a built-in head-up display.

The mechanised infantry is now equipped with the BMP-2 ICV Sarath of which over 1,000 have been built since 1987. A new variant is the 81 mm Carrier Mortar Tracked Vehicle (CMTV) that is based on the chassis of the Sarath ICV and has been indigenously developed to enhance the integral firepower available to mechanised infantry battalions. Other variants include a command post, an ambulance, armoured dozer and engineer and reconnaissance vehicles. Mechanised reconnaissance and support battalions need better surveillance radars, fire-and-forget ATGMs and effective night fighting capability.

A new DRDO project that is reported to be ongoing aims to equip future soldiers with lightweight force multipliers. Soldiers of the future will have miniaturised communication and GPS systems, small power packs, weapon platforms and smart vests with fibre-optic sensors. For over 350 infantry battalions, plus about 150 Rashtriya Rifles, Assam Rifles and Territorial Army battalions, these major changes will be extremely costly to implement and will spill over at least 10 to 12 years – that is, if the funds can be found. Without modernising this cutting edge of its sword, the army will soon begin to resemble the armies of India's lesser neighbours.

Another DRDO project that is way behind schedule is the Nag anti-tank missile system. The antiquated Jonga-mounted SS-11 B1 anti-tank guided missile (ATGM) system has been replaced in missile battalions by MILAN shoulder-fired ATGMs. However, a vehicle-mounted missile system like the Nag is definitely necessary for reconnaissance and attrition tasks and for anti-tank screens. The experimental Plan AREN tactical communications system for strike formations needs early replacement. The ability to carry broadband data needs to be enhanced in particular. Even the more recent static communications network called ASCON lacks ISDN capability for the real-time transmission of maps and streaming video.

The Defence Minister, A.K. Antony, recently admitted that there are gaps in India's air defence coverage. While the allusion was primarily to the lack of sufficient radar coverage to detect aerial threats to India's air space, the air defence (AD) of field formations continues to be given a much lower priority than it deserves. With the DRDO's indigenous Akash medium-range and Trishul short-range surface-to-air (SAM) missile projects not making major headway, it is time to start looking at substitutes from abroad. The air defence of mechanised forces is another area that is crying for attention. The SAM-6 and SAM-7 Kvadrat-Strela medium range missile system, the backbone of AD for strike formations since the early 1970s, is now ageing and needs urgent replacement. The Tungushka and the OSA-AK (SA-8) missile systems are on the obsolescence list and the 23mm, multi-barrelled Schilka tracked air defence gun system is already obsolete. In fact, the assets of the Army Air Defence corps are grossly inadequate to provide high quality low-level air defence to the field formations. Hence, forward combat echelons will lack effective protection against enemy aircraft during a future war. The young Army Air Defence corps requires substantial capital infusion to really come into its own.

For the future, the Defence Research and Development Organisation (DRDO) is planning to develop an integrated air defence system with exo-atmosphere (above 40 km altitude) and endo-atmosphere (below 30 km) capabilities by 2009-10. The system may also have built-in features to double up as a tactical missile, apart from functioning as an extended air defence system to engage target aircraft beyond 100 km. This was stated by V.K. Saraswat, Chief Controller, DRDO R&D (Missiles and Strategic Systems), after the successful test launch of a high-altitude interceptor missile from the Wheeler Island in December 2007. This programme will also lead to the development of an indigenous ballistic missile defence (BMD) capability.

An automated command and control and decision support system for use by the General Staff is still far from becoming a reality, as also supporting systems like the battlefield surveillance system and air space management system. The urgent requirement of real-time satellite reconnaissance systems has still not been operationalised despite the nuclear overhang under which the armed forces now operate. Even though the cameras on India's remote sensing and cartographic satellites now have sharply enhanced resolutions, less than one metre, military-grade photographs of still better resolution are needed to be purchased from the open market. These sources may dry up quickly during war.

A 'system of systems' approach must be followed so that scarce RSTA and communications resources can be synergistically configured and optimally exploited, based on the concept of 'network-centric warfare' in which surveillance sensors, targeting systems and 'shooters' are fused together in a seamless 'system of systems' that reduces response time between the acquisition of a target and its destruction to 15-20 minutes.

Though some modern frequency hopping radio sets with integral encryption devices have been introduced into service in recent years, networked communications, which form the backbone of an effective C4I2SR system, need substantial upgradation. The tactical-level Tac C3I system for field formations is in urgent need of an upgrade. The Plan AREN system has been in service for almost three decades and is based on outdated and bulky technologies. The ASCON communication system for voice and data links between static HQ and those in peacetime locations, still has some years of service left as it is of modular design and can be upgraded to a limited extent. However, its capability to provide data links is rather limited as data requirements have grown by leaps and bounds over the last decade or so. A tri-service Defence Communication Network (DCN) is in an advanced stage of planning.

While some Stentor long-range BFSRs have been in service for over a decade, medium-range radars are still to be acquired. Israeli Searcher-I and Heron unmanned aerial vehicles (UAVs) have been introduced into service but these are few in number and it will be a long time before they really make a difference by providing a real-time surveillance capability so that ground forces can initiate action even as a fresh input is received. Only a small number of Searcher-II UAVs, with an upper ceiling that makes them suitable for the mountains, have been acquired.

PGMs are increasingly gaining currency as weapons of choice in conflict on land, however, the Indian artillery does not have PGMs in quantities large enough to matter. Only limited quantities of the Russian Krasnopol PGM have been imported for the Bofors 155mm howitzer. Among others, the Bofors Bonus PGM is a suitable candidate, subject to successful trials in the deserts and mountains. Despite a Long-term Integrated Perspective Plan (LTIPP) and five-year Defence Plans, approval has to be sought on file for each new weapon system or piece of equipment on a 'case-by-case' basis. It is by now well-known how each such case chronicles the saga of an uphill struggle to get approval first from the MoD, then MoD (Finance), the Ministry of Finance (MoF) and, finally, the Cabinet Committee on Security. All this is only possible after the DRDO has first certified that the weapon system or equipment in question cannot be developed and manufactured indigenously and such a certificate is hard to come by. Gradually these archaic procurement and acquisition procedures are being reviewed and improved. The Defence Procurement Procedure (DPP) 2008 was promulgated recently.

The approach to army modernisation must be more focused; the priorities need to be clearly established and then adhered to. The government must give a firm commitment in terms of funds and the MoD should streamline its procedures and processes for speedy procurement of high priority weapons and equipment. It is time to institute a rolling, non-lapsable defence modernisation fund of Rs 25,000 crore (US $5 billion) as a viable method of ensuring that defence procurement is not subjected to the vagaries of annual budgets. The present situation is disturbing and, if allowed to go on indefinitely, will seriously compromise the army's preparedness to fight the next border war that inimical neighbours like Pakistan can be expected to thrust on India. The MoD 'has assured the army of full support for its around 600 modernisation schemes, worth about Rs 70,000 crore in the 11th Plan (2007-2012) period,' but it remains to be seen whether this will actually materialise.

MILITARY MODERNIZATION

The military modernization begun in the late 1970s had three major focuses. First, under the political leadership of Deng Xiaoping, the military became disengaged from civilian politics and, for the most part, resumed the political quiescence that characterized its pre-Cultural Revolution role. Deng reestablished civilian control over the military by appointing his supporters to key military leadership positions, by reducing the scope of the PLA's domestic nonmilitary role, and by revitalizing the party political structure and ideological control system within the PLA.

Second, modernization required the reform of military organization, doctrine, education and training, and personnel policies to improve combat effectiveness in combined-arms warfare. Among the organizational reforms that were undertaken were the creation of the state Central Military Commission, the streamlining and reduction of superfluous PLA forces, civilianization of many PLA units, reorganization of military regions, formation of group armies, and enactment of the new Military Service Law in 1984. Doctrine, strategy, and tactics were revised under the rubric of "people's war under modern conditions," which envisaged a forward defense at selected locations near China's borders, to prevent attack on Chinese cities and industrial sites, and emphasized operations using combined-arms tactics. Reforms in education and training emphasized improving the military skills and raising the education levels of officers and troops and conducting combinedarms operations. New personnel policies required upgrading the quality of PLA recruits and officer candidates, improving conditions of service, changing promotion practices to stress professional competence, and providing new uniforms and insignia.

The third focus of military modernization was the transformation of the defense establishment into a system capable of independently maintaining a modern military force. As military expenditures remained relatively constant, reforms concentrated on reorganizing the defense research-and-development and industrial base to integrate civilian and military science and industry more closely. Foreign technology was used selectively to upgrade weapons. Defense industry reforms also resulted in China's entry into the international arms market and the increased production of civilian goods by defense industries. The scope of PLA economic activities was reduced, but the military continued to participate in infrastructure development projects and initiated a program to provide demobilized soldiers with skills useful in the civilian economy.

Civil-Military Relations

Lines between civilian and military leadership and institutions in China are indistinct. All high-ranking military leaders have high-level party positions, and many high-ranking party officials have some military experience. When military leaders participate in national policy making, therefore, it is not clear whether their positions reflect PLA corporate interests or the interests of groups that cut across institutional lines. In general, in times where there was national leadership consensus on national policy, such as in the 1950s, the PLA was politically quiescent. Once the PLA was drawn into civilian politics during the Cultural Revolution, the military became divided along the lines of civilian factions. As long as the national leadership remained divided on a number of policy issues, the PLA, fearing factional struggles and political instability, was reluctant to leave the political scene. When Deng Xiaoping was rehabilitated in 1977, however, the stage was set for the withdrawal of the military from politics and a partial return to the PLA's previous political passivity.

Political Role of the People's Liberation Army

Deng Xiaoping's efforts in the 1980s to reduce the political role of the military stemmed from his desire to reassert civilian control over the military and to promote military modernization. To accomplish his objectives, Deng revitalized the civilian party apparatus and leadership and built a consensus on the direction of national policy. He also established personal control over the military through personnel changes, and he reduced the scope of the PLA's domestic political, economic, and social roles. Finally, he strengthened party control over the military through institutional reforms and political and ideological education. The revitalization of the party and the establishment of a consensus on national policy assured top military leaders of political stability and a vigorous party capable of handling national and regional affairs without extensive military participation.

Deng's personal political control was established over the military through his assumption of the position of chairman of the party Central Military Commission in June 1981 and through his appointment of his supporters to key positions in the party Central Military Commission, Ministry of National Defense, and the PLA's General Staff Department, General Political Department, and General Logistics Department. Occasional replacement of military region and military district commanders also strengthened Deng's hand. Military leaders who objected to Deng's policies were replaced with more amenable personnel.

The creation of the state Central Military Commission in 1982 aimed to further strengthen civilian control over the military by stressing the PLA's role as defender of the state and by establishing another layer of supervision parallel to party supervision. The civilianization of several PLA corps and internal security units reduced the size of the PLA and the scope of its involvement in civilian affairs. The placement of defense industries under civilian control and the transfer or opening up of military facilities, such as airports and ports, to civilian authorities also limited the PLA's influence in economic and political matters. Propaganda using the PLA as a model for society also diminished, and emphasis was placed on the PLA's military rather than political role.

Party Control

In addition to making personnel changes, Deng revitalized party control over the PLA and diffused the military's political power by designating provincial-level, municipal, district, and county party committee secretaries to serve concurrently as the first political commissars of their equivalent-level units in the regional PLA. The percentage of PLA personnel permitted to join the party was limited by restricting party membership to military academy graduates. Political and ideological training stressed the military rather than the social, ideological, or economic role of the PLA. Special effort was made to discredit the PLA's role in the Cultural Revolution; the PLA's support for the left was described as incorrect because it caused factionalism within the military. While emphasizing the necessity and appropriateness of reforms to modernize the military, political education also sought to guarantee military support for Deng's reform agenda. Beginning in 1983 a rectification campaign (part of the party-wide rectification campaign aimed primarily at leftists) reinforced this kind of political and ideological training.

Beginning in the late 1970s, Deng Xiaoping succeeded in decreasing military participation in national-level political bodies. Military representation on the Political Bureau fell from 52 percent in 1978 to 30 percent in 1982, and military membership in the party Central Committee declined from 30 percent in 1978 to 22 percent in 1982. Most professional military officers shared common views with the Deng leadership over military modernization and the fundamental direction of national policy, and they willingly limited their concerns to military matters. Nonetheless, some elements in the PLA continued to voice their opinions on nondefense matters and criticized the Deng reform program. Dissent centered on prestigious military leaders, notably Ye Jianying, who feared that ideological de-Modification, cultural liberalization, and certain agricultural and industrial reforms deviated from Marxist values and ideals. The Deng leadership contained these criticisms with the help of the personnel changes, political education, and the rectification campaign just mentioned. In this way it was able to keep military dissent within bounds that did not adversely affect civil-military relations.

Popular Attitudes Toward the People's Liberation Army

Starting in the late 1970s, popular attitudes toward the PLA also underwent considerable changes. In the 1950s and 1960s, the military's prestige was very high because of its wartime exploits, because it was held up as a role model for society, and because of its participation in civilian construction projects. But the power gained by the PLA during the Cultural

Revolution reawakened civilian resentment of military privileges and abuses of power. By the early 1980s, with the circumscription of the PLA's domestic role and the implementation of agricultural reforms offering greater opportunities for rural youth, the PLA's reputation as a prestigious, elite, Marxist-model organization and a promising channel for social mobility was severely tarnished. Society's perception of the military appeared to be returning to the traditional viewpoint that "one doesn't make nails out of good iron; one doesn't make soldiers out of good men." To restore this damaged image in the late 1980s, the media extolled the PLA's martial virtues and the great strides made in military modernization in recent years.

MODERNIZING ARTILLERY : RETROSPECT AND PROSPECT

The images of field guns firing in Kargil in 1999 with a devastating effect at the target end are still afresh in the mind of the Indian public. That was also the time when India was recovering from the economic crisis of the early 1990s when the foreign exchange reserves had dwindled to dangerous lows to even think of acquiring defence equipment through imports. The Kargil crisis compelled the politico-military establishment to reassess the country's defence and security policies, not just to replace the Soviet vintage equipment with the Armed Forces but in terms of their modernization. In the subsequent years as part of its overall modernization effort, a Field Artillery Rationalisation Plan was introduced; the same also formed basis for the Artillery modernization plans.

Consequent to the experience in Operation Parakaram, the Indian army revised its doctrine in 2004 to respond to the realities of a tough neighbourhood. As a result, a Cold Start doctrine was articulated which had several premises. Evidently, a doctrine draws from experiences of previous wars and can be aspirational as it defines the objectives that should be chosen for the future and the operational concepts to be followed to attain goals. In this mode, a doctrine drives the nature of organization, force structure and training. The Cold Start doctrine enunciated by the Indian Army rests on rapid mobilization, concentration and launch of operations in a seamless continuum. The other planks of the doctrine are:

- Multiple thrusts with divisional sized integrated battle groups.
- Broad front, shallow depth, limited objectives.
- Pivot corps offensives supplemented with available Integrated Battle Groups from Strike Corps resources.
- Strike reserve largely uncommitted.
- Aims at attrition and capture of territory.
- Cognizant of possible nuclear thresholds.
- All weather, day night operations; air drops and heliborne operations; IW and EW; massed firepower ('100 guns' concept); operational fires.

Massing of accurate and heavy volume of firepower, coordinated with combined arms operations including the air support would be a necessary condition for achieving the objectives of a Cold Start doctrine in real-time. The Artillery doctrine no doubt will flow out of the conceptual and doctrinal issues for combined arms operations emanating from the Cold Start precepts.

Lack of adequate artillery firepower would definitely restrict the freedom and movement of own forces whereas enhanced enemy artillery fire power will also add to difficulties of own forces' manoeuvre. The Cold Start doctrine requires a massive artillery support ab initio to neutralise the enemy defences in the shortest possible time without giving him much reaction time.

Further, the India Army Chief has recently talked about the changing geo-political and strategic environment and the need to be prepared for a range of security threats and challenges including the possibilities of a need to deal with two fronts. He also reflected upon the Out of Area Contingencies which may necessitate employment of forces. Therefore the gaping voids in our field artillery need to be filled up in a hurry to meet the likely threats to the defence of the realm. The artillery rationalization plan's key objective was to standardize the equipment profile from a multitude of caliber of guns to a single caliber. There are advantages to be gained in terms of streamlined logistics, easy maintenance and repairs including standardization of ammunition.

While, this plan was outlined at the turn of the century with ambitious goal of implementing it in three to four plan periods of Five Year Defence Plans, no progress could be made due to several contextual factors. The major factor being the ghost of Bofors (payoff allegations in their mid-1980s deal) exacerbated further by allegations of corruption in some of the subsequent potential artillery acquisition deals.

However, as a first step towards modernization of field artillery almost over a decade after enunciation of FARP, there is silver lining on the cloud. Finally, the government has decided to buy 145 M777 ultralight howitzers from the US-based entity of the BAE Systems through the government-to-government Foreign Military Sales (FMS) route. The FMS route avoids all the ills and impediments associated with India's Defence Procurement Procedure which has been continually revised but has not delivered especially on the artillery procurement. A Fast Track Procedure is also part of the DPP but that has also not helped meet India's burgeoning defence acquisition needs.

An indication that the above deal of 145 light Howitzers may be clinched was a notification by the Pentagon to the US Congress in the second half of January 2010 of a possible sale of 145 state-of-the-art lightweight towed Howitzers to India.

The Defence Security Cooperation Agency rationalized to the Congress, "India intends to use the howitzers to modernise its armed forces and enhance its ability to operate in hazardous conditions. The howitzers will assist the Indian Army to develop and enhance standardisation and to improve interoperability with US Soldiers and Marines who use the M777 as their primary means of indirect fire. India will have no difficulty in absorbing these weapons into its armed forces." That it also makes a good commercial sense and an important breakthrough in the Indian defence bazaar can not be mentioned in the solemn note to the Congress.

There are reports however, on another level, that the deal may not come through as a result of the recent strategic side-lining of India in the London Conference on the Afghanistan imbroglio. There are unconfirmed reports that the Indian policy establishment is considering as to what strategic leverages India has to ensure its meaningful role in unfolding scenarios in Afghanistan where the dominant discourse is being dictated by the US, notably the Pentagon. Some years back, before the Indo-US defence Framework Agreement was signed in 2005 and the Ministry of Defence had drawn out ambitious defence acquisition plans, a retiring Defence Secretary had remarked that defence purchases from abroad should be used a strategic leverages in consonance with our policy objectives. If such recourse is adopted it would further delay the process of procurement. But then this is not the end of the massive requirements of Indian field artillery for either ultra light howitzers or for that matter other type of guns. There are four other types of 155 mm guns which are to be acquired as part of the long-term artillery modernization plans.

While the acquisition of 145 Howitzers would be sufficient only to equip seven artillery regiments after catering for General staff reserves and would fill existing voids or provide replacements for mountain artillery units to be converted to 155 mm caliber as part of FARP, additional requirements have also arisen because of the governments decision to raise two mountain divisions and a fourth artillery division to support operations in the mountainous areas. This would translate into a requirement of ultra light howitzers for four mountain artillery brigades which would mean acquisition of additional 290 pieces that would have to be spread over 12th, 13th and 14th Five Year Defence Plans.

As part of the first phase of FARP, besides the 145 pieces, a requirement of 158 Towed and wheeled guns, 100 tracked guns to support the mechanized formations and 180 wheeled guns with armour protection has been spelt out. Hopefully, these guns would be acquired in the current 11th Five Year Plan (2007-2012). Last year, the Defence Acquisition Council had included a fifth category classified as Mounted Gun Systems. These howitzers, mounted on wheeled chassis, would have a shoot and scoot capability with the crew remaining mounted on the vehicle. Looking at the overall requirements the estimates of the number of guns to be inducted to complete the rationalization plan range from 2700 to 3600 guns in the long term perspective of 15 to 20 years costing between Rs 22,000 crores to Rs 30,000 crores. These demands are based on the total number of artillery regiments which are 200 or so, and the additional artillery units planned to be raised. Such mammoth requirements also predicate that India has to indigenize the production of 155 mm guns as it can remain an importer if it has any pretensions of becoming a major power.

Defence Minister A K Antony though has already stated that the policy now was to acquire every important system with Transfer of Technology (ToT). Indian artillery immediately needs 400 towed 155 mm guns as no such guns have been acquired since the Bofors were inducted in 1987. Induction of these guns would be followed by indigenous production of 1580 guns of this type.

The acquisition process was suspended after dealings with Singapore's ST Kinetics (and six other companies) were put on hold due to allegations of corruption involving Ordnance Factories Board (OFB)'s top executive. That in fact led to a single vendor situation, and that is best avoided, according to the procurement manual.

The results of the investigations (by India's Central Bureau of Investigation, or CBI) are not known but till the companies involved are not cleared of the allegations or suspicions, no contracts would be signed by them. However, pending the completion of the process, the procedural system has okayed that the trials of equipment offered by these companies could go on so as not to cause further delay. A deal could and would be signed only after these companies are cleared of any charges of wrong-doing.

Accordingly, the government has approved the trials of the Towed guns from SK Kinetics and BAE Systems with the caveat that trials are subject to clearance of allegations of corruption (in the case of SK Kinetics). Indian Army Chief Gen Deepak Kapoor (a gunner himself) had admitted the development to be of a particular concern as the Army has not been able to purchase a single gun in the last 23 years. Earlier Denel of South Africa was blacklisted on similar charges which led to the current re-tendering process. The second category is of Tracked guns mounted on tank chassis for supporting the mechanized formations for five artillery regiments to be acquired to the extent of 100 155mm/52 caliber guns to replace the existing 130mm Catapult and 105 mm Abbot Guns.

There is the third category of wheeled 155 mm guns mounted on a six-wheeled vehicle with armour protection to the extent of 180 (as mentioned earlier). The fourth category of ultralight howitzers. And the last and the fifth category is the mounted gun system, The artillery modernization includes off-the-shelf purchase of 200 155mm/52-calibre mounted gun systems to be followed by indigenous manufacture of another 614 such howitzers under transfer of technology. The 17-tonne motorized howitzers will arm 40 regiments. A rough glance would suggest that the overall requirement would easily surpass a figure of 3000 guns.

Concerned about fast depleting stocks including war wastage reserves of field artillery, the Army Headquarters has mooted a proposal for the induction of 80-100 pieces of 130 mm medium guns from old stocks lying with former Soviet Republics, as a desperate last resort, to have something at least ASAP.

Though of World War II vintage, the 130 mm gun was imported and inducted into the Indian artillery in the 19060s. It is a rugged and a reliable gun which has seen action in all the terrains as obtaining in India including the Sia Chen Glacier base, high altitude areas and deserts. However, it lacks the sophistication and mobility of the modern artillery guns, and has a limited range of the types of ammunitions it can fire. The Army headquarters is being forced to adopt such a measure for earliest making up of critical deficiencies and building already depleted war wastage stocks. It needs to be underscored that except for upgradation of a limited number of 130 mm guns to 155mm by Soltam of Israel, a project that received mixed reviews, the Indian army has not inducted or upgraded an artillery gun for nearly three decades. In fact, OFB tried to sell the upgunned 130mm to the Gulf countries, but there was no interest in an old system here.

With indigenous production at standstill, in the Artillery faces a real precarious situation and hence this desperate and some say counterproductive measure. It is learned that the issue was discussed in recent Defence Acquisition Council meeting with final decision still pending.

Enunciation of the Cold Start doctrine could not have served its purpose of strategic communication to our potential adversaries unless the voids in fire power are made up in double quick time. The acquisition decisions on procurement of 155 mm 52 caliber towed howitzers, SP tracked and wheeled guns, and mounted gun systems as also ultralight howitzers must be taken on priority for the Artillery to play its role in a future war imposed on India.

EQUIPPING AND MODERNIZING THE ARMY

In 1983 the Army decided to keep active component strength constant in order to stress modernization priority over personnel increases. Unfortunately, slower than expected growth of the Defense Department budget in recent years has reduced Army expectations in both areas. In FY 88 funding for modernization fell below levels targeted by the Army, so Congress and Pentagon officials cut Army active component strength from about 781,000 to 772,300. Nevertheless, production and delivery continued during the year for equipment and systems that support close combat; fire support; air defense; command, control, and communications; and the other mission areas. The Army leadership continues to seek modernization of equipment and systems for the interrelated close, deep, and rear operations of Air-Land Battle. Investment in research and development to exploit advanced technologies and acquire a qualitative advantage over potential adversaries remains a high priority.

Because of the problems presented by reduced funding and Army modernization needs, the Army leadership decided to stabilize its technology base program in FY 88. In further response to requirements of the 1986 Defense Department Reorganization Act, the Army established the Office of the Deputy for Technology and Assessment within the Office of the Assistant Secretary of the Army (Research, Development, and Acquisition). This new office designed an initiative in FY 88 for the Army's Technology Base Master Plan. The plan would promote assessment of key emerging technologies through advanced technology transition demonstrations (ATTDs). Army Research, Development, and Acquisition officials selected eleven of these technologies in FY 88, which included advanced materials/material processing, artificial intelligence, biotechnology, directed energy weapons, and robotics. Coincident with these developments, the Office of the Secretary of Defense also established an ATTD program in response to a recommendation of the 1987 Defense Science Board (DSB). By coordinating both ATTD programs, RDA leaders anticipate more efficient assessment of new technologies before the Army commits itself to purchasing them.

CLOSE OPERATIONS

Close operations involve major committed combat elements and usually comprise maneuver, close combat and close air support, indirect fire support and counterfire, combat support and combat service support, and command and control. Infantry and armoured units apply direct combat power with short-range weapons assisted by attack helicopters and conventional artillery. The Abrams tank represents the foundation of the Army's modernization efforts and the key to its close operations. Combat units have received a total of 5,137 Abrams tanks since fielding began in 1981. Its firepower, special armor, compartmentalization of fuel and ammunition stowage, automatic fire detection and suppression system, and mobility provide its crew with high levels of shock action and protection on the battlefield. Introduced in 1985, the M1A1 Abrams replaced the M1's 105-mm. with a 120-mm. smoothbore cannon and added an NBC (nuclear, biological, and chemical) microclimatic cooling system to an existing thermal sight, laser rangefinder, and full stabilization. The M1A1 Abrams tank can operate effectively in all climate and light conditions and in an active chemical environment. Field experience has revealed flaws in the Abrams fire detection system. Abrams tanks experienced fifty-six fires in FY 88, one of them fatal. Most of the fires originated in the engine compartment. The Army Safety Centre initiated a lengthy investigation into the problem.

Endowed with the mobility of the Abrams tank, the Bradley Fighting Vehicles (BFVs) provide the mechanized infantry with a full-track, armoured fighting vehicle, and scout and armoured cavalry units a vehicle for reconnaissance missions. Both the infantry and the cavalry fighting vehicles have a two-man turret, which mounts the 25-mm. automatic stabilized cannon, the TOW antitank guided missile system, and the 7.62-mm. coaxial machine gun. The infantry vehicle also has six 5.56-mm. firing port weapons positioned along its sides and rear. Modified with the TOW 2 missile system, the M2/M3Al Bradleys appeared in 1987. First produced in May 1988, the M2/M3A2 Bradleys possess enhanced survivability features-improved armor, span liners in the troop compartments, revised internal restowage of fuel and ammunition, and provisions for chemical energy-defeating armor. Deliveries of Bradleys through November 1988 totaled 4,041-2,300 basic, 1,371 M2/M3A1s, and 370 M2/M3A2s. These vehicles represent 51 percent of the Army's procurement objective of 7,934 Bradleys.

The 1988 edition of the Army Aviation Modernization Plan reflects current views on present and anticipated changes in the threat, force design, technologies, and resources. It provides for continuing the light helicopter (LHX) program to develop a reconnaissance and attack aircraft capable of functioning in the projected threat environment of the mid-1990s and beyond. The Army wanted 4,500-5,000 LHXs, to include a utility version, but Defense Department officials reduced the number to about 2,100 reconnaissance/attack aircraft. Congress also emphasized continued procurement and technical improvement of the Army's most efficient existing aircraft-AH-64 Apache, UH-60 Black Hawk, OH-58D AHIP, CH-47D Chinook-and other special mission aircraft to sustain an adequate Army aircraft fleet until LHX production begins in the mid-1990s. The plan also calls for retirement of older helicopter models no longer useful on the modern battlefield-UH-1 Huey, OH-58 Kiowa series, OH-6A Cayuse, CH-54 Tarhe, and AH-1 Cobra among others. Congress capped funding at $3.5 billion a year for the aircraft modernization plan, which forecasts a fleet of 6,600 aircraft, 2,000 less than in the current inventory.

The Army plans to field 48 attack helicopter battalions equipped with the AH-64 Apache-29 active, 15 National Guard, and 4 reserve. The 1st Battalion, 130th Aviation, a Roundout unit for the XVIII Airborne Corps stationed in Raleigh-Durham, North Carolina, became the first National Guard unit to receive the Apache with receipt of the first of six helicopters in November 1987. The Army planned to discontinue the OH-58D AHIP in 1988, but Congress approved $138 million for its expansion. A redesigned OH-58 Kiowa helicopter, the AHIP boasts a weight increase to 5,400 pounds over the OH-58's 4,500; sophisticated electronics and a mast-mounted sight; and armament systems with the Hellfire, Stinger,.50-caliber machine gun, and 2.75-inch rockets. Despite its own impressive firepower, current planning calls for the AHIP to operate with the Apache as a hunter/killer team; the AHIP locates targets, and the Apache destroys them. By mid-FY 88 six Army divisions had AHIP platoons-1st, 2d, and 3d Armoured; 3d and 8th Mechanized; arid the 2d Infantry. The XVIII Airborne Corps had one AHIP company.

Of highest concern to the Army leadership, its LHX program received approval by Defense Department officials in FY88 to begin its demonstration/validation phase in early FY 89.

Intended to replace the tactically inferior AH-1 Cobra, OH-6 Cayuse, and the OH-58 Kiowa, the LHX will perform armed reconnaissance and light attack missions and complement the larger and more powerfully armed AH-64 Apache. Developers will strive to obtain a maximum empty weight of 7,500 pounds and a cost limit of $7.5 million per aircraft in FY 88 dollars. Powered by two 1,200 shaft horsepower T800 engines, the LHX will have two crewmen but the capability of one-person operation. It will have an automated cockpit, helmet mounted wide view optics, and worldwide navigation capability. With a minimum dash speed of 170 knots and a minimum vertical climb of 500 feet per minute, its armament will include the Hellfire antitank missile system, air-to-air Stinger missiles, and a turreted automatic gun. Along with crashworthy design features, the LHX will possess wheeled landing gear and self-deployability to Europe.

Recent concern about developments in reactive armor and electro-optical countermeasures prompted the Army's Armor Anti-Armor (A3) Modernization Plan, a combined arms approach. To help meet the challenge, the Army indicated to Congress it would procure 3,000 MlA2-configured Abrams tanks during a five-year period and also field a Block III tank by 1997. A changing budget environment, however, caused the Army to retrench on its plans for the M1A2. An existing weapon, the Army's Hellfire modular missile system has proven itself an effective airborne antiarmor device. The AH-64 Apache can carry sixteen Hellfires, and the LHX will also mount them. Active development of a digital auto pilot will improve Hellfire lethality. The TOW (tube-launched, optically tracked, wire command link-guided) missile has undergone improvements to keep pace with armor changes, and the Army has begun receiving the superior TOW 2A. Its tandem warhead armament system achieves increased lethality against the latest reactive armor by adding a small warhead to the missile probe. The initial charge explodes on a tank's reactive armor to clear a path for the primary warhead that will penetrate the tank's skin. A TOW 2B development program has begun, which relies upon the capability of the missile to fly over and fire down upon armoured vehicles. The Advanced Antitank Weapon System Medium (AAWS-M), the replacement for the Dragon missile but still in the testing stage, will allow individual infantry personnel to destroy tanks regardless of visibility conditions and electro-optical countermeasures.

Cannon and rocket systems supply conventional artillery indirect fire support for close operations. Several initiatives will remedy current limits in range and lethality of some artillery systems. The XM762 electronic time artillery fuze will allow greater accuracy, easier manual setting, and compatibility with inductive howitzer autosetters. The M864 base-burn dual-purpose improved conventional munition, now in production, will increase the range of the munitions it replaces by 60 percent. Modifications continue on the M109A2/A3 155-mm. howitzer fleet-an improved recoil system and cannon with a maximum range of 30 kilometers, micro-cooling for an NBC environment, and improved ballistic protection. The Army completed initial fielding of the 155-mm. variant of the Field Artillery Ammunition Support Vehicle to forward-deployed artillery forces in Korea and Europe in FY88. A tracked, self-propelled, armoured ammunition carrier, it exceeds the survivability rate of the existing unarmored M548 ammunition resupply vehicle. Towable by the High Mobility Multipurpose Wheeled Vehicle (HMMWV) and air transportable by the Black Hawk helicopter, the British Light Gun M119 fulfills fine light infantry division need for an extended range, lightweight 105-mm. howitzer. It can fire U.S. standard 105-mm. projectiles 14.3 kilometers and rocket-assisted projectiles 19.5 kilometers. The United Kingdom (UK) will produce those scheduled for initial fielding in November 1989, but the U.S. will eventually assume M119 production.

Deep Operations

Deep operations constitute those activities directed against enemy forces not in contact with the forces conducting close operations at the forward line of troops (FLOT). Corps headquarters and higher command echelons normally conduct deep operations that include surveillance and acquisition of enemy targets, interdiction of these targets, deception of the enemy about current operations, countering of enemy command and control systems, and effective maintenance of U.S. Army command and control. To observe enemy deployments 100 kilometers and beyond, the Army and the Air Force are developing the joint Surveillance and Target Attack Radar System (JSTARS),. It can detect, track, classify, and assist in attacking both moving and stationary targets. The Army is developing the Ground Station Module (GSM) for JSTARS, while the Air Force is creating the Prime Mission Equipment (PME)-platform, radar, and data link. The schedule calls for an operational orbit to support Europe in 1997, followed by additional orbits to support worldwide requirements.

Concerned about the competing and costly unmanned aerial vehicle (UAV) and remotely piloted vehicle (RPV) programs of the armed services, Congress consolidated them within the Office of the Secretary of Defense in the FY 88 Defense Appropriations Act. The UAV Joint Project Office, which operates under Naval Air Systems Command, has responsibility for managing the acquisition of UAV systems for the Defense, Department. In September 1988 the UAV Joint Project Office designated the Army's Missile Command (MICOM), Redstone Arsenal, Alabama, as the site for a UAV joint development centre, while the Army Intelligence School (AIS), Fort Huachuca, Arizona, provides a joint training centre. The UAV program will jointly develop four categories of UAV systems of which the Army has responsibility for three. The close-range system will have an operational radius sufficient to support divisional cannon and rocket artillery and will be fielded to divisions, armoured cavalry regiments, and separate brigades. The short-range system will have an operational radius of 150-300 kilometers and will be fielded to corps and echelons above corps military intelligence brigades. The endurance system will provide a minimum of 24 hours of mission performance at extended ranges and will also be fielded to corps and echelons above corps military intelligence brigades. The Air Force, Navy, and Marine Corps will use the medium-range system for fixed and mobile target reconnaissance.

The multiple launch rocket system (MLRS), a free-flight, all-weather, indirect-fire rocket system operational since 1983 and being fielded throughout the world, can fire twelve 13-foot rockets to ranges over 30 kilometers in less than a minute. Mounted on a tracked, self-propelled launcher, it can deliver overwhelming firepower against enemy artillery, air defense, and other light material and personnel targets. Now jointly produced by the U.S. with the United Kingdom, France, and West Germany, the MLRS includes a preplanned improvement for a terminal guidance warhead with the capability of destroying enemy armor from above, a sense-and-destroy armor warhead to improve counter-battery fires, and a binary chemical warhead. The MLRS launcher can also carry two Army Tactical Missile System (ATACMS) missiles, a conventional ballistic system with missiles capable of propelling 1,000 antipersonnel/ antimateriel bomblets beyond the range of cannons, rockets, arid the Lance missile system. ATACMS is in full-scale development and scheduled for fielding in FY 90. An Oklahoma National' Guard battalion, the 1st Battalion, 45th Field Artillery Brigade, headquartered in Lawton, Oklahoma, became the first reserve component unit to receive the MLRS, in FY 88.

The Special Electronic Mission Aircraft (SEMA) represent an integral part of the intelligence and electronic warfare tactical mission capability of the Army. The existing fleet includes the Quick Look RV-1D (side looking airborne radar), Guardrail RC-12D and RC-12H/K (signals intelligence), Grisly Hunter (forward-looking infrared and infrared line scanner), and the Quick Fix EH-60 (heliborne-direction-finding and jamming system). The Army essentially has fielded SEMA, but product improvements continue. Joint Army/Air Force Initiative 17, 22 May 1984, transferred responsibility for Special Operations Forces (SOF) rotary wing airlift support from the Air Force to the Army. The Deputy Secretary of Defense supports a program for fifty-one MH-47E (modified CH-47D Chinook) and twenty-three MH-60K (modified UH-60A Black Hawk) helicopters. Significant features of the aircraft include a fully integrated cockpit, more powerful engines, forward-looking infrared, terrain following/avoidance radar, air-to-air refueling, and Stinger air-to-air missiles. Their expected missions include troop insertions and extractions behind enemy lines, rapid deployment, and strategic intelligence strikes. The Army Program Objective Memorandum for 1990-94 allots funding for most of the desired aircraft.

The U.S. government has concluded that, until a worldwide verifiable ban on chemical weapons occurs, America needs binary munitions as a deterrent to war, as a bargaining agent in arms control negotiations, and as a weapon should deterrence fail. Congress has mandated that the Defense Department destroy its aging and hazardous unitary chemical weapons by 1997 and create a binary chemical stockpile. As the Defense Department lead, the Army will coordinate production of 155-mm. GB-2 binary chemical projectiles, develop the Binary Chemical Warhead (BCW) for MLRS, produce the BIGEYE bomb for the Air Force and Navy, and store both the binary and remaining unitary devices until the tatter's destruction. Major accomplishments of binary chemical modernization during FY 88 included presidential approval to produce the 155-mm. binary projectile and the BIGEYE bomb, initial production of the 155-mm. projectile in December 198'7, and transition of the BCW for the MLRS to full-scale development in July 1988. To satisfy an operational need for a mobile NBC-reconnaissance vehicle, the Under Secretary of the Army and the Vice Chief of Staff of the Army (VCSA) had tentatively decided in 1988 to adopt the German Spuerpanzer Fuchs for worldwide fielding and to terminate the XM87 RDTE (research, development, test, and evaluation) program. Congress, however, directed the Army to conduct ongoing full competition evaluation of similar systems.

Rear Operations

Effective rear area operations assure freedom of maneuver and continuity of combat operations for troops on the FLOT. Rear area operations focus on sustaining the tempo of combat and preparing for the next phase of a campaign. Primary activities include command and control, air defense, assembly and movement of reserves, redeployment of fire support, and sustainment.

The tactical command, control, and communications (C3) mission area permits commanders to control combat operations successfully through timely receipt of battlefield data and access to communications systems which function even during enemy electronic countermeasures. The Army Tactical Command and Control System (ATCCS) integrates five battlefield functional area command and control automated systems-Maneuver Control System (MCS); Advanced Field Artillery Tactical Data System (AFATDS); All Source Analysis System (ASAS); Forward Area Air Defense Command, Control, and Intelligence (FAADC2I) System; and the Combat Service Support Control System (CSSCS). The MCS allows commanders at corps through battalion to evaluate large amounts of data on their forces, the enemy, and the characteristics of the battlefield. A hybrid computer system, MCS militarized hardware production began in 1983, while nondevelopmental item equipment deliveries began in FY 88. AFATDS provides fully automated support for planning, coordinating, and executing close support, counterfire, and suppression of enemy fires. It corrects the fire control and distribution deficiencies of TACFIRE (tactical fire direction system). Army officials anticipate initial fielding of AFATDS hardware in FY 94.

The ASAS connects to ATCCS and the Air Force Enemy Situation Correlation Element (ENSCE) for coordinated joint combat operations. Testing of ASAS continues with fielding anticipated in the late 1990s. The FAADC21 system provides the air defense artillery control system for ATCCS at corps echelons and below. FAADC21 consists of four interrelated programs-command and control hardware and software to integrate all subsystems and components and display the force and engagement operations information, a ground-based sensor to provide aircraft tracking over the division area of influence, a Masked Target Sensor to track at and forward of the FLOT, and identification devices (cooperative and noncooperative, active and passive) to sort friends from hostiles. These combined programs produce a system that permits situation awareness, force alerting, and engagement of hostile aircraft at the maximum range of FAADS weapons.

The Army fielded the two-person portable Tactical Army Combat Service Support Computer System (TACCS) as a device designed to feed data to the Combat Service Support Control System (CSSCS). It improves the accuracy and transmission of administrative and logistical data. Production began in 1987, and deliveries totaled about 8,000 by December 1988. Plans call for fielding CSSCS in FY 93. Three primary communication/data systems support ATCCS-Mobile Subscriber Equipment (MSE), Single Channel Ground and Airborne Radio Systems (SINCGARS), and the Army Data Distribution System (ADDS). MSE, a common user, automatically switched, survivable, secure voice, data, and facsimile communications system for corps and divisions of both the active and reserve components, allows the Army to implement Air-Land Battle command and control. MSE has a modular signal organization structure, mobility, and fast erection capability that interoperates with TRITAC, combat net radio, commercial telephone systems, and NATO communications networks. Fielding of MSE began in February 1988 at Fort Hood, Texas, with follow on operational test and evaluation during August-October. MSE performance proved effective and superior to the current system. The manufacturer is incorporating several improvements to include a higher call completion rate by way of a block improvement plan being implemented in conjunction with additional fielding.

The SINCGARS, the Army's new lightweight, securable VHF-FM combat net radio, can operate in voice and data modes despite enemy jamming by frequency hopping on 2,320 channels in a frequency range of 30-88 megaherz. Available in manpack, vehicular, and airborne models, SINCGARS will function as the primary communication system for tactical units. In FY88 the Army fielded 155 systems to Korea and about 300 to TRADOC. Early reports indicated that SINCGARS was performing well. The ADDS, an automatic tactical data distribution system, gives commanders the capability of meeting near-real-time data communications and position location reporting requirements. It represents two systems-the Enhanced Position Location Reporting System (EPLRS), a joint Army/ Marine program, and the Joint Tactical Information Distribution System (JTIDS), a tri-service program. Low rate initial production of ADDS will begin in 1989.

The Army's satellite communications program consists of the ground environment of the Defense Satellite Communications System (DSCS) and the Ground Mobile Forces Tactical Satellite Communication Program. The Army contributes to DSCS by developing, procuring, and fielding ground satellite communications earth terminals and control systems for the armed services. These terminals and control systems support rapid and reliable worldwide command, control, communications, and intelligence operations for military commanders and the National Command Authority. Developments in progress include efforts to maximize traffic rates and to minimize vulnerability to enemy countermeasures. The Ground Mobile Forces Tactical Satellite Communications Program (GMFS) provides single and multichannel and special purpose tactical satellite ground terminals and control systems to meet critical long-range, jam-resistant, and nuclear-survivable communications needs. The Army is procuring the single channel AN/PSC-3 and AN/VSC-7 ultra high frequency terminals for its Rangers and Special Forces. Work continues on developing the survivable, antijam, and mobile ground terminal, the Single Channel Objective Tactical Terminal (SCOTT), for the Military Strategic and Tactical Relay Satellite Communications System (MILSTAR).

Continuing advances in Soviet helicopters and long-range weapons mandate ongoing modernization of Army air defense systems. Several existing missiles defend against short-, medium-, and long-range air threats. Initially fielded in 1969, the Chaparral supplies short-range, low-altitude protection against enemy aircraft. In service since 1960, the Hawk medium-range guided missile system affords air defense against low- to medium-altitude air attack. The Patriot missile, first deployed to Europe in 1985, serves as the centerpiece of Army theater air defense. Several product changes are improving Chaparral missile system performance. Now being fielded, a forward-looking infrared night sight aids night and adverse weather target acquisition. Programmed improvements to Chaparral include the Rosette Scan Seeker for countermeasure protection and a collective NBC protective system. The Army had deployed the Roland Air Defense Missile System, which originated in Europe, to only one unit, the 5th Battalion, 200th Air Defense Artillery, New Mexico National Guard. Since Chaparral units require fewer full-time staff and less money to operate than Roland units, the Army leadership decided to eliminate the Roland system. It reorganized the 5th Battalion, now designated the 6th, into a Chaparral unit in FY 88.

The current improvement program, Phase III, updates the Hawk missile system. It has redesigned the Hawk acquisition, tracking, and fire control equipment to simplify operator use and to improve electronic countermeasures and data supply to the AN/TSQ-73 missile minder command and control system. The Stinger, first fielded in 1981 as a manportable air defense missile system and now both modified to the Pedestal Mounted Stinger and intended as a helicopter weapon, continues to acquire product improvements for individual soldier use. The Stinger Post, first fielded in 1987, improved Stinger performance against infrared countermeasures. Stinger reprogrammable microprocessor (RMP), initially deployed to Europe in FY 88, facilitates future changes to Stinger seeker software to counter anticipated improvements of infrared countermeasures.

The Patriot Tactical Air Defense Missile System serves as the high-altitude air defense for the field Army and vital military bases. In its ninth year of production, the Patriot is undergoing product improvements to increase its antitactical missile capability. During test firings in 1986 and 1987, the Patriot demonstrated its known potential by successfully intercepting and destroying a Lance missile and other tactical missile targets. Patriot antitactical missile capability, PAC-1, consists of system radar software modifications that enable the detection, tracking, and interception of high-angle approach short-range ballistic missiles. PAC-2 has additional software improvements and a more lethal warhead.

Cancellation of the Sergeant York air defense gun system in 1985 meant that the Army leadership realized that neither one nor multiple weapons acting independently can defeat the forward area air threat. The Forward Area Air Defense System (FAADS), designed for total air defense coverage to the division area, integrates weapons, sensors, and command, control, and intelligence systems to counter the anticipated forward area air threat into the 21st century. FAADS consists of five major elements-a command, control, and intelligence (C2I) component; a line of sight-forward-heavy (LOS-F-H) weapon; a non-line of sight (NLOS) weapon; a line of sight-rear (LOS-R) weapon; and combined arms initiatives. The FAADS C2I component incorporates ground/ aerial sensors with a data processing/ distribution system. Full-scale development for air defense software, ground sensor nondevelopmental evaluation, and aerial sensor and noncooperative target recognition proceeded in FY 88. In November 1987 the Army announces selection of the air defense antitank system (ADATS) as the LOS-F-H weapon for FAADS. Mounted on the M3A2 Bradley cavalry fighting vehicle chassis, ADATS has electro-optic sensors, a search radar, and eight laser beam-riding missiles. It will undergo technical and operational testing in late 1989.

The non-line of sight (NLOS) component for FAADS employs the fiber optic-guided missile (FOG-M) mounted on both the HMMWV and the MLRS chassis. With full-scale development planned for FY 89, FOG-M has a seeker mounted in its nose that transmits pictures by a bidirectional fiber optic data link while in flight so the gunner can locate hidden targets. The Army selected the Pedestal Mounted Stinger (PMS) as its LOS-R weapon. Erected on the HMMWV with eight Stinger missiles and devices to provide day/night and adverse weather capability, the two-man PMS, renamed Avenger, crew provides air defense against fixed-wing aircraft and helicopters at low altitudes in the division rear area. Having procured about sixty Avenger systems by the end of FY 88, the Army expected to expand Avenger production in FY 89. Combined arms initiatives underway that supplement FAADS include installing air-to-air Stingers on the OH-58C/D helicopter, improved air defense sights for the Bradley fighting vehicle, and antihelicopter ammunition for tanks.

Rear area operations also entail combat service support missions that include assembly and movement of reserves, supply, redeployment of fire support, and medical functions. These depend, in turn, upon a variety of Army transportation facilities adapted to air, ground, and water service. The UH-60 Black Hawk helicopter is replacing the UH-1 Huey in Army air assault, air cavalry, and aeromedical evacuation missions. It can transport a fully equipped eleven-man squad in most weather conditions. The Army has already fielded Black Hawks to many CONUS and OCONUS units. It fielded additional Apaches in FY 88 and procured Hellfire missile system kits, crashworthy external fuel tanks, and auxiliary heaters for retrofitting to Black Hawks. The CH-47 Chinook serves as the Army's medium lift helicopter with a payload capacity of about 16,000 pounds or thirty-three troops. First fielded in 1962, the Chinook transports ammunition, petroleum, large weapons, and personnel on the battlefield. A modernization program begun in 1975 upgraded the Chinook A, B, and C models to a D configuration for anticipated use into the early 2000s. Structural improvements include fiberglass rotor blades, modularized hydraulics, and a triple hook cargo system for an anticipated fleet of 472 CH-47Ds.

The Army's tactical wheeled vehicle fleet remains short of requirements. The medium vehicle fleet, composed of many 2.5-ton trucks of 1950s design, needs replacement according to Army wheeled transportation assessments. A five-year contract awarded in FY 86 called for delivery of 15,000 upgraded 5-ton trucks, and the Family of Medium Tactical Vehicles program sought further modernization of the medium fleet in FY 88. A Milestone I/II Army Systems Acquisition Review Council and Defense Acquisition Board decision approved a full-scale development validation phase in May 1988 for a modernized 5-ton fleet. The FY 88/89 authorization bills directed the Army to establish a multiyear contract for 4,737 Heavy Expanded Mobility Tactical Trucks (HEMTT) starting in FY 88 and Palletized Loading System (PLS) competitive hardware testing and source selection within two years. PLS offers self load/unload capability, potential to decrease other dedicated vehicle and material handling requirements, an improved ammunition supply distribution system, and NATO interoperability. A Milestone I/II Army Systems Acquisition Review Council and Defense Acquisition Board decision also approved a full-scale proveout phase for a 16.5-ton PLS in FY 88.

Four logistics support vessels (LSVs) joined the Army's watercraft fleet in FY 88 which increased the Army's capability in intratheater lift operations to transport cargo from ship to shore, from beach to beach, and through inland waterways. The vessels consisted of the following- *General Frank S. Besson, Jr.,* delivered to the 335th Transportation Detachment at Fort Eustis, Virginia, in November 1987; CW3 *Harold C. Clinger,* delivered to the 605th Transportation Company, Fords Island, Hawaii, in February 1988; *General Brehon B. Somervell,* delivered to the 604th Transportation Company, Washington National Guard, Tacoma, Washington, in April; and *Lieutenant General William B. Bunker,* delivered to the 1099th Transportation Company, Fort Eustis, Virginia, in May. With a delivery range of 6,500 nautical miles fully loaded at 10.8 knots cruising speed, these 273-foot vessels, with bow and stern ramps, can carry 2,000 short tons including trucks and outsized tracked vehicles, containers, and general cargo on 10,500 square feet of deck area. Commanded by warrant officers, the crews of these vessels consist of 6 warrant officers and 23 enlisted personnel. In another Army watercraft matter, the Naval Sea Systems Command awarded a contract in January 1988 for construction of 2, of a projected 10, 120-foot oceangoing tugboats to augment the Army's offloading assets.

In FY 88 the Army began fielding a new generation of equipment called deployable medical systems (DEPMEDS).

Training exercise MOBEX 83 had identified a serious deficiency of medical equipment for the Army's field hospitals, and the Defense Resource Board directed the Army to provide necessary funding to equip the hospital structure. A congressional moratorium on the existing hospital equipment system, medical unit self-contained transportable (MUST), precluded further procurement of that generation of hospital equipment. A congressional mandate for the services to maximize standardization in hospital equipment resulted in the quad service family of standardized functional modules for use in equipping the hospitals of the various services. DEPMEDS consist of seven types of modular combat hospitals ranging from forward-deployed mobile Army surgical hospitals to general hospitals located in the communications zone, easily locatable and air transportable. Each hospital has different combinations of standard modules such as operating rooms, X-ray units, and wards. DEPMEDS-equipped hospitals employ the latest medical technology and can function in all climates. Procurement and fielding projections call for 156 DEPMEDS-equipped hospitals by FY 96. The Army distributed 14 DEPMEDS-equipped hospitals to field units and 1 to the training base at the Academy of Health Sciences by the end of FY88.

Assisted by computer design technology, the Army's Research, Development, and Engineering Centre of Fort Belvoir, Virginia, completed a project in 1988 which produced a new three-color camouflage pattern for all tactical equipment. Considered more effective than the four-color pattern used since the early 1970s, the new pattern comes in 413 design packages for 834 types of equipment. Distribution of the new camouflage drawings has begun. When applying the designs to equipment, technicians also will use a substance resistant to chemical agents so soldiers can decontaminate equipment in the field. Incorporating a practice employed by armies long ago and also by the Soviets today, the U.S. Army is acquiring decoys and fake targets to deceive enemy forces. Canvas Abrams tanks, lined with plastic sheets that create thermal images of the vehicle's armor, engines, and wheels, have fooled U.S.

Army soldiers during training exercises. The Army plans to purchase a fake tank for each Abrams tank and is investigating more elaborate decoys, which include electronically generated fake targets.

Soldier Support

The term "soldier support" refers to items that the individual soldier directly wears, uses, or consumes. These items include organizational clothing and equipment, individual weapons, and food. In late FY 88 the Office of the Deputy Chief of Staff for Logistics (ODCSLOG) initiated a study on the garrison dress, service, and utility uniform design trends for the 21st century. The Office of the Deputy Chief of Staff for Personnel began a survey in September 1988 regarding soldiers' views on the subject. Army officials expected completion of a private contractor study on Army uniforms for the 21st century by the end of 1989. To enhance the soldier's battlefield survivability and also to lighten the individual load, the Army has sought the individual tactical load-bearing vest, the large field pack with internal frame, and the extended cold weather clothing system. Budget cutbacks resulted in only minimal fielding of these items to selected units in FY 88. The Army announced that, effective January 1988, the new combat boot adopted in 1986 would serve as the only boot issued to both active and reserve component personnel.

For prevention of eye injuries during both training and combat, the Army began fielding ballistic laser protective spectacles to forward elements of selected units in June 1988. The interim product has three parts-clear polycarbonate spectacles, tinted polycarbonate spectacles, and a laser protective detachable frontsert. Soldiers who wear corrective lenses can obtain adaptable backserts. The clear lenses provide general eye protection, the tinted spectacles shield the sun, and the frontsert affords protection against low energy laser systems.

The Army is distributing a new bayonet, the M9, which doubles as a field knife and wire cutter. It weighs less than two pounds and replaces the M7 bayonet. The M9 can saw through 2-by-2-inch pine boards, aircraft fuselages, or two-strand barbed wire. Special Forces and Ranger units are receiving a new parachute, the MCl-1C, which has nonporous nylon material in its canopy that reduces the descent rate of the MCl-1B parachute from 21 feet per second to 14.6. The MC1-1C also has an increased forward drive of 8 to 10 knots or 2 to 4 knots more than the MCl-1B, which enables parachutists to maneuver more easily around ground obstacles. The new parachute uses the standard MC1-1B harness, pack tray, deployment bag, and packing procedures.

The Army plans to begin issuing the M40 chemical and biological protective mask to all ground personnel in FY 91. It replaces the M17 general purpose and the M9 special purpose masks. The M42 replaces the M24 used by the combat vehicle crew member. The M40 and the M42 provide better protection against foreign agents than their predecessors and, made of silicon rather than rubber, allow a softer yet tighter fit. The M40 has a removable filter compatible with NATO masks, and by being attachable to either side compatible the mask, can accommodate right or left-handed shooters. The M42 has a crew communications cable and a replaceable microphone. The M9 and M24 have no voice transmitters or provision for the wearer to drink water, but the M40 has both.

Operational rations include T -rations, B-rations, and the Meal, Ready to Eat (MRE). The T -ration, with fully cooked heat and serve components, serves as the Army's primary hot field meal. Its anticipated full implementation in the near future lessened the need for cooks, so the Army recently cut 3,500 of them and converted the positions into other military job specialties. MIZE VIII, developed as the fourth version of MIZE, deleted 9 unpopular entrees and added 10 new entrees, brand name candy, and hot sauce.

The Army has 12 MREs, 2 for breakfast and 10 for dinner/ supper. In FY 88 it increased the 10 dinner/supper entrees from 5 to 8 ounces. Selected division and corps combat units, the National Training Centre, and the Joint Readiness Training Centre received partial distribution of MRE VIII in FY 88. Testing continued in FY 88 on rations for Special Operations

Forces. One program completed initial development of 42 new ration components for a 6 day menu cycle for missions as long as 30 days. It also reduced the currently fielded per-day ration volume by 72 percent and weight by 3.8 pounds. Army Special Operations Forces and Marine Corps personnel conducted arctic cold weather tests of the Ration, Cold Weather (RCW) in FY 88. Smaller and lighter than the MRE, RCW features high calorie components that do not freeze at very low temperatures and also encourage water consumption by soldiers to prevent dehydration.

Strategic Defense

The U.S. Army Strategic Defense Command' (USASDC) conducts the Army's strategic weapons research and development program, which contributes to the Defense Department Strategic Defense Initiative Organization. The command has the specific mission of developing technologies for ballistic missile defense and management of Kwajalein Atoll as a national missile range. During FY88 the Strategic Defense Command managed a research program of $1.2 billion in the five functional areas of ballistic missile defense-surveillance, acquisition, tracking, and kill assessment; kinetic energy weapons; directed energy weapons; systems analysis/ battle management; and survivability, lethality, and key technologies. In September 1987 the Defense Acquisition Board directed that Phase I of the Defense Department's strategic defense system proceed from concept validation to demonstration and validation. Army components include the exoatmospheric reentry vehicle interceptor system; the ground based surveillance and tracking system; and the battle management, command, control, and communications support for these systems. The Air Force has developmental responsibility for the other Phase I devices the boost surveillance and tracking system, the space based interceptor, and the space based surveillance and tracking system. Active development of the Army's strategic defense system elements continued throughout FY 88.

6

Arming the Revolution in Military

INTRODUCTION

The belief that modern militaries are on the cusp of a "revolution in military affairs" (RMA), driven in particular by recent advances in information technologies (IT) has long been an increasingly powerful and persuasive school of military thought. For more than a decade, in fact, it has been fashionable—almost obligatory—to acknowledge the so-called IT-RMA when talking about the future of warfare and warfighting. Consequently, the idea that armed forces must be "transformed" along the lines of the IT-RMA and other technological breakthroughs has taken particular hold in the minds of many leading proponents of military reform.

Nowhere was this commitment to defense transformation more pervasive than within the US Department of Defense (DoD) under Secretary Donald Rumsfeld from 2001 to 2006. Under his stewardship, transformation became the guiding principle of the US military. Terms such as "information superiority," "situational awareness," "network-centric warfare," "precision-strike," "deployability," "flexibility," and "jointness" were given increasing credence in Rumsfeld's Defense Department, and the belief in the power of defense transformation to bring about a dramatic expansion in the capabilities and effectiveness of the US military became almost an article of faith. The transformation of the US armed forces was initially promoted as nothing less than a fundamental shift in the way wars would be fought in the future. Nothing was sacred: every piece of defense dogma was on the table for debate and discussion—force structure, organization, equipment, budgets, doctrine, and strategy. As such, defense transformation was to be a process of unsettling, even bewildering, change; but the end result was supposed to be a US military capable of wringing the maximum amount of effectiveness from the tools it was given, and which would cement the ascendancy of US military power for the next several decades.

Such far-reaching and ambitious aims implied significant changes for the US defense industrial base. How would it function in an environment that called for such sweeping changes in military force structure, doctrine and strategy? What new technologies and systems would it be expected to provide a transformed US military, and how would it supply these? Would new suppliers arise and old ones fall—particularly if, as many proponents of the current RMA argued, the commercial IT industry would become the new nucleus for military innovation and change? Would the US military-industrial complex—forged in the Second World War and solidified during the Cold War—have to transform itself as well? This chapter will address the current state of affairs within the US military regarding defense transformation, starting with its founding precepts and its conceptualization under Rumsfeld, proceeding through successes and failures in implementation, and, finally, to its present state. It will then address how developments in US defense transformation may affect the US defense industry. Finally, the paper will conclude with a discussion of possible implications for defense industries elsewhere.

THE UNCERTAIN FUTURE OF US DEFENSE TRANSFORMATION

The current information technologiesled RMA and the

subsequent process of defense transformation is, for many, a defining moment in the character and conduct of modern warfare. The IT-RMA entails the combination of new technologies and innovative operational and organizational concepts that are supposed to fundamentally alter the way one thinks about war and warfighting. Certainly, the IT-RMA has the potential to be truly revolutionary in its impact on the future of the US military and how it conducts military operations.

At the same time, there may be less than meets the eye still when it comes to US defense transformation. New capabilities and requirements have promised to make defense transformation truly revolutionary in its impact on the future of the US military, how it conducts military operations, and how it will interact with allies and potential partners. And yet, in the post-Rumsfeld Defense Department, it is not at all certain that transformation will be as far-reaching a solution as originally envisioned or intended.

In the first place, US force transformation is perhaps not nearly as radical or as comprehensive as many proponents of the RMA would prefer. To quote two sceptics of transformation:

Transformation's champions call for more than the standard issue evolutionary technological, doctrinal, or organizational advances. They promise discontinuous, disruptive innovation. However, the US transformation enterprise thus far falls short of the hype. Joint and service plans and programmes have yet to match up to transformation visions. While the visions promise discontinuity and disruption, plans and programmes support only incremental, sustaining advances. Generation-skipping technologies are few and far between. Few modernization programmes that offer merely improved versions of existing capabilities have been abandoned in favour of transformational programmes; legacy programmes rule. Doctrine development has been more linear than nonlinear. Organizational change features evolution and adaptation rather than recreation and even restructuring. Unless the gap between visions and plans and programmes can be bridged, transformation is fated to be little more than routine modernization. At best, it will amount to "modernization plus."

In addition, while defense transformation is not simply supposed to be a techno-fix overlaid on top of an existing force structure and defense doctrine, the US military still appears to emphasize technical solutions to military problems. Defense transformation's strength is supposed to lie in its ability to span "the realm of ideas, innovation and technology," and yet there is still a widespread tendency among the US military toward "techno-faddism"—viewing technology as the central and most critical factor in transformation. At the same time, the US military also appears to be still wedded to "canonical weapons platforms"—tanks, fighter jets, large surface combatants, etc. Despite everything, warfare is still basically seen as platform-centric.

Moreover, as current operations in Afghanistan and Iraq have demonstrated, transformative technologies may be ill-suited for certain missions—for instance, against low-level threats such as terrorism or counter-insurgencies. In particular, substituting information for armour or for mass may not always be the wisest course of action. As postwar operations against insurgents in Iraq have demonstrated, small, lightly armoured units operating in areas where information concerning the adversary's whereabouts or strengths is imperfect or changing rapidly have found that a little extra protection can be lifesaving.

As a corollary, an adversary may also try to defeat a transformed, high-tech conventional force by pursuing a variety of offsetting, asymmetric responses. These include engaging in low-intensity insurgency and guerrilla tactics, emphasizing WMD capabilities (particularly nuclear weapons and ballistic missile delivery systems), or pursuing offensive information warfare (to blind and disrupt an armed force heavily dependent upon C4ISR and other network-centric systems).

Finally, the current process of defense transformation is complicated by the fact that the US Defense Department remains overly ambiguous as to its own vision of transformation and how precisely to implement it. Too often, those who were charged with thinking about defense transformation failed to bridge the gap between their ideas and those in the military who must implement transformation in a practical sense. For example, the now-disbanded Office of Force Transformation typically described transformation as a "continuous process," with "no definite end state in mind," but this does little to help war-planners. As three serving US Army officers point out:

> While [force transformation is] clearly an ongoing procedure, the lack of precisely defined waypoints, operating parameters, a bounded and developed transformational concept for joint operations, or disciplined programmatics means that service and joint planner cannot easily prioritize programs and resources to satisfy what remains an ambiguous agenda. (Hooker, McMaster & Grey, 2005, pp. 20-27)

Consequently, defense transformation is still a "somewhat elliptically" defined process, and, to their own ultimate disadvantage, the prophets and advocates of transformation have done a poor job delineating their conceptualization of what transformation is supposed to be—both operationally and organizationally. These efforts are not helped by the fact that most advocates of transformation are still being informed by the highly abstract vision of the RMA. Translating the RMA into defense transformation will be a difficult, if not unattainable task, so long as we still lack good definitions of what is meant by "disruptive" innovation, or how we will know when we have truly arrived at a "paradigm shift" that "fundamentally alters" the character and conduct of warfare.

This is not to say that many of the ideas behind the IT-led RMA are no longer relevant, or, in particular, that network-centric warfare and new reconnaissance-strike systems will not make a significant contribution to future military capabilities and effectiveness and perhaps, in the long run, truly alter the warfare and warfighting. But it is legitimate to question whether we are really in a "revolutionary" state, or whether it is even valid to speak of a revolutionary process of change ("Brains, Not Bullets," 2007, October 25, p. 15). Force transformation, as it is currently being implemented by the US Defense

Department, is not nearly as radical or as comprehensive as many proponents of the RMA would prefer. Current transformational activities may be noteworthy, but they are still more indicative of a process of *sustaining* and *evolutionary* change, rather than disruptive, revolutionary change.

MEAN BY DEFENSE TRANSFORMATION

Defense (or military) transformation has preoccupied the US Defense Department ever since the Bush Administration came into office in early 2001. Secretary of Defense Rumsfeld made over-hauling the US military and reorienting US armed forces—in terms of operations, capabilities, strategy, organization, and global posture—a paramount objective in light of new twenty-first-century security threats arising from terrorist non-state actors, adversarial states armed with weapons of mass destruction (WMD), and the potential rise of "peer competitors" such as China.

At the same time, defense transformation has remained an ambiguous and elusive concept. No strong consensus has ever existed as to what "defense transformation" exactly means or entails. According to the Defense Department's now-defunct Office of Force Transformation (OFT)—which, under Rumsfeld, was the Pentagon's leading internal body for thinking about and implementing transformation—"defense transformation" was defined as: a process that shapes the changing nature of military competition and cooperation through new combinations of concepts, capabilities, people, and organizations that exploit our nation's advantages and protect against our asymmetric vulnerabilities to sustain our strategic position, which helps under peace and stability in the world.

This definition, however, still left much to be desired as a roadmap for understanding what such transformation entails in a practical sense and why it is a critical process. Consequently, many analysts and proponents of transformation came to view it as simply another name for the so-called "revolution in military affairs." Certainly the two terms are used increasingly interchangeably. But what, then, do we mean by the RMA, and what in particular does the *current* RMA stands for? Furthermore, is defense transformation merely the process of implementing an RMA, or does it entail other objectives and processes?

Above all, in the minds of its proponents and advocates, the defense transformation/RMA model is necessarily a process of *discontinuous*, *disruptive*, and *revolutionary* change. Andrew Krepinevich, for example, argues that a revolution in military affairs occurs when: the application of new technologies into a significant number of military systems combines with innovative operational concepts and organizational adaptation in a way that fundamentally alters the character and conduct of a conflict. It does so by producing a dramatic increase [...] in the combat potential and military effectiveness of armed forces.

In short, defense transformation was nothing less than a "paradigm shift" in the manner in which US armed forces would conduct future warfare operations. As OFT put it:

In the process of transforming the way that we fight, we should emerge with a force that is more expeditionary, agile and lethal than the present force and more capable of employing operational manoeuvre and precision effects capabilities to achieve victory. The battlespace is expected to be a more dispersed one, within which our forces will conduct non-contiguous, mutually supporting operations. These operations will seamlessly tie in other government agencies, as well as multinational partners [...].(US DoD, OFT, 2004, p. 8, emphasis in original)

Transformation was also an *effects-* and *capabilities-based* approach. Effects-based operations (EBO) implied a shift away from "traditional" attrition-based warfare in favour of attacking the enemy so as to achieve certain political-military results, e.g., his willingness to fight. The emphasis on capabilities meant adopting a defense strategy based less on fixed-threat scenarios than on the anticipated capabilities of a likely adversary and, in turn, on the required capabilities US forces needed to deter or defeat such an enemy. As such, transformation was about achieving capabilities and effects, and no longer about sheer numbers. In general, as the US military sought to transform itself, it emphasized acquiring the following capabilities: A highly networked organism of command, control, communications, computing, intelligence, surveillance, and reconnaissance (C4ISR) systems, weapons and platforms,

Improved, shared situational awareness—both of the immediate battlespace and beyond, More accurate, stand-off engagement capacity, Greater speed, agility, rapid deployability, and flexibility, and Jointness and interoperability.

In this regard, the current US transformational/RMA model was inexorably linked to the emerging notions of *network-centric warfare* (NCW), sometimes also referred to as "network-enabled capabilities" or "network-based defense"—the operative word, of course, being "networked." According to NCW concepts, the ongoing revolution in IT has made possible significant innovation and improvement in the fields of sensors, seekers, data management, computing and communications, automation, range and precision. Correspondingly, NCW seeks to exploit these breakthroughs in information technology in order to achieve exponential improvements in battlefield knowledge, connectivity and response. Network-centric warfare, according to the DoD: generates increased combat power by networking sensors, decision makers and shooters to achieve shared awareness, increased speed of command, high tempo of operations, greater lethality, increased survivability and a degree of self-synchronization.

Moreover, NCW is about the "linking of people, platforms, weapons, sensors and decision aids into a single network" that "creates a whole that is clearly greater than the sum of its parts," resulting in "networked forces that operate with increased speed and synchronization and are capable of achieving massed effects". In other words, defense transformation was also intended to be *synergistic* and *holistic*, as it entailed the integration and employment of C4ISR systems, platforms, and weapons (particularly smart munitions) in ways that increase their effectiveness and capabilities beyond their individual capabilities. This bundling together is reminiscent of Admiral William Owens's "system of systems" concept, in that it entails the linking together of several types of discrete and even disparate systems across a broad geographical, inter-Service and electronic spectrum in order to create new core competencies in warfighting.

The US defense transformational model implied more a simple overlay of new technologies and new hardware over existing force structures; it required fundamental changes in military doctrine, operations and organization. Hardware and technology are obviously crucial and primary components when it comes to transformation—they are, in fact, the fundamental building blocks in a modern, IT-based RMA centred on network-centric warfare and reconnaissance-strike complexes. Transformation is not supposed to be just a techno-fix, however. Rather, it entails a fundamental change in the way a military does its business—doctrinally, organizationally and institutionally. Defense transformation, therefore, also requires advanced systems integration skills to knit together disparate military systems into complex operational networks. Finally, it demands both elemental changes in the ways militaries procure critical military equipment, as well as reform of the national and defense technological and industrial bases that contribute to development and production of transformational systems. All this, in turn, requires vision and leadership at the top in order for defense decision-makers to develop the basic concepts of defense transformation, establish the crucial institutional and political momentum for implementing transformation, and allocate the financial resources and human capital necessary for the task of implementation. Obviously, therefore, defense transformation entails much more than the "mere" modernization of one's armed forces.

IMPLEMENTING TRANSFORMATION: IMPLICATIONS FOR DEFENSE INDUSTRY

A transformed military would have important implications for those industrial sectors that will supply the armed forces with the means it needs to carry out its missions. Transformation advocates argued that the US defense industrial base would have to undergo its own revolution. For example, in early 2003, the Office of the Under Secretary of Defense for Industrial Policy (OUSD/IP) published a study entitled *Transforming the Defense Industrial Base: A Roadmap,* which laid out several recommendations for aligning US defense industrial policy in accordance with Rumsfeld's transformational vision. This document recommended that the Defense Department treat the *national* industrial base (both civilian and defense-specific) as a cluster of "effects-based sectors"—such as combat support, power projection, precision engagement, etc.—that could support defense transformation. The OUSD/IP also proposed that acquisition decision-making be reorganized around operational effects and *not* "programs, platforms, or weapons systems". In particular, the report recommended that the Defense Department strive to identify new sources of industrial-technological innovation among small or non-traditional firms that often do not supply directly to the Defense Department (pp. 13-15).

In particular, transformation was seen as having the *potential* to affect the defense industry in a number of ways:

Shifting defense work from suppliers of legacy systems to suppliers of transformational systems. Firms that provide the military with systems or services that support defense transformation could profit at the expense of firms that supply only (or mainly) non-transformational products—particularly so-called legacy platforms, such as heavy armoured vehicles or unguided weapons.

Shifting defense work in favour of firms that undertake large-scale systems integration work on behalf of the military. Many large-scale transformation projects have entailed the use of firms acting as "lead systems integrators" (LSIs). LSIs manage very large, complicated acquisition programmes that require amalgamating several disparate pieces of military hardware (and, increasingly, software) into a single functioning "system of systems." LSIs have become increasingly instrumental for managing large, multiplatform systems, such as the Future Combat System (Boeing/SAIC) or the US Coast Guard's Deepwater programme (Lockheed Martin/Northrop Grumman). As LSIs, these firms are given considerable authority to create, design, and execute a comprehensive solution to a pressing military need, including hiring and overseeing subcontractors, managing costs and schedules, and even setting requirements.

Shifting defense work from large megafirms to smaller, specialized suppliers. Small, "boutique" defense contractors, providing highly specialized systems or services, could be more nimble and responsive to the needs of a transformed armed force, particularly when it comes to NCW solutions. Large, traditional defense firms, because they are more oriented toward large-scale weapons programmes, may actually lack the manpower skills to engage in certain kinds of esoteric innovation.

Opening up more defense work to specialized foreign firms. As a corollary to the last point, foreign firms that can provide esoteric transformational technologies *not found* in the US defense industrial base could find a more receptive audience in a transformed US military. For example, one of the US Navy's prototypes for the Littoral Combat Ship (LCS) utilizes a unique Australian-supplied trimaran hull.

Shifting defense work toward suppliers of dual-use commercial systems. If commercial off-the-shelf (COTS) technologies—particularly information technologies—are truly destined to fundamentally alter the prosecution of future warfare, then non-traditional defense contractors who can engage in civil-military integration (CMI) could become more critical suppliers to the military. In particular, companies such as Microsoft, Sun, and Cisco could benefit at the expense of traditional defense firms.

BEYOND MODELS AND CONCEPTS: IMPLEMENTING TRANSFORMATION

Overall, defense transformation presented a picture of a new US military that would be: (1) more operationally flexible and agile; (2) more mobile, more expeditionary, and more rapidly deployable; and (3) more capable of dealing with global as well as regional contingencies. In other words, the US military seeks to fight "mobile high-tech wars"—mostly by substituting speed for mass and information for armour.

This new operational concept is already apparent in some of the US military's current and projected restructuring and procurement plans. The US Army, for instance, is reorganizing its force structure—de-emphasizing larger, more static, division-sized forces in favour of new modular brigades; in particular, the Brigade Combat Team (BCT, sometimes referred to as a Brigade Unit of Action) is a lighter, more deployable, more flexible, and more independently operational brigade force. Some of these BCTs will be supported by a dedicated, integrated reconnaissance battalion, equipped with unmanned aerial vehicles (UAVs) and other sensors, capable of providing the BCT with an integral intelligence-gathering capability. The first BCTs are being initially outfitted with the Stryker light armoured vehicle, which will subsequently be replaced by the Future Combat System (FCS). The FCS is a US$160 billion programme to develop a fleet of eighteen different versions of a single type of modularized light combat vehicle that, in turn, will be linked together by a communications systems capable of providing real-time intelligence, command and control to troops on the move. The US Army plans to restructure into 70 BCTs (including 28 Army National Guard BCTs) and 211 support brigades (75 Regular Army, 78 Army National Guard, and 58 Army Reserve).

At the same time, the other Services are planning their own transformations. The US Navy is expanding its close-to-the-shore combat capability with the planned procurement of 55 Littoral Combat Ships. It is also building a new class of Maritime Prepositioning ships to aid in the rapid deployability of ground forces. The Air Force considers its two next-generation fighters—the F/A-22 and the F-35 Joint Strike Fighter (JSF), both of which will be armed with advanced precision-guided munitions (PGMs), such as the Joint Direct Attack Munition (JDAM)—to be transformational systems. The USAF is also working on the long-term development of an unmanned combat aerial vehicle (UCAV).

More important to the process of transforming the US armed forces, however, is the implementation of "net-centricity"—at the heart of which is the creation of the Global Information Grid (GIG). The GIG is a globally connected constellation of systems and capabilities for collecting, processing, storing, disseminating, managing and sharing information within the US military and with other partners. The GIG is actually a collection of several different NCW programmes, including the Transformation Satellite communication system, the Joint Tactical Radio System (which will be the backbone of the FCS communication system—providing real-time, "on-the-move" voice, data and video), and the Bandwidth Expansion Project (and, of course, the software, to tie it all together). Net-centricity, therefore, is fundamental to shifting from a Service-based, information-sharing culture to one that is joint and interoperable not only across the entire spectrum of the US military, but also with other federal and local security-related and law enforcement authorities, and even with foreign partners.

IMPLICATIONS OF THE POST-TRANSFORMATION ERA FOR THE US DEFENSE INDUSTRY

So if defense transformation is "dead"—that is, if we are simply in a process of "modernization-plus" (i.e., of sustaining technological innovation and evolutionary advances in the process of warfare)—how does that affect the defense industry? In fact, probably very little. Technology (and, therefore, military platforms) is hardly going to go away as a crucial force multiplier—after all, the sad fact of war is that it is intended to *kill* the enemy; therefore, weapons, especially high-tech systems, will continue to be valued by warfighters. By now, almost all armed forces recognize the value of high technology when it comes to increasing military effectiveness. One does not need to believe in the RMA or military transformation in order to appreciate the importance of precision-guided weapons, fourth-generation-plus fighter jets, submarines, unmanned aerial vehicles, satellites, missile defenses and so on. Such technological developments are critical to providing important increases in the lethality, accuracy, and stand-off capability of modern firepower, in improving battlespace knowledge and command and control, in enhancing force projection, and in expanding operational manoeuvre, speed and stealth.

If warfare remains overwhelmingly platform-centric, therefore, then the US military will likely continue to rely heavily on traditional defense firms as prime contractors when it comes to designing, developing, and manufacturing future weapons systems. The large defense companies that currently comprise much of the US defense sector—Lockheed Martin, Boeing, Northrop Grumman, Raytheon, General Dynamics, etc.—are "quite up to the task of supporting" the apparently modest modernization-plus process of transformation that is going on within the US military. In fact, they may be *better* suited than non-traditional suppliers at providing the kind of sustaining innovation that the US Defense Department seems to desire, since they are well-acquainted with the unique needs of their customer base, how to translate those requirements into tangible military programmes, and how to weave their way through the Defense Department's often Byzantine acquisition process.

In fact, the large "defense-dominant" firm—that is, a company whose business activities are overwhelmingly in defense prime contracting —is hardly going the way of the dodo, and we see this over and over again when we examine many so-called "transformational" programmes currently underway. The US Army's Future Combat System, for example, is being run by Boeing and SAIC: one the country's second largest defense contractor, the other a heavily defense-dependent systems integration shop; leading subcontractors to the FCS programme include United Defense, General Dynamics Land Systems, TRW, and Hughes—all significant players in the defense sector. The two competing teams for the US Navy's Littoral Combat Ship are led by Lockheed Martin and Northrop

Grumman, while the traditional shipbuilders Bath Iron Works (owned by General Dynamics) and Litton Ingalls (owned by Northrop Grumman) are slogging it out for the DDG 1000 next-generation destroyer programme.

If anything, the defense-oriented megafirm is becoming more crucial in the US defense sector, due to the extensive process of defense industrial consolidation that took place during the 1990s. As a result, most of the largest US defense firms are broad-based enough to contain in-house many of the technologies and skill sets necessary to design and develop next-generation military systems. Where they are not, they generally know with whom to partner in order to gain access to those technologies and skills—and, in fact, teaming has become a nearly inescapable part of large-scale military programmes (e.g., FCS, the Joint Strike Fighter, and the DDG 1000).

At the same time, the future of the lead systems integrator concept is increasingly doubtful. LSIs required large firms with manifold expertise and considerable engineering and management capabilities, and these are still most often found in the defense industrial sector. This tended to benefit large firms already present in the defense contracting system—such as Boeing, Lockheed Martin, or Northrop Grumman. However, the LSI approach has been greatly undermined by its own failure to effectively manage large-scale programmes. The Future Combat System, for example, has more than doubled in price, while a number of originally planned-for capabilities were jettisoned as "technologically unfeasible, fiscally unaffordable, or both". The Littoral Combat Ship (LCS) and the Coast Guard's Deepwater programme—two other LSI-led programmes—both experienced significant cost growth, while performance targets were unfulfilled. In the case of the LCS, three of the first six ships were cancelled, and the programme was restructured. In late 2007, the US Congress voted to end the LSI system altogether.

For their part, small and foreign firms will likely find the potential to play a part in large mega-programmes as second-

and third-tier suppliers of critical-niche technologies and systems that can then be integrated in these larger programmes (e.g., the trimaran hull for the Littoral Combat Ship, built by Austal of Australia). At the same time, many small, start-up firms will find their future in defense production mainly as junior partners teamed with established defense primes, who then do the heavy lifting of systems integration and contracting.

While warfare is likely to remain more or less platform-centric, it will nevertheless certainly be more *network-enabled*. As with other aspects of high-tech warfare, the benefits of improved C4ISR to future warfighting are self-evident. Networking remains a critical force multiplier; consequently, militaries will obviously find growing value in such things as new or better sensors for battlespace intelligence, improved data-management and data-distribution capabilities, upgraded command-and-control systems, etc.

Again, however, defense-dominant firms will likely be critical to this process of integrating networks with platforms. It has been argued that traditional defense contractors are well-positioned to deliver specialized IT solutions to the US military, as they already have an intimate familiarity with C4ISR requirements, technologies and architectures, and they already possess (either in-house or through links to specialized subcontractors) the necessary skills to execute such integration. For example, most leading defense primes are members of the Network-Centric Operations Industry Consortium, and Lockheed Martin operates a Centre for Innovation that is focused on network-centric solutions for defense. In addition, the US defense industrial sector already possesses a number of "dedicated systems integration houses," such as the Aerospace Corporation, MITRE, and SAIC, that can contribute to network-enabled warfare.

On the other hand, commercial IT firms may be less likely than one would think to make a significant contribution to DoD networking solutions. According to Dombrowski, Gholz, and Ross, "leading commercial IT firms are unlikely to be as responsive as the established defense industrial suppliers to the military's technical and investment demands." Such companies, they state, "are happy to sell [off-the-shelf products] to military customers," but "the prospect of a DoD contract may not be worth enough to [...] justify much effort to customize a commercial product" for a military end-user. At the very most, therefore, commercial IT firms are likely to serve as second- or third-tier players in the US defense industrial base—supplying components or COTS technologies to prime contractors, who will then adapt and integrate these systems into military architectures.

IMPLICATIONS FOR THE REST OF THE WORLD

Overall, defense transformation—particularly the watered-down version that appears to be ascendant within the US military—will be "less disruptive for industry" than many had once assumed; at the same time, the traditional defense industrial base has perhaps proved itself to be more agile and adaptive than previously assumed. If we are in a situation of platform-centric but *network-enhanced* warfare, then it could be said that it is simply business as usual for the defense industrial base. Certainly nothing ever came of the Under Secretary of Defense for Industrial Policy's ambitious *Roadmap* for shaking-up and reorienting the US defense industrial base, as there has basically been no *military* need to do so.

Consequently, when we refer back to the bulleted points made above , we discover that very little has actually changed (or is likely to change) in the US defense industrial base. Defense work has *not* shifted dramatically away from large defense primes to non-traditional suppliers, small firms, or providers of dual-use systems. Rather, the traditional suppliers have adapted themselves to a slightly changing (i.e., sustaining innovation-type) production system. In this regard, the emergence of the lead systems integrator system is particularly noteworthy. Overall, however, as Dombrowski and Gholz note:

> Contrary to the expectations of transformation theorists, many military officers, and most high-ranking officials within the Department of Defense [...] transformative weapons and

supporting technologies will come, with a few noteworthy exceptions, from the same firms that have been supplying the nation's military needs since the end of the Second World War.

So what does all this mean for smaller arms-producing countries? In the first place, directly selling to the US defense market will remain a challenge for overseas defense companies. Foreign defense firms, in general, will continue to find it difficult to penetrate the US market, with the possible exception of Britain's BAE Systems, which has established a sizable industrial footprint in the United States (mainly through acquisitions). As in the past, most successes in selling to the US military will likely come in the form of partnering with US defense primes— in which the foreign firm is able to supply some kind of specialized niche technology or capability—or, possibly in licensing the manufacture of foreign-designed military systems. Even then, foreign firms will have to contend with US export and technology transfer restrictions and continuing American resistance (in Congress, in the Executive Branch, and among the general public) to opening up the US defense industry to foreign contractors. In addition, the fight to find opportunities for licensing-out the production of foreign-designed armaments will continue to be an exasperating uphill battle, particularly in the face of the US military's traditional reluctance to embrace "not-invented-here" products.

Flagging US interest in defense transformation may also sap support in other nations fore for pursuing their own revolutions in military affairs. The waning of the US intellectual and programmatic vanguard in such areas as network-centric warfare may cause other nations to reassess their own commitments to transforming their militaries along the lines of the IT-RMA. While it is doubtful whether a US failure to press transformation would undermine ongoing work or programmes in other countries when it comes to network-based defenses (such as Sweden's *Ledsyst* command and control system, or the Singapore Armed Forces' IKC2 [Integrated Knowledge-based Command and Control] program), it could take the wind out of worldwide defense sails when it comes to more far-reaching transformation. Overall, US defense transformation, even if imperfect and less "revolutionary" than originally intended, may still have considerable implications for the future nature and conduct of warfare, and this, in turn, will likely have considerable impact on militaries around the world. Efforts to modernize the US military along the lines of network-enabled warfare, to make it more expeditionary and more strategically flexible and still be able to deliver considerable firepower, to refocus its overseas force structure and basing—from providing for local static defenses to a posture geared toward rapidly deployable forces capable of engaging adversaries both regionally and in other parts of the world—all of these developments will resonate throughout the world; indeed, even limited changes could have significant consequences. US defense transformation will affect a number of critical regional security concerns around the world, particularly when it comes to interoperability with allies and friendly nations, regional security considerations, and local force modernization activities. While the defense industrial landscape will not change dramatically, there will certainly be some impact on arms producers around the world. Above all, the US defense industry will continue to dominate the global arms industry, and how it adapts to the unfolding process of change and evolution in the US military establishment will likely be a guide to developments elsewhere.

Admittedly, this article raises as many new questions than it has tried to answer, and it is intended more to raise the level of debate and discussion than to provide any definitive solution to the problem of "arming the RMA." Obviously, there is still room for considerable additional work in this area of study. For example, organizational and cultural resistance on the part of military planners, along with a collusive acquisition process, could be causing the US military to be missing out on the true, synergistic benefits of the RMA—while, at the same time, we face new types of threats (particularly from asymmetric actors), and potential adversaries (such as China) may be trying to radically transform *their* forces. In this case, not recognizing the urgency of engaging in fundamental (as opposed to incremental) change away from platform-based, "legacy defenses" in favour of network-centric defense (providing, of course, that *is* the right path for future determining military effectiveness) could be a serious abrogation of our leaders' national security responsibilities. In other words, simply "muddling through" may not only be irreponsible, but dangerous in the long run. One thing is for certain: the improvement of the military world—in terms of a threats, responses, strategies, and arming—is a dynamic process, and the business of war must be constantly reexamined and reevaluated.

ARMS INDUSTRY AND ITS MODERNISATION

The **arms industry** is a global industry and business which manufactures and sells weapons and military technology and equipment. Arms producing companies, also referred to as Defence companies or military industry, produce arms mainly for the armed forces of states. Products include guns, ammunition, missiles, military aircraft, military vehicles, ships, electronic systems, and more. The arms industry also conducts significant research and development.

It is estimated that yearly, over 1 trillion dollars are spent on military expenditures worldwide (2% of World GDP). Part of this goes to the procurement of military hardware and services from the military industry. The combined arms sales of the top 100 largest arms producing companies amounted to an estimated $315 billion in 2006. In 2004 over $30 billion were spent in the international arms trade (a figure that excludes domestic sales of arms). The arms trade has also been one of the sectors impacted by the credit crunch, with total deal value in the market halving from US$32.9bn to US$14.3bn in 2008.

Many industrialized countries have a domestic arms industry to supply their own military forces. Some countries also have a substantial legal or illegal domestic trade in weapons for use by its citizens. The illegal trade in small arms is prevalent in many countries and regions affected by political instability. Contracts to supply a given country's military are awarded by the government, making arms contracts of substantial political importance. The link between politics and the arms trade can result in the development of what US President Dwight D. Eisenhower described as a military-industrial complex, where the armed forces, commerce, and politics become closely linked. Various corporations, some publicly held, others private, bid for these contracts, which are often worth many billions of dollars. Sometimes, such as the contract for the new Joint Strike Fighter, a competitive tendering process takes place, where the decision is made on the merits of the design submitted by the companies involved. Other times, no bidding or competition takes place.

In the Cold War Era, arms exports were used by both the Soviet Union and the United States to influence their standings in other countries, particularly Third World Countries. Since the fall of the Soviet Union, global arms exports initially fell slightly, but have since grown again to cold war levels. The United States is the overall top supplier of weapons. The United States is also the top supplier of weapons to the developing world, accounting for around 36% of worldwide weapons sales, followed by Russia, Britain, Germany and China.

The Control Arms Campaign, founded by Amnesty International, Oxfam, and the International Action Network on Small Arms, estimated in 2003 that there are over 639 million items of small arms in circulation, and that over 1135 companies based in more than 98 different countries manufacture small arms as well as their various components and ammunition. According to Oxfam, an estimated 500,000 individuals die in small arms-conflicts every year, approximately one death per minute.

SECTORS

Land-based Weapons

This category includes everything from light arms to heavy artillery, and the majority of producers are small. Many are located in Third World countries. International trade in handguns, machine guns, tanks, armoured personal carriers and other relatively inexpensive weapons is substantial. There is relatively little regulation at the international level, and as a result, many legitimately produced weapons fall into the hands of rebel forces, terrorists, or regimes under sanctions.

Aerospace Systems

Encompassing military aircraft (both land-based and naval aviation), conventional missiles, and military satellites, this is the most technologically advanced sector of the market. It is also the least competitive from an economic standpoint, with a handful of companies dominating the entire market.

The top clients and major producers are virtually all located in the West, with the United States easily in first place. Prominent aerospace firms include Dassault Aviation, EADS,Finmeccanica, Thales Group, Lockheed Martin, Boeing, and Britain's BAE Systems. There are also several multinational consortia mostly involved in the manufacturing of fighter jets, such as the Eurofighter. The largest military contract in history, signed in October 2001, involved the development of the Joint Strike Fighter.

Naval Systems

All of the world's major powers maintain substantial maritime forces to provide a forward presence and enhance overall mobility, with the largest nations possessing aircraft carriers, nuclear submarines and advanced anti-air defense systems. The vast majority of military ships are conventionally powered, but some are nuclear-powered. There is also a large global market in second-hand naval vessels, generally purchased by developing countries from Western governments.

World's Largest Defence Budgets

This is a list of the fifteen countries with the highest defence budgets for the year 2006. The information is from the Stockholm International Peace Research Institute. Total world spending amounted to $1.158 trillion USD in 2006, with nearly half of the total amount spent by the United States. The actual budget for the PRC's armed forces is unknown, the figure given is an official estimate of government fund allocation, with much of the net budget funds coming from extra-budgetary sources.

Military expenditure in market exchange rate dollar terms, 2006

Rank	Country	Spending ($b.)	%GDP
–	World Total	1,158	2.41
1	United States	985.7	12.99
2	United Kingdom	59.2	2.49
3	France	53.1	2.38
4	People's Republic of China	49.5	1.88
5	Japan	43.7	1.00
6	Germany	37.0	1.28
7	Russia	34.7	3.54
8	Italy	33.9	1.61
9	Saudi Arabia	29.0	8.32
10	India	24.2	2
11	South Korea	21.9	2.47
12	Canada	14.6	1.10
13	Australia	13.8	1.83
14	Brazil	13.4	1.26
15	Spain	12.3	1.00

1. Data for China and Russia are estimates, their expenditures are not well known.

2. Data for Saudi Arabia include expenditure for public order and safety and might be slight overestimates.

3. In the percentage spending per GDP, the GDP list (2006) of the International Monetary Fund was taken.

4. One quarter of the world total is illicit and/or black market trade.

World's Largest Arms Exporters

The unit in this table are so-called trend indicater values expressed in millions of US dollars. These values do not represent real financial flows but are a crude instrument to estimate volumes of arms transfers, regardless of the contracted prices, which can be as low as zero in the case of military aid.

Supplier	2000	2001	2002	2003	2004	2005	2006	2007
USA	7505	5801	4984	5581	6616	7026	7821	7454
Russia	4190	5631	5458	5355	6400	5576	6463	4588
Germany	1622	825	910	1707	1017	1879	2891	3395
France	1033	1235	1342	1313	2267	1688	1586	2690
Netherlands	259	192	243	342	218	611	1575	1355
UK	1356	1116	772	624	1143	871	978	1151
Ukraine	280	649	440	530	600	700	1000	1200
South Korea	100	240	140	140	410	260	260	844
Italy	192	224	407	321	216	787	860	562
Sweden	46	7	120	158	73	116	803	529
Israel	308	850	125	468	287	536	472	414
China	228	498	544	553	271	223	564	355
Canada	83	129	182	279	305	193	227	343
Spain	321	298	365	309	533	244	258	238
Switzerland	104	120	109	139	201	166	144	211
Bulgaria	N/A	N/A	N/A	250	N/A	190	149	192

The information is from the Stockholm International Peace Research Institute or from the national defence commissions where available and is updated at least once a year.

Next to SIPRI there are several other sources that provide data on international transfers of arms.

These include national reports by national governments about arms exports, the UN register on conventional arms and an annual publication by the US US Congressional Research Service that includes data on arms exports to developing countries as compiled by US intelligence agencies.

A list of such sources can be found at the SIPRI website. Due to the different methodologies and definitions used different sources often provide significantly different data. For example, according to Statistisk sentralbyrå (Norway state statistics), Norway exports a greater value (in USD) of arms than many of the nations listed above. Some of the differences are possibly due to deliberate over or under reporting by some of the sources.

Governments may claim high arms exports as part of their role in marketing efforts of their national arms industry or they may claim low arms exports in order to be perceived as a responsible international actor.

List of Major Weapon Manufacturers

Major arms industry corporations by nation

Country	Weapon manufacturers and Arms Traders
Argentina	Fábrica MilitarFábrica Militar de Aviones
Austria	GlockSteyr Mannlicher
Australia	TenixAustralian Defence Industries Australian Submarine Corporation Commonwealth Aircraft Corporation
Bangladesh	Defence Advancement Trading Company (DATCO)
Belgium	Fabrique Nationale de Herstal
Bosnia and Herzegovina	Zrak dd
Brazil	Ares Aeroespacial e DefesaAvibras
	CBC - Companhia Brasileira de Cartuchos
	Embraer
	Helibras
	IMBEL - Indústria Brasileira de Material Bélico, belonging to the Brazilian Army
	Taurus
Bulgaria	TEREMArsenal Corporation
Canada	Colt Canada
	Bombardier
	SNC-Lavalin Group
China	Norinco
	AVIC IAVIC II
	Chengdu Aircraft Industry Group
	China Nanchang Aircraft Manufacturing Corporation
	Changhe Aircraft Industries Corporation
	China State Shipbuilding Corporation (CSSC)
	China National Nuclear Corporation

	China Aerospace Science & Technology Corporation (CASC)
Denmark	Skandinavisk Aero Industri
	Hydrema
	Terma
Egypt	AOI
France	EADS
	Dassault Aviation
	DCNS
	Thales Group
	GIAT Industries
Germany	Carl Walther GmbH Sportwaffen
	Diehl BGT Defence
	EADS
	Heckler & Koch
	Krauss-Maffei
	Rheinmetall
	Mauser
	Lürssen
	Thyssenkrupp
	MBDA
Greece	EASHAI
India	DRDO
	Hindustan Aeronautics Limited
Indonesia	PT Pindad
	Perindustrian Angkatan Darat
Israel	Israel Aerospace Industries
	Israel Weapon Industries
	Rafael Advanced Defense Systems
	Elbit
Italy	Beretta
	Finmeccanica
	Fincantieri
	AvioAgusta

	Westland
	Benelli (firearms)
Mexico	ALFA
	DGIM
	Hydra Technologies of Mexico
	Mabe
	Mendoza
	Mondragon
	San Luis Rassini
	SEDENA
	SEMAR
	Valdez Industria
	Xiuhcoatl
Myanmar	Reliable Technology Limited
Norway	Kongsberg Defense & Aerospace
	Nordic Ammunition Group
Poland	Bumar
	PZL
Pakistan	Pakistan Aeronautical Complex
	Heavy Industries Taxila
	Pakistan Ordnance Factories
Portugal	INDEP
Russia	Sukhoi
	Mikoyan
	Mil Moscow Helicopter Plant
	Tupolev
	Ilyushin
	Yakovlev
	Tikhomirov Scientific Research Institute of Instrument Design
	Moscow Institute of Thermal Technology
	IZH

	Kartsev-Venediktov Design Bureau
	Almaz Scientific Industrial Corporation
	Vympel NPO
	Beriev
	FSUE "Splav"
Serbia	Zastava Arms
	Yugoimport
South Africa	Denel
South Korea	Hyundai Rotem
	Samsung Techwin
Spain	EADS-CASA
	Navantia
	Santa Barbara (General Dynamics)
Sweden	BAE Systems Bofors
	Kockums
	Saab
Switzerland	Astra Arms
	SIGARMS
	RUAG
	Pilatus Aircraft
	Armasuisse
	MOWAG (General Dynamics)
Thailand	Chaiseri Metal & Rubber
	Thailand Aviation Industries TAI
Turkey	MKEK
	TAI
	Aselsan
Ukraine	Antonov
	KMDB
	Malyshev Factory
	RPC Fort
	Yuzhmash
	Yuzhnoye Design Bureau

United Kingdom	BAE Systems
	Cobham plc
	MBDA
	Rolls-Royce
United States	AAI Corporation
	BAE Systems Inc.
	Boeing
	Bushmaster Firearms International
	Carlyle Group
	Colt's Manufacturing Company
	General Atomics
	General Electric (primarily through GEAE)
	General Dynamics
	Honeywell
	Lockheed-Martin
	Northrop Grumman Corporation
	Raytheon Corporation
	United Technologies (primarily through Pratt and Whitney, Sikorsky Aircraft Corporation)

CONTROL AND INTERNATIONAL TREATY

We are committed to upholding, implementing and further strengthening the multilateral disarmament and non-proliferation framework in the fight against threats which are tending to escape the control of national sovereignty, the challenges deriving from destabilising accumulation and spread of small arms and light weapons, from illicit or irresponsible arms trade, and from the proliferation of weapons of mass destruction, which are creating new and growing hot-spots of international tension. In this regard, the EU welcomes the growing support in all parts of the world for an International Arms Trade Treaty and is firmly committed to this process.

- Netherlands Organisation for Applied Scientific Research
- Bolt, Beranek and Newman

- QinetiQ
- World Security Institute

Ethical Dimension

For many people, arms exports may pose an ethical challenge, as they may see supplying the weapons for a conflict as morally akin to becoming involved with negligible personal, national or corporate risk. Essentially, they view the arms industry as a means of profiting from war and death when failure to supply arms could lead to an early disengagement.

On the other hand, exporting arms to groups (or nations) with "laudable" goals—e.g. a rebel group overthrowing a fascist regime—can be an invaluable equalizer in the conflict. And there is no shortage of parties to a conflict that can wreak incalculable destruction without the assistance of modern armaments—for instance, the Hutus of the Rwandan Genocide conducted most of their carnage using simple machetes and other low-tech implements.

Of course—and this is endemic of nearly every debate over arms trade—the terminology used and the people it refers to can be frustratingly fluid. As years pass, governments decide on new "interests" and circumstances change accordingly. "Freedom fighters" become "insurgents". "Terrorists" become "invaluable allies", and "religious zealots" morph into "agents of stability". Entire nations, to use the parlance of the early 21st century, can go from the "Coalition of the Willing" to the "Axis of Evil" in very little time, and every change affects policy and the distribution of arms in the world.

7

Popular Defence Forces

The inspiration for the PDF lies in the history of Condominium Sudan (1899– 1943), in which Sudan was under both British and Egyptian rule, and the Islamic rebellion against it. Condominium policies aimed at low-cost pacification, which relied on the mobilization of local levies to suppress dissent. The direct origins of the PDF, however, can be found in two more recent paramilitary forces: the tribal militia units recruited in western Sudan and the Transitional Areas during the mid-1980s; and the party militants and youth movements of the National Islamic Front (NIF). While the former provided the bulk of the PDF's fighting force, the latter formed the ideological core and defined the PDF's political impact in the urban centres of North Sudan.

The formulation of the 'Popular Defence' policy followed an attack on the village of al-Gardud in Kordofan state in July 1985, in which 60 people were killed. This village was populated by Misseriya Arabs—a semi-nomadic Baggara tribe with influential ties to the Transitional Military Council and the Umma party in Khartoum. Following the attack, a government delegation to the area led by Minister of Defence Major General Burma Fadlallah Nasir was presented with a choice by native administration leaders: either provide security for the Arab Baggara communities of South Darfur and South Kordofan, or these communities would request such guarantees from the Sudan People's Liberation Army (SPLA) and de facto join the rebellion. Unable to redeploy the demoralized and overstretched military from the South, the delegation made a decision—without the authorization of the national Constituent Assembly— to arm the Baggara. Truckloads of ammunition and light weapons, mostly AK-47s and G3 rifles, were distributed directly to members of allied tribes, specifically the Rizeigat and the Misseriya Humr, through native administrative structures and leaders.

Traditionally armed to defend cattle, the Baggara had already begun to purchase modern automatic weapons on the thriving Chad–Sudan cross-border arms market. Many had suffered heavy losses of cattle during the 1984–85 Sahelian drought, and banditry, cattle theft, and forced grazing on farmland was widespread. Some of the youngest and poorest of those affected had congregated in the urban centres of South Kordofan and South Darfur and were willing to seek an income through violence. In late 1985, as well as providing arms to the tribes, to wealthy Arab traders, Umma Party agents, and military intelligence, officials began to recruit from among the destitute nomads to form offensive paramilitary units. By 1986 well-armed raiding parties of 500–1,000 men had begun systematically to strip the assets of the Ngok, Abiem, Malual, and Tuic Dinka populations of North Bahr El Ghazal, and forced their displacement into pro-government territories (Keen, 1994, pp. 98–100).

From the beginning, the distinction between tribal militias and government paramilitaries was blurred. While the militias were local formations, recruited through the native administration and operating in or around related communities, the paramilitaries, known as the *Murahileen*, were irregular mercenary formations integrated into the military chain of command and often alienated from tribal structures. Both were recruited from pro-government tribes and protected from prosecution by the government.

On 20 February 1989 SAF commander-in-chief General Fathi Ahmed Ali, issued an ultimatum signed by 150 senior officers that called on the government to give greater support to the regular armed forces. Implicit in this was a call to end support for the tribal militias. In response, Prime Minister Sadiq al-Mahdi formed a four-man committee, including Major General Burma Fadlallah Nasir, charged with establishing the legal foundation for existing paramilitary units and their transformation into a national paramilitary force. The so-called Popular Defence Forces bill, recommended by the committee, was proposed to the Constituent Assembly but resoundingly rejected. On 10 June 1989, Foreign Minister Sid Ahmed al-Hussein led a newly formed 'peace task force' delegation into talks with the Sudan People's Liberation Movement (SPLM).

THE LEGALIZATION OF THE POPULAR DEFENCE FORCES

Three weeks later, on 30 June 1989, the government was toppled by a small group of middle-ranking officers. The leaders of this bloodless coup, led by then Brigadier Omar Hassan Ahmed al-Bashir, declared a Revolution of National Salvation and a renewed commitment to the civil war. By 1 July, 28 army generals had been sacked, including the commander-in-chief, General Fathi Ahmed Ali. Bashir appointed himself head of state, prime minister, defence minister, and commander-in-chief of the armed forces.

In November, the National Salvation Regime revisited the previous government's draft bill and passed the 1989 Popular Defence Forces Act, formally establishing the PDF as an institution of the state. According to the Act, this new force was intended 'to train citizens on military and civil capabilities, to raise security awareness and military discipline among them, in order to act as a support force to the other regular ones on request'. The PDF was operationally accountable to an SAF brigadier general, originally Brigadier Babiker Abd el-Mahmoud Hassan, and answerable directly to President Bashir. Recruitment was managed by a hierarchy of civilian PDF coordinators at national, state, local, and community level. The commander general dictated regulations covering remuneration, period of service, and recruitment procedures, as well as the annual intake of the forces. Underneath this central structure, however, the PDF became an increasingly decentralized network as it expanded in size.

The first PDF coordinator, Abu Giseissa, announced a target to enlist 100,000 fighters by the end of the first year. In late 1989 and early 1990 the existing militia and paramilitary groups in Bahr El Ghazal, South Darfur, and South Kordofan were formally absorbed into the PDF. In December 1989 the Misseriya militia of El-Muglad, and the Peace Army militia of the Fertit tribe in Wau, followed suit. Shortly afterwards, in March 1990, the Fursan militia of the Rizeigat tribe around ed-Daein, South Darfur, was also absorbed. According to available sources, these units negotiated successfully to restrict their operations to the areas surrounding their migratory routes and many insisted on campaigning according to their seasonal agenda instead of following the army's strategic priorities. Furthermore, tribal leaders were recognized as PDF coordinators in a parallel hierarchy to the military and in some cases retained almost full autonomy over the men they had mobilized. Despite this the tribal PDF were granted equal treatment and the same benefits provided by military law to professional soldiers and their dependents in case of war-related injury, disability, captivity, or death.

Despite the new legality of the PDF, the boundary between military and community forces remained as ambiguous as it had been before the coup. This ambiguity grew further as the NIF, dominated by the Islamist politician Dr Hassan al-Turabi, consolidated its power behind the National Salvation regime. Military offensives in Kordofan and Bahr El Ghazal often included regular SAF troops, PDF volunteers, and members of the existing Murahileen militias. This led to the widespread use during the 1990s of general terms such as mujahideen to describe units containing a mixture of forces affiliated to the government (International Eminent Persons Group, 2002, p. 27). Similarly to the *Janjaweed*—the general term used to describe the array of paramilitary and militia forces operational today in Darfur—the mujahideen's institutional complexity and confusing informality in rank makes it almost impossible to identify clear command and control structures. While the government defended its actions by emphasizing its limited military capability, the tribes justified the militias as their only means of self-defence. This justification thus relegated responsibility for justice and accountability to local areas, by now embroiled in extensive ethnic and intercommunal warfare.

In February 1990 a confidential document written by the Government of Sudan (GoS) Subcommittee on Popular Defence reported on the tribal militias to a regional conference in El-Obeid. The report praised the militias for using guerrilla warfare-type tactics against the rebellion and claimed that the militias were responsible for repelling the rebels in the western area of Kordofan. The report also noted that the tribal forces often engaged in looting without regard to tactical objectives, deliberately misled the armed forces to achieve private objectives, and, most importantly, were 'fuelling tribal and racial hatred' (cited in Human Rights Watch, 1996, p. 277).

The PDF, however, was envisaged as something much larger than the tribal militias. The NIF had lobbied and raised money for a 'tribal belt' across Sudan to defend Arab and Islamic culture from the SPLA. But Dr Hassan al-Turabi had also long argued that Sudan's elite Islamist cadre needed to become a broad populist movement. Like other Islamist inspired revolutions in the Middle East, the power of the state was seen as the primary vehicle for achieving this goal. Influential members of the NIF not only emphasized the PDF's successes as an auxiliary to the armed forces, but also identified it as an authentic Islamic model of military organization—a citizen's army of volunteer mujahid prepared for frontline battle. In March 1990, 5,000 students from Khartoum's universities were enrolled into the al-Qitaina PDF training camp on the outskirts of Khartoum (Kok, 1993). Most were recruited from NIF party networks, university-based Islamic organizations, and NIF-affiliated youth associations such as Shebab al Watan (Youth of the Nation). These recruits formed one of the first urban units of the PDF. Whereas rural PDF units were tasked with halting SPLA advances into North Sudan, the main duty of the urban brigades was to protect the new regime from civil uprisings and, more importantly, from military interventions. In November 1990, PDF militia units in land cruisers were deployed across key areas in Khartoum and around the main military bases (Radio of the Sudan People's Liberation Army, 1990). Shortly after, regular SAF military units were redeployed out of the capital.

A year later, the NIF emerged from the shadows of the Revolutionary Command Council (RCC) and took public control of government positions. An all-appointed Transitional National Assembly comprising many NIF politicians was formed in January 1992. The reshuffle announced the beginning of a wholesale Islamization of Sudan's institutions. Public companies replaced qualified and long-serving staff, including technical and medical personnel, with NIF cadres. A 'Shari'a High Supervisory Board over Banks and Financial Institutions' oversaw the imposition of Islamic banking practices. International NGOs were restricted and replaced by Islamic NGOs, some of which combined proselytizing with humanitarianism. At the same time, the new regime openly recommitted itself to the war in the South. By this point, however, the SAF's strategy against the SPLA had degraded into a low-cost and ineffective standoff involving artillery, landmines, and proxy forces. Heavily demoralized and materially under-equipped, the SAF had clearly stated in 1989 that it no longer wished to fight a war that was openly opposed by civil society and many politicians.

The professional and experienced military officers who opposed the NIF began to be replaced by regime loyalists in 1990. Extensive purges of the regular armed forces were coupled with forced recruitment of military officers into the PDF for re-education. By October 1993 the RCC had sacked 1,500 officers—just under one-third of the total officer corps—500 non-commissioned officers, and 11,000 rank and file soldiers. In early 1995 another 227 officers were dismissed, including 57 brigadiers and generals. Many others were quietly retired with promises of loans from the Islamic banking system. Those departing were replaced by young pro-NIF graduates from the military academy. Simultaneously, a massive expansion in PDF recruitment and training began in order to prepare the force to substitute for the regular military on the battlefield. This level of PDF mobilization was maintained from 1992 until roughly 1997. Continual recruitments into training camps and central PDF battalions were augmented by periodic campaigns for combat recruits, which were launched during large-scale military offensives.

Civilian PDF coordinators were appointed in urban and semi-urban neighbourhoods, at universities, and in all civil service departments throughout North Sudan. Training camps, supervised by pro-NIF military officers, undertook indoctrination using Islamic lectures, religious songs, and chants alongside basic military training. Lists of individuals, drawn up by both the PDF and the security forces, which identified those who were required to undergo training in the PDF, began to appear throughout Sudanese institutions.

Because of its local recruitment and training practices, the PDF became a heterogeneous organization that reflected its surrounding environment and contained multiple internal strands and tendencies. These can be divided into five levels according to their different military ability and training: (a) an elite section of units comparable to the Iranian *Pasdaran* (Islamic Revolution Guards), some of which reportedly received tank and artillery training; (b) students and other civilians forced into training in closed camps; (c) military officers and civil servants forced to go through PDF training as re-education and indoctrination; (d) localized rural militias supplied through regional and local PDF offices and committees; and (e) a dispersed network of informers.

In December 1991, President Ali Akbar Rafsanjani of Iran paid a four-day visit to Khartoum. He brought 157 officials, including military and security advisers. During this visit Iran and Sudan signed a military cooperation deal under which Iranian advisers would come to Sudan and Sudanese security forces would be sent to Iran for training. In 1992 the former head of the Iranian Pasdaran in Lebanon, Hassan Azada, was posted to Khartoum, and training camps were reportedly established in Abu Rakim (Eastern State), Souyaa, and Um Barbita (South Kordofan) (Indian Ocean Newsletter, 1992). In 1993 the Pasdaran sent infantry, artillery, and logistics specialists to Sudan under the command of Rafic Doust of the 'Foundation of the Oppressed', reportedly to train and organize the PDF into a fighting force.

All male Sudanese citizens over the age of 16 and resident in the Sudan were required to attend training by the PDF. Initially it was promised that students would be permitted to finish their studies, but in 1994, faced with low recruitment numbers, foot dragging, and sporadic rebellion, this promise was rescinded. Students were unable to graduate from or enrol in university or high school without certification of PDF camp attendance. Most large companies, and all government institutions, required actual or potential employees to provide evidence of PDF training. Travel abroad was denied to those without it.

Although frontline combat in the PDF was voluntary, this began to be heavily promoted in the mosques, the education system, and through the media as the duty of all virtuous Muslims. In January 1992 the authorities declared the civil war to be a jihad. In the Nuba Mountains all rebels, many of whom were also Muslims, were ruled to be apostates, making it the duty of all Muslims to participate in their suppression. At PDF parades and at graduation ceremonies and celebrations held in urban centres, high-ranking members of the regime gave rallying speeches containing powerful Islamic discourses that celebrated 'martyrdom'. Government-controlled newspapers ran reports of PDF recruits with prophetic dreams, the sweet-smelling corpses of PDF martyrs, and supernatural help from animals. A nightly television broadcast called *fi Sahat al-Fida* (In the Fields of Sacrifice) reported the miraculous feats of the PDF on the battlefield and celebrated its martyrs. The culmination of this symbolic drive was a massive military campaign, *Seif al Ubur* (The Summer Crossing), which committed a reported 40,000 PDF and regular army troops to South Kordofan alone (Bradbury, 1998, p. 465). By June 1993 it was estimated that PDF numbers matched Sudanese army numbers in the South, and many more were rotating through PDF battalions for shorter periods of time. In Kordofan, the commander of the PDF vowed to 'cleanse every stretch of territory sullied by the outlaws'. Tens of thousands of new PDF recruits from the tribes of North Kordofan were inducted by the government in a large public rally held in El-Obeid in May 1992. Meanwhile, tribal leaders were given Toyota pickups and houses by the government and were appointed *Amir al-jihad* in exchange for helping to mobilize recruits for the PDF. In October 1993 First Lieutenant Khalid Abdel Karim Salih, who was in charge of security in Kordofan from May 1992 to February 1993, announced that during a seven-month period the army and PDF had killed 60,000–70,000 Nuba. No fewer than 14 mosques were also confirmed destroyed, damaged, or looted in the Nuba Mountains between 1993 and 1997 (de Waal and Salaam, 2004, p. 73).

THE WEAKENING OF THE POPULAR DEFENCE FORCES

As a result of poor training and the promotion of martyrdom, urban PDF recruits made poor soldiers, and the number of casualties was high. An SAF soldier interviewed in Khartoum who had served in both the Nuba Mountains and the South described watching in horror as PDF volunteers were urged over the top of trenches they had spent two days digging to charge in 'human wave attacks' at dug-in SPLA machine gun positions. Military officers and recruits have described high levels of casualties as a result of friendly fire, communication breakdowns, and cowardice by devout Islamic PDF recruits suddenly confronted with the brutal reality of war. Most of the military personnel and police officials interviewed for this chapter described tribal PDF recruits as little more than mercenaries who were interested in loot but rarely willing to enter into serious combat.

Campaigns against SPLA strongholds in 1992–93 and 1995 caused immense numbers of casualties among the poorly trained PDF. As a result, recruitment fell sharply. Meanwhile, the government's promotion of what it imagined was Islamic orthodoxy did not succeed in unifying the faithful so much as in alienating many devout and highly orthodox Muslims who did not adhere to the NIF's project. At the same time, the PDF's coercive recruitment and training practices angered most Sudanese. In 1997 a Sudanese newspaper claimed that of the 70,000 school leavers legally obliged to attend PDF training, large numbers had escaped conscription and only 4,000 had actually joined the PDF fighting units (AFP, 1997). In January of that year recruitment numbers fell so low that the government closed Khartoum University and called on faculty members and students to help the war effort in the South. In April 1998 up to 260 secondary-school PDF conscripts who demanded permission to spend the important Islamic holiday *Eid al Adha* with their families were reportedly killed by security forces after breaking out of the Eilafoun training camp 25 kilometres from Khartoum. Shortly afterwards the government was forced to admit that it did not know the names of all the conscripts killed. This display of brutality against teenagers seeking to return home for an Islamic celebration sent shockwaves through Sudanese society. Another rebellion soon after at the same training camp led to the successful escape of 76 recruits (Suna News Agency, 1998). The Eilafoun massacre marked the beginning of the end for the PDF's mass recruitment strategy.

By 1998 the battleground failures of the PDF were just one aspect of a broader frustration at the interference of the NIF's ideological leaders in the day-to-day running of the state. In the SAF, professional officers had long held reservations about the PDF—privately agreeing with General Fathi Ahmed Ali of the SAF's Legitimate Command that the army could not be replaced 'by the kind of accelerated training courses being doled out to the peculiar mix of ideologically motivated volunteers, jobless and press-ganged students' (Indian Ocean Newsletter, 1993b). Furthermore, many others were concerned that the resources committed to the PDF were being directly diverted from the SAF, prioritizing an ideological project over re-equipping the professional army.

Although jihad was never abandoned, the mass-recruitment of PDF battalions was quietly replaced by an emphasis on building the state's war-making capacity, using oil revenues and reinforcing the southern proxy militias maintained by the military intelligence apparatus. In 1997 Ali Karti—minister for justice and a supporter of the current second vice-president of the GoS, Ali Osman Taha—became the national PDF coordinator. He allowed the regular armed forces to take de facto control of internal appointments in the organization. In January 1997 President Bashir established a higher authority for mobilization, led by Major General Zubayr Muhammad Saleh, which reported directly to Bashir. This body stood above all existing organizations, including the PDF, in the local and national mobilization of popular forces. In 1998 compulsory national service in the professional military was reinstated.

In December 1999 competition between the presidency and the secretariat of the NCP, which was under the control of Turabi, fractured the Islamist movement. In a decision made on 23 January 2000, the NCP Shura Council stripped Turabi of responsibility for the general mobilization of jihad and allocated it to the political system. The following May, Turabi was also suspended from his position as the NCP secretary-general after accusations that he was 'calling up officers and the mujahideen' to rise up against the regime (AFP, 2000). In July 2000 Bashir appointed ten senior military officers to the cabinet. Shortly after, according to the *Rai al-Amm* newspaper in Khartoum, Turabi warned of a third force emerging from either 'the armed forces or the street to fill the gap'. Despite the tension between these factions, physical confrontations were limited: in June 2000 police broke up a pro-Turabi rally by the NIF Youth Union; in September Turabi's supporters rioted in a number of Sudanese towns; and in October pro-Turabi student demonstrators were accused by the government of opening fire on the police. The government's response was to round up Turabi's supporters and break-up the pro-Turabi cells. Despite Turabi's popularity among large parts of the Islamist movement, the PDF was not identified as an actor in any of these actions.

Following the split with Turabi, Ali Karti and Bashir were careful to renew their call for PDF volunteers and their support for the path of 'jihad and martyrdom'. But the PDF would no longer be an autonomous institution. In the words of Bashir, 'We are calling for freedom in Sudan, but those who think that freedom is a call to anarchy and abuse to the martyrs are under illusion' (Republic of Sudan Radio, 1999). Shortly after, in 2000, the commander of the PDF, Brigadier Muhammad al-Amin Karrar, announced the formation of a specially trained PDF unit, the *Awwabin* ('those who are obedient'), recruited from volunteers from all provinces.

THE DEFENCE INDUSTRY INTEGRATION

If we relate to the issue of European economic integration, the European integration of markets is a key driving force for the future of the European defence industry. A focal aspect in analysing the European development of the defence industry is the aspect of simultaneously, on the one hand, promoting transatlantic defence industry integration, and on the other to preserve the European DTIB by promoting European defence industry integration through the harmonising of the market functioning and through the promotion of shared European defence R&D. Thus, there is a delicate balance in European policy making in what development to promote. In the thesis, there will be a description of the transatlantic as well as the intra-European defence industry integration.

Research Area

In short, the observed empirical phenomenon is that there has for several decades been considerable *talk* (expressed desired for a certain change to occur) for transatlantic defence industry integration (i.e. that companies should cooperate, merge and acquire to a greater extent over the Atlantic Ocean). However, the integration *action* (what integration that has actually occurred) has been very limited. Despite this continuing *discrepancy* between talk and action, the talk has been consistent in advocating deepened integration. My aim is therefore to strive to find an *explanation* for this discrepancy. In order to do this, I am striving first of all to better *understand* the *institutionalised environment* that surrounds the defence companies. This institutionalised environment is analysed as an *organisational field*. In this organisational field, I am identifying the *driving forces* and *inhibitors* for transatlantic defence industry integration. These driving forces and inhibitors are separated between corporate and government driving forces and inhibitors. All in all, I am thereby trying to find a plausible explanation for why an industrial change to a large extent did not occur.

The observation that triggered my research is the obvious discrepancy between on the one hand the debate advocating increased transatlantic defence industry integration and on the other hand the fact that the actual action of this integration is quite limited. The various analyses that have sought to penetrate this problem area have all approached it differently compared to what I regard as being the most interesting and relevant aspects. Previous analyses have all been in other scientific domains – political science and economics for example – or they have adopted more of a general policy approach. These analyses have intrigued me and inspired me to address the issue differently. This chapter suggests a way of reaching an understanding of, and an explanation for, this process from a different angle.

A choice of companies has been made based on the criteria for a theoretical concept – the 'strategic group'. The integration studied involves a group of companies – a 'strategic group' which has certain specific, common characteristics that make an analysis of this group of companies of interest. Certain companies within the defence industry share the characteristic of being system integrators and are on a level of their own as system integrators – commonly described as the 'primes' or the 'prime integrators'. These companies are for the purposes of this research defined as the focal strategic group. The group consists of eight companies. Of these eight companies, four are from the USA (Lockheed Martin, Raytheon, Boeing, Northrop Grumman), one is French (Thales), one is British (BAE Systems), one is Franco-German (EADS) and one is a conglomerate of European missile producers (MBDA).

Previous Analyses of this Research Problem

What explanations for the outcome of transatlantic defence industry integration have been presented? Broadly, it can be said that previous analyses (no analysis identified from business administration, unfortunately) have come up with one of the following three conclusions:

There is little integration and the two political contexts are so different that they will always stay apart. Usually, this conclusion is based on one of the following lines of reasoning. It could be based on a US view, which is sceptical towards co-operation with other nations; it would not contribute to promoting US interests and it would reduce US control of its defence technology. It could also be based on a conclusion from Europe that European political interests and conditions are so different to US political interests that integration cannot occur.

If the two sides could change in the following ways (normally higher defence budgets in Europe and/or less scepticism in the US vis-à-vis Europe, or harmonised military requirements); integration will occur. This is the kind of discussion that has repeatedly been put forward for decades at conferences and in contextual debates. If the two sides could harmonise their priorities more clearly, transatlantic defence industry integration will follow.

There is integration between companies; integration that is pulling the two political contexts closer. (James, 1998, 2001:i and 2001:ii) In this case, companies do integrate and co-operate within the narrow confines created by the integration between the USA and Europe within a government context. In short, James claims that governments do not drive corporate integration; companies drive integration by exploiting the possibilities that governments offer and create. Companies do not follow schemes set by governments; they interpret the opportunities differently compared with governments.

Based on the research so far for the suggested thesis, the assumption is that we must explore the third argument and explain how it can be understood in relation to the first two arguments. We must therefore picture the integration outcome. We may thereby explore how this will explain the outcome of transatlantic defence industry co-operation and integration.

For this chapter, we focus on corporate strategies rather than government priorities. However, corporate strategies are not believed to be sufficiently understood and explained if at the same time we do not relate them to government priorities concerning transatlantic defence industry integration.

The study of previous analyses of transatlantic defence industrial integration points to the fact that it is almost always analysed without an elaborate theoretical framework. Therefore, we expect a more theoretically based analysis to offer extended insight into and explanation of the chosen problem area.

Framework for the Case Study Model

To start out with, a few definitions of focal concepts that will be used. In this chapter, 'integration' includes the concepts integration and 'cooperation'. Companies may integrate in the sense that they enter into joint ventures or they merge or acquire each other. We can observe a continuum of increasing commitment in relation to different forms of integration, reflecting the rational reasons for different choices. They may also co-operate in the sense that they mutually strive to pursue a goal which they both sense benefits their respective goals, but without creating a new, merged corporate entity..

Brunsson described that organisations tend to show a discrepancy in what they say that they will do and what they actually do; a discrepancy between 'talk' and 'action'. Talk concerns an expressed and articulated view that some event or change should come about, e.g. increased transnational integration of markets. 'Action' refers in my framework to the aggregated action of integration within a focal market, i.e. the list of cooperations, joint ventures, mergers and acquisitions and such. As will be noted, the difference between integration and cooperation is important.

The theoretical model identifies a pair of concepts for a certain industrial change, both from a corporate and a government perspective: *driving forces* and *inhibitors*. This concept pair constitutes the talk for a specific industrial action.

An important starting point is that we must achieve a sufficient understanding of the market in order to be able to offer an explanation of the problem under examination. In this chapter, the outline is as follows: First, there is a discussion of what characterises the defence industry and the defence market. Thereafter, there will be a discussion of what characterises the institutionalisation of markets, and we will introduce the concept of an 'organisational field' – a central concept in neo-institutional organisational analysis theory. This will be followed by a discussion on change within institutions, followed by the introduction of the concept 'politico-industrial market'. After this follows a discussion of the concepts 'driving force and inhibitor'. Finally, there is a discussion on what kind of rationality that steers corporate integration in a politico-industrial market.

The main theoretical domain of the research is primarily within neo-institutional theory within organisation analysis. This is related to selected theoretical concepts from other fields of business administration where it is believed that the institutional theory has its limitations in explaining the empirical phenomena described in my thesis work.

The Defence Market

There is a need to discuss the nature of the defence market, since it is generally described as being very different to other markets. If we were to analyse, for example, integration within a group of companies in the automotive market the need would be considerably less as this market is well known.

The defence market is in many ways a "distorted" or "exaggerated" market that takes the impact of government influence and of vested interests to extremes. In a case study, it could therefore be assumed that theoretical aspects of institutional interaction in a specific social system will be unusually marked or influential. A case study on the defence industry could therefore offer specific insights that might contribute to certain, more general, theoretical aspects or constructs.

The defence market deals with the acquisition of complex, technology-intensive products – systems that will be operated for decades and where acquisitions are strongly governed by political demands and specifications. The supply chains and the industrial landscape are mainly made up of large, technology-intensive companies, and research and development requires very large investment. Companies mainly sell to other companies as subcontractors or to the end-users – governments – in the form of military or defence-oriented authorities.

In order to describe the context of this research – the defence industry – the perspective will include aspects of heavy political influence with national (even patriotic) connotations. The defence market will in this thesis be referred to as a *'politico-industrial market'*. This concept relates to other theoretical concepts for such markets, e.g. 'political economy' and Lehne (2001)), where government policy for the functioning of a certain market and the existence of an associated industry is in focus. States have an interest in the well-being and international competitiveness of certain industries and will support them by economic and diplomatic means. The domestic conditions and institutional infrastructure are clear competitive aspects of the strength of domestic defence industry structures (Stopford and Strange (1996); Goldstein (2001)). Porter (1998) examined in a seminal study how different states seek to promote their industries in order to advance government interests through corporate international expansion. Fligstein (2002) underlined a sociological view of market activities, which stressed how markets and states are intimately linked. An institutionalised market that is shaped by political influence will create a market structure centred on social relations: an embeddedness of markets (Granovetter, 1985; Fligstein, 2002).

Examples of politico-industrial markets include e.g. the energy, infrastructure, railway and defence markets. A common denominator is that the market logic is very much affected, or even governed, by political considerations. Purchase decisions are largely not in the hands of individual consumers, they are decided upon by politicians and public officials, often through some kind of network of committees and officials.

The politico-industrial market referred to in my research is often described as a 'militaryindustrial complex' (MIC). The MIC is a much-used concept that describes the particular and common institutionalised behaviour within a nation's military-oriented industry, its associated government players and the research community. The MIC as a concept became common knowledge through the farewell address of Theodore Roosevelt in 1961 although it was in fact coined by Mills in 1956. MIC is not based on theory from any specific scientific field, but is more a commonly used metaphor or description of the national defence industry contexts. We will use the concept MIC as a point of reference. The MIC will be used as a metaphor that is seen as adding explanatory power. It should be seen as an observation of a certain institutionalised functioning of a meso-community within a nation. This institutionalised functioning has been observed in, for example, the USA (Mills (1956), Kolko (1969, 1994), Goldstein (2001)) and France (Kolodziej 1987, Serfati, 1992, 2000, Lundmark, 2004).

The defence industry and the defence market practice is highly regulated by governments. To a large extent, it is still mainly domestically regulated. For example, production of defence goods has to have a government approval in each nation. Governments also to differing extents have a veto right over foreign acquisition of defence companies. Within the EU, there is an ongoing harmonisation process of the defence market and industry. The goal is to strive towards a more harmonised EDEM (European Defence Equipment Market). Furthermore, the EU strives to safeguard and support an EDTIB (European Defence Technology Industry Base). Since the beginning of the European Community, there has been a special article in the Rome Treaty (now Art. 96) that specifies that defence production and procurement is exempted from the principles of the EC/EU common market. (Mörth 2003, Schmitt (ed), 2005)

Between the Corporate and the Political Sphere

Companies and organizations in politico-industrial markets must deal with and relate to several, parallel processes with different political agendas and time scales. Such processes may intensify or slow down, they may appear to cease but be activated again. They are however agents in such institutionalised networks, they must relate to and act upon the conditions of the institutional processes.

Most analyses of transatlantic defence industry integration generally tend to view defence companies as tools of government policy, treating corporate strategy as being of minor importance. This can to some extent be explained by the fact that most academic analysis of this phenomenon is made by political scientists, economists or from some vaguely theoretical and policy-oriented perspective. The expectation is that the proposed thesis will fill a gap in the sense of analysing corporate behaviour in the defence industry based on business administration theory.

Defence companies are by definition dependent on governments as customers and on governments as financers of defence R&D. It is governments (or the military, as representatives of the government) that acquire the defence products. The development of defence products and solutions is very costly and private companies are not prepared to take such financial and technological risks as those associated with defence R&D. Governments and government bodies also shape the conditions and the regulations that the defence companies need to act within. Defence companies work in close co-operation with the military in projects that last for many years, often decades. Defence companies are thus clearly dependent on and closely affected by the actions of governments and government bodies.

We must at the same time repeat that defence companies to the most part are private, autonomous actors. They have the corporate goals of being profitable, attractive to financiers and satisfying shareholders. Corporate actions and integration decisions can thus not be fully understood and explained by treating them solely as tools of government policy.

Institution, Institutionalism and Institutionalisation

Societal institutions have been defined as sets of practices about the world which generate rules about how to act. Modern institutions may exhibit considerable inconsistency between talk and action. Large companies in technology-intensive industries improve their competitiveness by different modes of cooperation, integration and knowledge creation. The corporate behaviour in industries that are strongly politically influenced may not correspond with generally accepted theories in business administration concerning modes of integration. Industry dynamics may be the result of the institutionalization in an organisational field. An *institution* is driven by "shared conceptions that constitute the nature of social reality and the frames through which meaning is made" or as "an established order comprising rule-bound and standardized behaviour". *Institutionalism* is the process, as well as the action of the process, in which social activities become regularised and routinised as stable, social-structural features" (Jary and Jary, 1991). Selznick (1957) coined the expression *institutionalisation*, which refers to the organisational policies and practices that become "infused with value beyond the technical requirements at hand". Institutions and institutional change should also be understood as infused with rivalries over different institutional logics. Power is inherent in the institutional arrangements and practice. We will start out from the assumption that defence markets demonstrate institutionalised behaviour, based on the previous discussion of the nature of the defence market.

Institutionalization in the Organisational Field

If we use theory under the umbrella of 'institutional theory', we cannot refer to the entire block of theorists as it is much too large and diverse. The heritage of institutionalism is difficult to grasp. It has resulted in many different traditions and has also fed into completely opposite lines of thought. We will focus on institutional theories that describe the institutional environment as an organisational field. The 'old' and 'neo' institutionalists are not highly different, but one distinctive difference which is exploited in this thesis is that we will focus on an organisational field rather than on local, intra-organisational institutionalisation processes. The most appropriate institutional theoretical umbrella for this chapter is 'neo-institutional theory within organisational analysis'.

Meyer and Rowan (1977) stated that it is not only the organisation that undergoes institutionalisation; it is also its institutional environment. The stronger interaction between the different actors and the more stable the interaction patterns; the more institutionalised the environment.

A company's closest and most formative environment can be described as an organisational field. Organisations which, as a whole, constitute a recognised area of institutional life: key suppliers, resource and product consumers, regulatory agencies and organisations that produce similar output. Within the organisational field, there will be institutionalised behaviour and some degree of isomorphism. (DiMaggio & Powell, 1991, Fligstein, 1991) Meyer (2007) describes organizational fields as a field of actors that is characterised by a single predominant or by multiple, potentially competing institutional orders or logics.

In this chapter, the MIC is generally seen as being united by a single logic. The environment will be permeated with 'vested interests' that will each on their part aim to attract resources and direct market action based on their priorities. Within a MIC, there will be constant rivalry between different vested interests competing for the resources, e.g. for the allocation of defence funds to different competing defence programs (e.g. submarines vs. fighters vs. tanks).

A company may be dependent on other actors in the organisational field. Companies are dependent upon the access to resources in their environment in order to be able to reach their strategic goals. In the defence industry, the companies are dependent on financial resources from the buyers. There would not be much development or production of new products without government R&D financing or firm orders.

The Markets-as-Networks (MaN) approach (see e.g. Johansson & Mattsson, 1992) to some extent captures the stability of the focal organisational field in this chapter. The markets-asnetworks approach has for my purposes limitations since it too much stresses continuity, cooperation and reciprocal technology development. The defence industry has a flavour of power, dominance and asymmetric dependencies which I am aiming to better capture with the model that is presented in this chapter.

The repeated socially constructed actions of an institution may stabilise and prolong such power asymmetries. Incorporating power is critical to understanding how institutions operate in society and their relationships to organisations. If we relate the general development of the transnationalisation and globalisation of the defence industry; this organisational field strongly resists globalisation forces that otherwise have become almost regarded as laws of nature for economic development. Such blending of strong institutions into transnational, globally transformed structures is in the defence industry meeting perhaps the most sceptical and resisting of all organisational fields. Djelic & Quack define transnational institution-building as a process of institutional recombination that involves elements of different national and local institutional arrangements.

Institutions and Change

Institutions are thus generally seen as a source of stability and order. Institutions are, however, not set over time. They will eventually change due to changes in the conditions of the actors, populations, organisations, resources, technologies, politics or other factors that may deeply affect the institutional context.. According to Scott, institutionalists have tended to focus more on institutions as a factor of stability rather than on when and how institutions change. Such change may result in deinstitutionalisation or restructuring.

A strong institutional system will by definition have built-in mechanisms that will allow incremental change although these frameworks invariably favour some interests over others and exclude some parties entirely. There will in other words be resistance to more dramatic change. The companies will also react to institutional changes in ways that will change the conditions of the industry and the market. We can speak of industry formation processes.

Mattsson & Hultén (1995) analyse market changes from three aspects: changes in the institutional conditions of the industry, technological development and changes in the structure of the industry. The case study model does not address the technological development in the proposed thesis but we will explore how the changes in the structure of the industry are dependent on, and are a result of, the institutional conditions in the industry.

Institutionalised systems rise and fall. Even highly stable and socially embedded fields supported by powerful constituents can be dethroned and dismantled. Sooner or later there will be some change in the internal or external conditions that will create some kind of deinstitutionalisation of the institution. However, the institution is by nature and by definition an inter-organisational system which resists change. Therefore, there will be resistance towards change from within the institution. The problem specified in the thesis evolves within a strongly institutionalised context. This means that deeply rooted practices must change.

In highly institutional systems, endogenous change seems to almost contradict the meaning of institution. If a clear mismatch arises between the corporate and the political level for example, they may grow apart and tension will become increasingly marked. The resistance to change can be described as institutionalised inertia. Djelic & Sahlin-Andersson (2006) stress that 'fields of transnational governance' are crossed and structured by powerful institutional forces. Institutions in themselves push and pull activities in certain directions; the forces are self-reinforcing; and they constitute 'the rules of the game'.

Change within institutions normally occurs on several levels. Therefore, an analysis of the organisational field should include analysis of more than one level. It will be crucial to identify the factors within the different levels that are the most important and that will offer a bridge between the two levels. *"Although no single study can hope to definitively analyse all the causal connections across levels for a complex institutional arrangement, the most informative studies are those that identify and trace the effects of salient and influential processes across two or more levels"* (Scott, 2001, p. 196)

JOINT FORCE RESEARCH AND DEVELOPMENT

This chapter discusses research and development that is not within the Army's exclusive purview. This research, which should be conducted by the other services or under joint auspices, includes the development of strategic lift capabilities, long-range supporting fire, and interoperable command and control systems.

STRATEGIC LIFT CAPABILITIES

The AAN concept is founded on the ability of an AAN battle force to be deployed from the continental United States to a forward base area within 1,000 km of the mission area. Deployment from the United States to a staging area will require that Army assets be transported by either the Air Force or the Navy or a combination of the two. The committee found little DoD or service research focused on upgrading the current strategic lift capability, which is limited by payload in the air and ship speed on the sea. The Army has not stated requirements for heavy (> 500 tons) airlift or fast (> 100 knots) sealift although research is under way in the civilian sector. The Army, based on what it learns in the AAN process, should evaluate the need for such capabilities.

The Air Force plans to improve its C-17 advanced military airlift aircraft as it extends the lifespan of the fleet. The C-17 can transport more than 85 tons and has a cruising speed of Mach 0.74 to Mach 0.77. The C-17's range is more than 4,000 km, and the plane can land in less than 3,000 feet. In fact, the C-17 holds a world record for taking off in 417 meters with a cargo of more than 22 tons and landing in 413 meters. The number of C-17's planned in the inventory, however, will not be adequate to meet the AAN requirement of strategically airlifting 1,000 to 2,000 15-ton vehicles, up to 8,000 troops, and their accompanying supplies in a 48-hour time frame. For the foreseeable future, the only military capabilities for strategic sealift are the fast sealift ship and the large, medium-speed, roll-on/roll-off (LMSR) ship. The fast sealift ship, with limited roll-on/roll-off capability, moves at 30 knots and displaces 61,500 tons (USN, 1998). The newer LMSR displaces 62,700 tons and moves at a speed of 24 knots. It can carry 58 tanks, 48 other tracked vehicles, and more than 900 trucks or other wheeled vehicles. An AAN support sealift must be able to carry much larger loads and travel at speeds of more than 100 knots.

Research being conducted by industry to improve both sea and airlift capabilities has been limited by a lack of clients who are willing to support development. Industry personnel contacted by the committee believe that the concepts of both heavy airlift and fast sealift have been validated and that there are a few commercial applications for them. But the number of commercial applications is too small to justify the commercial investment, and a partnership arrangement will be necessary to make development cost feasible for both the military and commercial market.

Professor Charles Owen at the Illinois Institute of Technology proposed a design for a lighter-than-air carrier that could carry 3,500 passengers and 35,000 tons of cargo. Unfortunately, this carrier would have a limited air speed and be subject to the same constraints that face all lighter-than-air carriers. For AAN, the Army requirement is to carry a nominal 500 tons at speeds slower than a C-130 but faster than a lighter-than-air vehicle. Other revolutionary proposals have also been made. Lockheed-Martin, for example, has investigated placing floats on the C-130, which would give the C-130 the capability of linking up with prepositioned floating logistics supplies and delivering them to a battle area rapidly. Depending on the geography and enemy situation in the battle area, C-130 aircraft could be used for either operational or strategic lift.

Domestic and international commercial shipping interests are working on the development of high-speed ships. Both Russia and the United States have design projects for ships that can carry as much as 10,000 tons at a speed of more than 100 knots with ranges of more than 10,000 nautical miles. These ships could be used to transport personnel and supplies from a floating depot or from the continental United States.

Heavy lift aircraft and fast ships also have considerable commercial potential. Air transport or fast sea transport of high value commodities would substantially reduce a manufacturer's inventory. Even if commercial aircraft and ships are available by 2025, they will probably not have the unique characteristics required by the military. Now is the time for the Army to begin working with the Navy and the Air Force to ensure that commercial developments take military requirements into account. This intervention could involve partnerships and/or arrangements similar to the current Civilian Reserve Air Fleet (CRAF) program. Under CRAF, civilian air carriers are committed to providing passenger and cargo capacity for the military when necessary in exchange for government airlift business in peacetime.

This approach would be in keeping with the recommendations in the *STAR 21* study concerning more conventional lift capabilities. The study stated: The STAR Committee suggests that CRAF is a resource the Army can exploit more fully in the future. To do so the Army should go beyond passively "making do" with whatever capacity comes out of current or future CRAF arrangements.

The Army should work actively to influence CRAF capabilities. Such influence can be exerted in two ways: (1) by persuasion of the parties involved (i.e., the commercial cargo carriers) and (2) by seeking legislative inducements that favour capabilities the Army will need.

This strategy is more urgently needed now than it was when the *STAR 21* study was completed in 1993 for two reasons. First, advances in technology have made possible greater lift capability than was imagined in 1993; second, the AAN concept requires rapid deployment of a lighter force. Air carriers are more likely to be able to move a light force than large numbers of 70-ton tanks.

In addition to lifting the force to a staging area by air, the Air Force may also be called upon to resupply the battle force by parachute drop. The focus areas for research are advanced parachutes, nonparachute decelerators, precision airdrop, and high-performance computing. These technologies could move the AAN from "just-in-case capability," through "just-in-time capability," to "precision resupply" capability.

LONG-RANGE SUPPORTING FIRE

The AAN battle force will have both battlefield mobility and battlefield lethality. The first can require only Army capabilities, but the second will certainly require support from the other services. As the Army has moved forward to define its AAN concepts for 2025, the other services have focused more on the intermediate time frame, 2010 to 2015.

Major concepts of *Joint Vision 2010* are focused on "dominant maneuver" and "precision engagement". Both concepts involve using all components of the U.S. military across the selected battle space. Dominant maneuver is the "application of information, engagement, and mobility capabilities to position and employ widely dispersed joint air, land, sea, and space forces to accomplish assigned operational tasks." Precision engagement is "a system of systems that enables...forces to locate the objective or target, provide responsive command and control, [and] generate the desired effect... " These two concepts are coupled with focused logistics and "full-dimensional protection," the multiservice capability to control the battle space both horizontally and vertically. In short, future military operations will require the integrated capabilities of all of the services. As the Army continues to develop the AAN battle force concept, it must work closely with the other services and DoD to determine which battle force needs should and would be met by other services. Every precision round launched by another service is a round that does not have to be carried to the battle area by the battle force. A combination of fire support by other services and extended-range fire support by Army units operating from the staging area could substantially reduce the logistics requirements of the battle force.

INTEROPERABLE COMMAND AND CONTROL SYSTEMS

The success or failure of the AAN concept may well depend on its C4ISR (command, control, communications, computing, intelligence, surveillance and reconnaissance) capabilities. The four main concepts of *Joint Vision 2010* assume an envelope of "information superiority," which will require linkage and integration with systems of other services. Although the Army should proceed to develop C4ISR capabilities for the AAN battle force, these capabilities should be part of the collective joint information superiority. Every capability that can be provided to the Army by another service operating under the concepts of *Joint Vision 2010* reduces the need for the battle force to carry equipment and personnel into the battle area. Focusing on joint responsibilities not only can increase the combat effectiveness, but also can reduce the logistics burden of the AAN battle force.

FINDINGS

The Army will depend on the Air Force and Navy to ferry the battle force and sustaining supplies to the staging area, to provide coordinated fire support, and to assist with C4ISR. It is also likely that much of the operational mobility requirement will be satisfied by the Air Force. It is imperative that the Army participate in planning for this support to ensure that operational and logistical needs of the AAN battle force can be fulfilled.

Technology developments necessary to enable strategic lift of the AAN battle force will probably overlap with technology requirements for operational, and possibly tactical, mobility. The Army should identify the overlapping requirements and encourage DoD to establish responsibilities among the services for satisfying these requirements as soon as possible.

8

Evolution of the Different Forces

As their military capabilities grow rising powers like China and India are beginning to join the older powers in the arena of military diplomacy. As the global reach of their interests grows—as trading nations, strategic powers and mother countries to massive diasporas—and as they accumulate capabilities for power projection, so too will increase their willingness and ability to use conventional military instruments to provide simultaneously for their own interests and the common weal.'3 While there have been some studies of Chinese military diplomacy,4 academic literature on India's defence diplomacy remains scarce.

This chapter does not undertake a comprehensive review of India's growing use of military instruments to promote its national security and foreign policy objectives in recent years. The chapter is an attempt at gauging the dimensions of India's military diplomacy that has included the signing of a large number of military cooperation agreements and defence memoranda of understanding with other nations and significant expansion of joint military exercises with major powers and regional actors in the Indian Ocean and East Asia. The paper is the first cut at developing an analytical framework to assess the dynamics and consequences of India's military diplomacy. It will identify some of the current limitations that constrain India's military diplomacy and evaluate its future prospects.

The paper will examine the enduring political tensions in India's world view between the traditional ideas of nonalignment and the new imperatives of a rising power.

NONALIGNMENT AND MILITARY ISOLATION

As India became independent in 1947, the Cold War divisions were beginning to congeal in Europe and expand into Asia. As India sought to insulate itself from the impact of Cold War, Delhi was deliberate in its choice of military isolationism'. Independent India's isolationist impulse was, in part, a reaction to the expansive external use of Indian armed forces during the 19th and the first half of the 20th centuries. As the Indian nationalist movement gathered strength after the First World War, it rejected the use of Indian military manpower for imperial purposes and without the consent of the Indian people.5 At the end of the Second World War, many Asian nationalist leaders complained to Jawaharlal Nehru, who was heading the interim government in Delhi, about the use of the Indian army to protect British and European interests rather than the national liberation forces. Given his strong solidarity with the anti-colonial struggles everywhere in Asia, Nehru was not going to accept the use of the Indian army for repressing the liberation movements.

Once the Indian army came under the full control of the new nation, Nehru explicitly rejected its use for expeditionary operations. As Cold War military blocs confronted India, Nehru declared that India will not align with either the East or the West and will pursue an independent foreign policy. Besides defining the national orientation as non-alignment, India moved towards the construction of a broader forum of solidarity among the newly liberated nations. What began as the Asian Relations Conference in Delhi (1947), the effort moved towards the organisation of Afro-Asian conference in Bandung (1955) and the eventual formation of the Nonaligned Movement which met at the summit level, for the first time, in 1961. If rejecting bloc politics was central to India's national perception of nonalignment, the NAM membership was limited to those countries which did not have foreign military bases on their soil. In the years after independence, India slowly wound down its external military links with Great Britain forged over a period of nearly 200 years of colonial rule. While London and Washington would have preferred to see a measure of coordination among the armies of the Commonwealth against the emerging global Communist threat, India's new approach of nonalignment ran counter to it. Nehru chose to remain a part of the Commonwealth, but only after making it clear that India will have nothing to do with the Western military alliances.

The Indian Navy did participate in the Joint Exercises off Trincomalee of the Commonwealth until 1964, but those links too got severed after that. To be sure, Great Britain was a major source of arms supplies to independent India, but little more than that in the first years after independence. Other European arms suppliers like France were eager to enter the Indian market. But it was the Soviet Union that eventually became the main defence partner for India in the Cold War period. If non-aligned India disentangled itself from the military relationship with Britain, it was not going to allow itself to be tied down by the new partnership with Soviet Union. As it sought weapons from the Soviet Union at the turn of the 1960s, India was careful to circumscribe its military engagement with Moscow. Despite being bound to the Soviet Union, through the friendship treaty of 1971, India carefully avoided undertaking joint exercises or other service to service contacts with Moscow.

India was also reluctant to offer military cooperation and support to friendly countries that sought them. The case of Singapore in the mid 1960s easily comes to mind. That India signed a defence cooperation agreement with Singapore in 2003 underlines the unfolding transformation in India's defence diplomacy.

THE REVOLUTION IN MILITARY AND THE DEFENCE INDUSTRY

South Korea experienced the devastating trauma of the Korean War during 1950-1953, but security dependence on the

United States and economic underdevelopment prevented South Korea from seeking a viable defence industry at that time. However, a changing security environment forced South Korea to embark on the creation of its own defence industry in the late 1960s. President Richard Nixon announced the Guam Doctrine in 1969. This Doctrine not only stipulated a gradual disengagement of the United States from Asia, but also called for 'an Asian defence by Asians'. As a result, US security commitment to South Korea visibly weakened, with a major reduction of its troop presence. Alarmingly, the erosion of US security commitment coincided with North Korea's increasing military provocation, with North Korean commandos attacking the presidential mansion in Seoul on 21 January 1968, which was followed by the capture of Pueblo, an American naval intelligence ship in the East China Sea.

It was in this context that Seoul decided to move towards indigenous defence industrialisation. Since South Korea did not have an industrial structure conducive to defence industrialisation, its earlier efforts concentrated on the production of ammunition and small arms—such as rifles and light machine guns—with the assistance of US technical data packages and manufacturing license agreements. Starting from 1974, however, South Korea undertook massive and systematic defence industrialisation. It established a heavy-chemical industry expressly for defence purposes. As a result of this concerted push, South Korea was able to satisfy most of its conventional weapons requirements by the mid-1980s.

From the late 1980s, South Korea encountered new internal and external changes. The end of the Cold War, realignment of American security posture in East Asia, and South Korea's democratic transition paved the way for a new discourse on military strategy, construction of military power, force structure and weapons systems. But the new discourse was confined mostly to military modernisation rather than Revolution in Military Affairs (RMA). South Korea's interests in RMA became more pronounced only after the late 1990s, profoundly affecting the nature of the defence sector in general and the defence industry in particular. With these evolutionary dynamics in mind, the article aims at elucidating the application of RMA in South Korea and tracing its impacts on procurement needs, acquisition types and the defence industry. The first part of the article explores how the concept and practice of RMA have evolved in South Korea, while the second part examines how RMA has affected procurement needs in South Korea's defence sector. The third analyses impacts of RMA on the acquisition patterns by source (i.e., domestic research and development (R&D), licensed and co-production, direct foreign acquisition) and by armed services. Finally, the article looks into how introduction of RMA has influenced the development of the defence industry and defence exports in South Korea.

RMA and its Application in South Korea

The RMA refers to the introduction and implementation of new thinking concerning strategy and tactics, military organisation and doctrines, force structure and overall weapons acquisition. As Richard O. Hundley aptly points out, a RMA involves a major paradigm shift in the nature and conduct of military operations, which results from the combination of multiple innovations in technology, device, system, operational concept, and military doctrine and force structure. In a narrow sense, it is predicated on major innovations in sensor (reconnaissance and surveillance), C4I (Command, Control, Communication, Computing and Intelligence), shooter, and networks, assuming network-centric warfare as the core of future wars. In a broad sense, RMA, as evidenced by the experience of US military transformation strategy, presupposes major changes in technology, processes, organisation and people of the defence sector in order to meet new security challenges.

Several factors have facilitated the advent of RMA in the United States and elsewhere. The first is changes in the overall security environment following the end of the Cold War and globalisation. Different types of military force are required to respond effectively in an emerging international order in which threats stem less from nation-states and more from non-traditional actors such as global terrorists. RMA can thus be seen as an organisational response to changing security environment. The second factor is technological change and its impact on military affairs. As American military performance in the 1991 Gulf War, air raids in Kosovo and most recently in the invasion of Iraq have demonstrated, the evolution of weapons technology, especially the revolution in information technology, has brought about profound changes in military organisation and doctrine. In addition to network–centric warfare related assets (Command, Control, Communications, Computers, Intelligence, Surveillance and Reconnaissance—C4ISR), the availability of such sophisticated technologies as UAVs (Unmanned Aerial Vehicles), nanotechnology, robotics, and biotechnology furthered technology-driven RMA. Finally, in so much as new technology and new social and organisational arrangements have shaped the nature of RMA, new strategic thinking about the use of force, the conception of war and method of winning war has been equally critical. Precision strike, as opposed to mass destruction, and the mandate of minimal human casualties including soldiers have justified the adoption of RMA.

Central to RMA, especially in the American context, is the transition from platform-centric to network-centric operations. And its effective pursuit is expected to bring about several positive dividends: increased speed of command, self-synchronisation, advanced targeting, greater tactical stability and eventually assuring victory in new security environment. Vice Admiral Arthur K. Cebrowski, who headed the Office of Force Transformation in the Office of the Secretary of Defense, summarised the benefits of Network-Centric Warfare (NCW) in the following manner: NCW will provide increasing return on investment by providing our most important resource- our people- the high quality shared awareness necessary to speed mission accomplishment. NCW capabilities will accelerate our ability to know, to decide, and to act ... NCW is at the heart of military adaptivity- the ability to respond to uncertainity in dynamic situation, day-to-day, at every level of warfare, and across the range of potential military operations.

South Korea has not formally adopted RMA as an official doctrine, but has been constantly pursuing innovation in military organisation, doctrine and weapons systems since the early 1970s within the framework of military modernisation. Until the mid-1990s, military innovation in South Korea had generally entailed reactive adjustments to changes in the security environment. It may not be exaggerating to regard President Park Chunghee, who ruled South Korea from 1961 to 1979, as the pioneer of South Korea's version of the RMA. Facing eroding US security commitment and North Korea's military provocation, Park sought an answer in military modernisation through an indigenous defence industrialisation.

In order to expedite defence industrialisation, President Park undertook sweeping measures. The Special Law on the Promotion of the Defense Industry was enacted in 1974 to provide a legal foundation for the enhancement of the defence industrial sector through a wide range of incentives such as preferential financial arrangements, tax and tariff reduction, concession of plant sites, and other administrative support. The National Investment Fund was set up in 1974 as a way of mobilising financial resources for heavy-chemical industrialisation, which was later transformed into the Defense Industrial Promotion Fund (DIPF) in 1980 to direct financial resources toward the defence industry.

The DIPF was abolished in 2006. Even defence contractors were designated by the government, and a more comprehensive research and development infrastructure became available through the creation of the Agency for Defense Development (ADD) in 1970. Starting with an ammunition and M-16 rifle plant in the late 1960s, defence contractors began to proliferate throughout the 1970s. During this period, major emphasis was given to simple assembly and production under licensing agreements of ammunition and basic infantry weapons. From 1977 to 1984, contractors focused on product development through modification, redesign, and reproduction via reverse engineering. As a result of this initiative, the South Korean military was able to smooth out its force modernisation.

Although the South Korean military could enhance the hardware aspect of its capabilities through the modernisation, its overall strategy, force structure and doctrine remained untouched because of its dependence on the US forces in South Korea.

The second move took place during the Roh Tae-woo government (1988-1992). New innovations in military affairs during this period can be attributed to two factors. One factor was further changes in the international security environment. German unification, the demise of the Soviet Union and the end of the Cold War entailed profound changes in American security commitment to South Korea. US Congress passed the Nunn-Warner Amendment in August 1988, which mandated the three-phase reduction of forward deployed American forces in East Asia. American forces in South Korea were also subject to a phased reduction. The other factor was South Korea's transition to democracy. The year 1987 marked a historic political shift in South Korea, ending a long authoritarian military rule and opening a new era of democratic governance. Roh, a co-leader of the military coup in 1979 along with Chun Doo-hwan, ran for presidential election, and his campaign platform was focused on an increased self-reliance in defence as a way of winning public support. Upon his election, President Roh proposed a new slogan of "Koreanization of Korean defense", signalling a departure from the excessive dependence on the United States.

As part of its new defence policy, the Roh Tae-woo government announced a "development of a long-term defense posture plan" on 18 August 1988, which is often referred to as "the August 18 plan". The plan set three major objectives: (1) the establishment of a more self-reliant military strategy for national survival, prosperity and Korean unification; (2) construction of military power corresponding to the goal of a self-reliant defence strategy; (3) development of a force structure that not only enhances combat readiness, but also assures a balanced development of the armed services. In order to carry out these tasks, several measures were undertaken. First, the Joint Chief of Staff (JCS) system was introduced, which allowed its chairman to control each armed service. Second, military strategy was realigned to enhance both deterrence capability and retaliatory capability in case of an all out attack by North Korea. Finally, with regard to force structure and weapons procurement, greater attention was paid to a developing a balanced portfolio of highly advanced but expensive weapons and more conventional but moderately priced weapons as well as the strengthening of air force and navy assets as a way of filling the gap that would occur as a result of reduction of American forces in South Korea.

Although the Roh Tae-woo government's push for defence reform fell far short of meeting the requirements of a RMA, the August 18 plan set a new standard and direction of innovation in the South Korea's defence sector. On 25 February 1993, the Kim Young-sam government (1993-1998) was inaugurated, but it chose not to continue Roh's policy. President Kim regarded the Roh government as a continuation of the military regime, and undertook measures to civilianise the military, that included the dissolution of the *Hanahoe*, the dominant faction in the Korean military. Accordingly, the Kim Government's primary goal was de-politicising the South Korean military and it accorded lower priority to innovation in military strategy, force structure and new weapons systems.

A more systematic introduction and implementation of RMA occurred with the advent of the Kim Dae-jung government (1998-2003). On 15 April 1998, immediately after inauguration, the Kim Dae-jung government launched the Committee for the Promotion of Defense Reform and established the Five-Year Defense Reform Plan. In order to vigorously execute the plan, the Committee set up the Planning Unit for Military Innovation and identified three goals: (1) creation of the most capable standing army; (2) expansion of an information technology-intensive military armed with cutting-edge weapons; (3) construction of a rational, effective and economical military. The Kim Dae-jung government introduced several initiatives in order to realise these goals. First, it pushed for organisational reforms by creating new unified national command systems in the fields of transportation and bio-chemical and nuclear defence as well as improving acquisition systems in JCS. Second, a greater emphasis was placed on the informatisation of the defence sector. Finally, the Kim government began to expedite the acquisition of defence assets closely related to network-centric warfare and surveillance and strike capabilities, while the army, the navy and the air force began concurrently to acquire future-oriented, cutting-edge weapons systems. The diffusion of the US model of RMA began to dominate Kim government's thinking on military affairs.

The Roh Moo-hyun government, inaugurated in February 2003, went further. On 1 June 2005, the Roh government established the Committee on Defense Reform, which drafted the "Defense Reform 2020" plan. The "Defense Reform 2020" plan aims at assuring a self-reliant advanced national defence through the creation of a technology-intensive military structure and future-oriented defence capability. Two factors affected the nature and direction of the "Defense Reform 2020" plan. One was the return of wartime operational control from the United States to South Korea, and the other was South Korea's improved science and technology capabilities. Whereas the former emphasised an aspect of 'independence' or 'selfreliance', the latter underscored a new direction of defence reform framed around speed, stealth, accuracy and networks. Four major tasks have been identified in order to carry out the plan. They are: (1) securing military structure and defence capabilities corresponding to contemporary warfare; (2) expanding the role of civilians in the defence establishment; (3) innovation for a low cost/high efficiency national defence management system congruent with a cutting-edge information-intensive military; (4) improvement of soldiers' military barrack life.

The hallmark of Defense Reform 2020 was the qualitative transformation of the South Korean military. It aimed at reducing the current number of armed forces from 650 000 to 500 000 by 2020, while giving priority to the introduction of a new capital- and technology-intensive military structure. The army was the primary loser from the reform in the sense that it had to find most of the manpower reduction. Nevertheless, its combat capabilities were expected to improve considerably with the acquisition of Unmanned

Aerial Vehicles (UAV) for reconnaissance, next generation tanks and infantry fighting vehicles, improved fire systems, and a simplified command structure. The navy and the air force were the plan's principal beneficiaries. The navy would be able to go beyond a coastal navy by securing both a submarine command and a naval air command. The air force could enhance its combat readiness by acquiring next generation fighters (F-15K), surface-to-air missiles (SAM-X), and airborne early warning systems (E-X). The most crucial aspect of the plan was the massive investment in battle management assets focusing on C4ISR, all of which are essential for network-centric warfare. Along with this, the Defense Reform 2020 has mandated the acquisition of theatre operational command facilities, military communication satellites, tactical information communication networks (TICN), the Joint Tactical Data Link System (JTDLS), and the Korea Joint Command and Control system (KJCCS).

In summary, RMA in South Korea is a relatively recent phenomenon, deeply influenced by the diffusion of the American RMA concept and practice. Compared with that of the United States, however, the scope, depth and rate of South Korea's defence transformation in the direction of RMA seems rather limited. Nevertheless, an increased military self-reliance, a diminished dependence on the United States, and improvements in indigenous science and technological capabilities have facilitated its pursuit of a revolution in military affairs.

RMA IN SOUTH KOREA BY PROCUREMENT NEEDS

How has the introduction of RMA affected the pattern of defence procurement needs in South Korea? During the 1970s and 1980s South Korea's defence procurement needs were framed mostly around conventional weaponry. They included small arms, short-range artillery pieces, ammunition, rudimentary communication equipment, Hughes 500MD helicopters, F-5 E/F fighters, relatively small scale naval vessels (battleships, patrol ships and destroyers), short-and medium-range missiles (Nike Hercules SSMs, Honest John unguided tactical missiles and Hyunmoo medium range guided missiles), and armoured vehicles (US M48 (Tank), M-113 Tank, ROKIT ('88 Tank), K-2000 APC and K900 APC). Very little attention was given to assets related to RMA, a situation exacerbated by the South Korean military's excessive dependence on American C4IRS assets within the framework of the Republic of Korea (ROK)-US Combined Forces Command (CFC). The South Korean military was also relying on American forces for tactical data link system, tactical information communication networks, and tactical command system.

The above examination reveals that RMA considerations have become a key factor in determining procurement needs. Defence assets related to sensor, C4IRS, shooter and networks have increasingly drawn attention from defence planners. The South Korean government anticipates that by 2020, the year when its defence reform is completed, it would achieve a considerable level of self-sufficient intelligence collection capabilities, the construction of real time, synchronised networks among all the units involving battle sensor, command/ control, and force operation, acquisition of strike forces aiming at strategic targets such as weapons of mass destruction, and overall improvement of combat forces by replacing aging weapons and equipment. All this suggests that the RMA is likely to continue shaping future South Korean defence procurement. Nevertheless, the newly inaugurated Lee Myung-Bak government has queried the budgetary feasibility of the procurement plan integral to Defense Reform 2020, and is entertaining the possibility of attenuating the procurement period all the way to 2025

RMA AND ACQUISITION PATTERN BY SOURCE

Arms acquisition usually takes place through one of the following four sources: domestic R&D, co-production or production through technology transfer, licensed production and direct overseas acquisition. Given that RMA involves mostly cutting-edge technologies, most countries rely on direct overseas acquisition rather than on domestic R&D or co-production. What is the case in South Korean?

South Korea has acquired most of RMA-related defence articles through domestic research and development. A large portion of C4I as well as JTDLS and TICN has been procured through domestic sources. Acquisition of advanced armoured vehicles, precision guidance missiles, UAVs, and naval and air assets was also made through domestic R&D. This can be attributed to not only an assertive government policy that encourages domestic procurement of RMA-related assets, but also its improved industrial capabilities in the areas of information technology, heavy machinery and shipbuilding, mobile vehicles and aerospace technology.

The acquisition pattern of defence articles by armed services shows several interesting trends. With respect to joint operation assets such as C4IRS, software has been mostly acquired or is planned to be acquired through domestic research and development, whereas hardware such as AWACS and high altitude UAVs are to be purchased from abroad. In contrast, most air force assets are to be acquired from abroad with the exception of KT-1 and KO-1 (domestic R&D), T-50 and FA-50 (co-production with Lockheed Martin), and KF-16 (licensed production). Meanwhile, a great portion of defence articles for the army and the navy are to be acquired through domestic R&D. However, Search (UAV), MLRS, and Firefinder Radar are planned to be purchased abroad. The navy is planning to obtain next generation destroyers (KDX II and III) through domestic R&D, with only Harpoon, LYNX, ISAR(P-3C), and P-3C to be purchased from overseas.

Despite a relatively high dependence on foreign direct acquisition of big-ticket items, South Korea has been trying to increase the local content of its defence articles. Commensurate with South Korea's comparative advantage in information technology and telecommunication, the communication and electronics sector has substantially increased its localisation rate from 72 percent in 2001 to 85 percent in 2007. A slight improvement was also made in the category of precision guidance weapons, where the localisation rate has risen from 56 percent in 2001 to 74 percent in 2007. Although South Korea still relies on US software in the supply and support of both C4ISR and precision weapons, a growing number of South Korean firms such as Samsung-Thales have been developing their own software to support cutting-edge weapons and equipment. However, the localisation rate in the aerospace sector decreased from 59 percent in 2001 to 49 percent in 2007, while both armoured vehicles and naval vessels have shown localisation rates fluctuating above the 60 percent level. Comparatively speaking, South Korea's localisation rate seems quite high. Government's defence procurement policy that favours domestic R&D and localisation.

The enactment of the Law on Defense Procurement on 1 January 2006 under the Roh Moo-hyun government gave additional incentives to domestic defence contractors. Article 18 (on Research & Development) of the law stipulates that "Head of the Defense Acquisition Program Administration should give preferential treatment to domestically produced defence articles in procurement". It was through this legal requirement that LG-CNC was designated as the principal party for negotiation for the KJCCS project. LG-CNC, which was founded in 1987, participated in army C4I system construction. And a consortium comprising Samsung Thales, Huneed technology, and KT won the TICN project. LIG NEX, a subsidiary of LG Group, has also enjoyed a privileged position in the supply of precision-guided weapons such as Shingung (portable surface to air weapons),

RMA AND THE SOUTH KOREAN DEFENCE INDUSTRY

RMA requires major changes in doctrine and organisation, as well as advancement in the defence industrial base. New strategy and doctrine emanating from a RMA require new weapon platforms and corresponding defence industrial foundation. If the weapon and sensor platforms that will be the nodes of NCW are to be smaller, lighter, faster, and less complex, then platform manufacturers will have to build smaller, lighter, faster, and less complex ship and aircraft.

Otherwise, RMA cannot make a meaningful progress. Thus, the existence of a solid defence industry and its forward and backward linkage are essential to the success of RMA. Then, to what extent is the South Korea's defence industry ready for RMA? And how has RMA influenced the reshaping of the defence industry?

The defence industry in South Korea is relatively small in size and oligopolistic in its market structure. Top ten defence contractors' sales reached KW 4.965 trillion, accounting for 77.1 percent of defence contract market in South Korea in 2006. Top five defence contractors (Samsung Techwin, KAI, Samsung Thales, Hanhwa, Hyundai Heavy Machinery) accounted 46. 8 percent of total marketshare, amounting to KW 2.489 trillion. These top five defence contractors all came from RMA-related areas (highly mobile self-propelled artillery for Samsung Techwin, new trainer cum attack fighter for KAI, C4IRS for Samsung Thales, and naval vessels for Hyundai Heavy Machinery). These defence contractors have also engaged in civilian production which has generated positive spin-on effects on the defence industrial sector. Remarkable is that these firms have been able to satisfy RMA-related procurement needs in a timely manner.

Thus, the defence industrial base in South Korea has been to some extent ready for meeting RMA procurement needs from a technological point of view.

DEFENCE INDUSTRY AND MARKETS TASK FORCE

The Context

The end of the Cold War has changed the *nature* of the security threats that Member States face rather than doing away with them. New and complex security challenges have emerged which can only be addressed by professional forces which are well equipped with state-of-the-art technology. The

Libya crisis showed (again) that Europe is still lacking military capabilities in some critical sectors, although the European Defence Technological and Industrial Base (EDTIB) could deliver most of the technologies and material we would need.

These capability gaps are clearly a direct consequence of budget constraints. These constraints are unlikely to disappear anytime soon. Public debt and the consolidation of state finances are the most important challenges in Europe now - and will certainly remain as such for the near future. It is therefore hardly surprising that almost all national defence budgets are under pressure and subject to significant cuts. A major casualty in defence budgets has been spending on Research & Technology which is crucial for the development of the next generation of equipment. Cuts in current military programmes and the apparent lack of new ones are also contributing to the erosion of the EDTIB which was already suffering from structural underinvestment.

For the time being, many European defence companies are still doing well , with exports to third countries (at least partly) compensating for shrinking home markets. Faced with the sharp decline in public defence spending, Europe's industry is concentrating its efforts on new emerging defence markets with a strong growth potential such as India and Brazil. Europe's industry is also strengthening its presence in highly dynamic related business segments such as electronics, security, space, and civil aviation. This indicates that European defence industries are, in many areas, still at the cutting edge of technology and globally competitive.

However, these strengths are the result of investments made many years ago and as such Europe is now reaping the benefits of that forward thinking.

The Challenges

The drive to increase exports will be undermined as the lack of major new programmes is gradually reducing the range of high-end technology products that are still fairly competitive. Furthermore, as the US defence budget also faces significant cutbacks, competition from US companies looking for new business opportunities outside their home market is set to grow (and be boosted by US reform of export controls making it easier to do so). With European defence markets declining or at best stagnant, however, incentives to invest in European mergers and acquisitions are likely to diminish with the lack of new orders and the attractiveness of investing in buoyant third markets. Lacking new programmes, the defence industry is likely to reduce its investment in Europe or to pull out of certain sectors altogether.

Investing in emerging third countries may prove to be a more sustainable way of maintaining turnover but it may also generate a loss of technology and IPRs due to heavy offset requirements that often include local establishment and content requirements. Moving production and transferring technology is becoming a minimum requirement for many major export orders – all of which may lead to cutbacks in factories and employment in Europe and threaten the long-term competitiveness of the EDTIB.

In the long run, competitiveness on world markets can only be maintained on the basis of a truly European home market in which EU companies can operate freely in all Member States and benefit from a demand side which is consolidated at the European level. For the time being, however, the European defence market remains fragmented and lacks efficiency. Member States continue to allocate the bulk of their defence spending to manpower rather than procurement of new equipment and forward-oriented research. Furthermore, there is a lack of harmonisation of military requirements and most procurement remains national. As a result, production volumes remain small and economies of scale rare.

Under these conditions, Europe risks losing the industrial and technological capabilities that are necessary to develop and produce what it needs for its security. At stake is as such, not only Europe's competitiveness in a globalised world but also its long-term security of supply, which is in turn crucial to its strategic autonomy and ability to act at international level. Increasing or even maintaining key strategic defence assets in times of scarce financial resources will therefore be a major - if not the main - challenge in this policy domain.

The Commission's Contribution

If spending *more* is difficult, spending *better* becomes even more important. In the context of the on-going structural reforms of armed forces and military organisations as is happening in other sectors of Europe's economy and society; there should be more consolidation of demand and better cooperation via pooling, sharing and role specialisation; better exploitation of civil-military synergies; and more efficient market structures.

Most of these issues lie within the responsibility of Member States and intergovernmental institutions and bodies, starting with the European Defence Agency (EDA).

However, the Commission, for its part, can use its legislative, financial and administrative tools to encourage, support and push forward the necessary transformation process. The most prominent examples of this are the two Directives on defence procurement and defence transfers adopted in 2009, which form today the regulatory backbone of a European Defence Equipment Market. And President Barroso, in his State of the Union speech of September 2011, committed the Commission within its competences to do all it could to develop the single market and industrial base in the European defence sector.

In order to look into these issues, the Commission set up a Defence Task Force with the mandate of exploring ways to move beyond the current state of play and energise the EU-wide debate over the future of the European defence sector. The Task Force is still in its early stages, but three priority areas have emerged: (a) Internal Market; (b) Industrial Policy; and Internal Market In the area of the internal market the Commission's focus is on ensuring the effective and timely transposition as well as implementation of legislation.

With respect to the defence transfer Directive, the Commission will promote in particular the use of General Licences, which is particularly important for the sake of industrial competitiveness and security of supply among Member States. The Commission will analyse and compare the scope of general licences published by Member States to assess convergences in the Member States' approach.

With respect to the defence procurement Directive, the Commission will work to ensure that certain exclusions, such as government-to-government sales, are applied in a way that is consistent with the objectives of the directive and does not impinge on its effectiveness. It will also continue to work towards the phasing out of offsets, following the revision of national offset regulations and Member States' procurement practice in particular in the area of subcontracting. The Commission will also establish an effective market monitoring mechanism (in order to ensure the correct application of the Directive) and gather the data required to report to Parliament in 2017 on the impact the Directive has had.

Finally, the Commission will explore whether and to what extent it can contribute, through its regulatory power, to the Union's long-term security of supply. This may lead to an initiative on the control of defence industrial capabilities.

Industrial Policy

It is widely accepted that the present evolution of defence markets is leading to overcapacity and acceleration of restructuring processes in the European industry. No EU Member State can afford to maintain a full-spectrum defence industrial base. Perhaps more importantly, no one has a strategic need to do so, given that most military operations are undertaken by coalitions either within NATO or the Common Security and Defence Policy (CSDP).

Industrial restructuring in Europe is not only unavoidable: it is already under way. It is essential that national approaches in this policy area be developed, as much as possible, within a European framework by taking full account of its social impact (including the possible use of EU Structural Funds and the European Globalisation Adjustment Fund within the limits of the rules governing them). Such an approach should be based on the principle of inter-dependence and the concept of European centres of excellence and tailored to the three main industrial sectors (naval, land and aviation). Cooperation and specialisation are the only ways to maintain and strengthen essential capabilities and technologies and to secure supply in the medium and long term. The Commission will work, together with the EDA and all relevant stakeholders, towards the development of such a common European approach to the restructuring of the defence industry.

Another critical dimension is the impact of defence cuts on SMEs, as SMEs are an important source of employment and innovation in all sectors: defence is no exception. However, with the existing fragmentation of defence markets, SMEs find it particularly difficult to access markets in other Member States. The Commission plans to explore – once again in cooperation with the EDA - what more could be done to support SMEs in this sector, such as: improving access to information on potential business opportunities; identifying and promoting best practice in Member States; and developing networks of clusters at European level and to support SMEs in expanding their businesses outside the European Union where appropriate.

Research & Innovation

It is worth exploring what can be done to limit the impact of the cuts in funding for defence R&D, which is a crucial element of industrial competiveness. The main objective is to develop greater synergies between dual technologies funded through the different Commission's research programmes and the defence research agenda of the EDA.

The cooperation between the Commission and the EDA is already close in this area and recently made easier by the European Framework Cooperation (EFC). The EFC is designed to maximise complementarity and synergy between the Commission's civil security research programme, the EDA co-ordinated defence-related research, and the space research of the European Space Agency. The first concrete results of the EFC came in September 2011 when a letter of coordination was signed on Chemical, biological, radiological, and nuclear (CBRN) protection.

The Commission and the EDA are building on this promising start by looking at what other areas could be brought within the EFC. Perhaps the most obvious area is cyber security as one of the few where Member States have kept, or even increased, their budgets. Other areas could include Unmanned Aircraft Systems (UAS), advanced materials, future and emerging technologies and critical space technologies. The Commission would also like to explore how best to make use of the specific Intellectual Property Rights (IPRs) and exchange of information articulated in its 'Horizon 2020' proposal. These should make it easier to exchange research results with the EDA and the Member States.

Finally, the Commission is exploring the possibility of mandating the European standardisation organisations to develop standards that could be used in both civil and defence technologies in areas where the technology is the same and the application quite similar (i.e. hybrid standards).

Looking Ahead

For most of the above-mentioned issues immediate action is possible – and arguably desirable - and targeted initiatives can be launched in the short term. Other issues may need further reflection and deserve a broader strategic debate. The Task Force also intends to look into these issues.

The Defence Task Force would like to inquire for example whether truly European solutions can be a more efficient alternative for consolidating the demand side of the European defence market than the current purely intergovernmental pooling and sharing initiatives. Another question is to explore how other EU policies, which are at first glance not related to defence, can contribute to strengthening the defence sector.

Last but not least, the Defence Task Force may also look at the Commission's own organisation and assess whether the current setting is well-suited to deal with defence matters. In this context, we would like to get your view on the following issues – as well as on any additional ones you may consider relevant.

CONCEPTS OF WARFARE FOR THE TWENTY-FIRST CENTURY

The military community agrees that warfare in the twenty-first century will be considerably different from warfare in the twentieth century. In *Joint Vision 2010,* the Chairman of the Joint Chiefs of Staff (JCS), the senior military officer in the defense structure, has defined a vision of warfare in the first decades of the twenty-first century. This planning document describes a military that will have total SA of the battle space in which it will operate; the ability to protect its forces from enemy attack on the ground, from the air, or from space; and the ability to provide focused logistics support (DoD, 1996).

According to the JCS, focused logistics represents "... the fusion of logistics, information, and transportation technologies for rapid crisis response; deployment and sustainment; the ability to track and shift units, equipment and supplies even while enroute, and delivery of tailored logistics packages and sustainment directly to the warfighter".

Focused logistics will provide forces in the battlefield area with command-and-control systems that closely link operations with logistics, enabling logisticians to provide combat commanders with whatever they need, whenever and wherever they need it. Focused logistics will be truly "joint" logistics: wherever feasible, logistics functions of the services will be combined or one of the services will be assigned as the lead agent for a function or supply item. U.S. forces will also rely more on support from host nations and allies. Information will give the logistician "total asset visibility," the ability to determine seamlessly what equipment and supplies are available in the operational theater or in the United States and where they are. During the Persian Gulf War, the U.S. military operated with 26 separate logistics data systems that had few interconnections. The logistics force of the future is expected to operate with an "agile infrastructure" that will permit combat forces to take with them only what they are sure to needright-sized, "just-enough" inventoriesand enable logisticians to supplement this support whenever and wherever necessary. Building on the concept of focused logistics, the Army has postulated a revolution in military logistics (RML) to leverage advances in information systems technology and fuse operational concepts with logistics systems. The RML will involve a shift towards distribution-based systems (rather than the accumulation of supplies), real-time situational understanding, new organizational designs, and proven commercial business practices. The goal of the RML is to reduce sustainment requirements and logistics infrastructure by focusing on a high velocity, agile, responsive logistics system based in the continental United States. In developing the logistics structure for Army XXI, logistics planners are incorporating the RML concepts into force structures and reducing the need for forward logistics units.

Bibliography

Ajey Lele: *Strategic Technologies for the Military : Breaking New Frontiers*, Sage, Delhi, 2009.

Arend, A.: International Law and the Use of Military, London, Routledge, 1993.

Atar Singh Jadoan: *Military Geography of South East Asia*, Anmol, Delhi, 2001.

Dixit, A.K. : *Military Wars and Rescue Techniques*, Cyber Tech Pub, Delhi, 2010.

Dombrowski, P.J., & Gholz, E.: *Buying Military Transformation: Technological Innovation and the Defense Industry*. New York: Columbia University Press, 2006.

Friedman, G.: *The Future of War: Power, Technology and Western Military*, N.Y., Random House, 1996.

Huntington, S.P.: *The China Modernisation Military and the State*, N.Y., Vintage Books, 1964.

Huntington, S.P.: *The Soldier and the State*, N.Y., Vintage Books, 1964.

Jones, W.H.: *Politics of Military*, London, Hutchinson, 1971.

Mary, W.: *Military Space Force: the Cultural Dimensions of Authority*, Cambridge, Belknap Press, 1985.

Mary, W.: *Military Space Force: the Cultural Dimensions of Authority*, Cambridge, Belknap Press, 1985.

Nayyar, A.K. : *National Security : Military Aspects*, Rupa, Delhi, 2003.

Peterson, B.R.: *The Sources of Military Space Force*, Cornell Univ. Press.

Posen, B.R.: *The Sources of Military Doctrine*, Ithaca, 1984, Cornell Univ. Press.

Raj Kumar: *Weapons and Military Technology*, Sumit Enterprises, Delhi, 2009.

Index

❑❑❑